S0-BJL-175

Transforming Democracy

DATE DUE

SUNY Series in Political Party Development
Susan J. Tolchin, editor

Transforming Democracy

Legislative Campaign Committees and Political Parties

Daniel M. Shea

STATE UNIVERSITY OF NEW YORK PRESS
in cooperation with
The Center for Party Development
Washington DC

SCCCC - LIBRARY
Rivos Mall Dr.

Published by
State University of New York Press, Albany

1995 State University of New York

All rights reserved

Printed in the United States of America

No part of this book may be used or reproduced in any manner whatsoever without written permission. No part of this book may be stored in a retrieval system or transmitted in any form or by any means including electronic, electrostatic, magnetic tape, mechanical, photocopying, recording, or otherwise without the prior permission in writing of the publisher.

For information, address State University of New York Press,
State University Plaza, Albany, NY 12246

Production: Christine Lynch
Marketing: Nancy Farrell

Library of Congress Cataloging-in-Publication Data

Shea, Daniel M.
    Transforming democracy : legislative campaign committees and
political parties / Daniel M. Shea.
        p.   cm.
    Includes bibliographical references and index.
    ISBN 0-7914-2551-7 (alk. paper). — ISBN 0-7914-2552-5 (pbk. :
alk. paper)
    1. Political parties—United States—States.   2. Political
consultants—United States—States.   3. Campaign management—United
States—States.   I. Title.   II. Title: Legislative campaign
committees.
JK2276.S47 1995
324.2747—dc20   94-32958
                                                                      CIP

10 9 8 7 6 5 4 3 2 1

For Christine, my companion

Contents

Tables   ix

Figures   xi

Preface   xiii

Introduction   1

Chapter 1   Some Background on State
             Legislative Campaign Committees   17

Chapter 2   Possible Explanantions for the Growth
             of State LCCs   31

Chapter 3   The State of Party Organizations:
             Decay or Resurgence?   47

Chapter 4   Theory, Data, and Method   69

Chapter 5   New York State: A Case Study   83

Chapter 6   The State-Level Relationship   113

Chapter 7   The County-Level Relationship   137

Chapter 8   Conclusion   165

Appendix A   The New York State Instrument   185

Appendix B   State Party Chair Survey   197

Appendix C   County-Level Instrument   205

Notes   213

Bibliography   223

Index   235

Tables

1.1   States with Legislative Campaign Committees   18

2.1   Correlation between Party Organization Strength
      and Legislative Campaign Committee Strength   33

2.2   Logistic Regression of Factors Leading to the
      Creation of State Legislative Campaign Committees   45

2.3   OLS Regression of Factors Contributing to the
      Strength of State LCCs   45

3.1   Contrasting Attributes of Rational-Efficient and
      Party-Democracy Models of Party   61

5.1   Level of Interaction with LCCs by Party of Chair
      (In Percentages)   102

5.2   Perceived Likelihood of Assistance From LCCs
      Controlled by Party*   107

5.3   "Whose Wishes Do the LCCs' Actions Represent?"
      Controlled by Party   108

5.4   "How Do You See LCCs in State Party Structure?"
      Controlled by Level of Exposure and Party   109

5.5   Perceived Objectives of LCCs, Controlled by
      Level of Exposure and Party   110

6.1   Formal Linkages between LCCs and State Party
      Committees Controlled by Party of Respondent   116

6.2   Amount of Effort Expended on Certain Activities
      by the State Committees   119

6.3   Financial Interdependence between LCCs and
      State Party Committees   120

6.4 Bivariate OLS Regression with LCC Resources ($) as Independent Variable and Ten-Point Cooperation Scales as Dependent Variables   121

6.5 Cooperation between LCCs and State Committees on Tangible Candidate-Directed Activities   125

6.6 Bivariate OLS Regressions between Level of Party Competition and Candidate-Directed Interdependence Scales   125

6.7 Correlation Between Measures of Project Interdependence and Legislative Professionalization 1   128

6.8 Perception of LCC Activities: Do They Undertake the Following?   130

6.9 Respondent's View of LCC, Controlled by Party   132

7.1 Exposure to LCCs, Controlled by State   146

7.2 Levels of Strategic Cooperation, Controlled by State   150

7.3 County-Level Project Interdependence   152

7.4 Multivariate OLS Regressions, with Institutional Support and Candidate-Directed Interdependence as Dependent Variables   154

7.5 Objectives of County Party Committees   156

7.6 Amount of Effort Respondent's County Committee Places on Certain Projects   157

7.7 Correlation between County Committee Concerns and Perceived LCC Interests   159

7.8 How County Chairs See LCCs in Their State   161

7.9 Correlation of LCC Involvement in General Party-Building Activities and Relationship between Party and LCC   163

Figures

6.1 State Party Committees Included in the Sample   114

7.1 Dimensions Used to Select the Four States:
LCC Resources and Party Organization Strength   140

xi

Preface

Party politics was an important part of my formative years. My father, Dennis Shea, chose teaching government as a career and found time to aid local, and occasionally state and national, Democratic candidates. Among many posts, he is perhaps proudest of having served on Robert Kennedy's staff in 1968. My mother, Rosemary Shea, embraced a similar path, spending several years as county party chair and as a delegate to state and national party conventions. Her tenacity, grit, and sense of purpose have helped set a high standard for party activism in Central New York.

It seemed only natural to follow in their footsteps and after receiving a Master of Arts in Campaign Management, I returned to New York State to join the cause—this time with the Democratic Assembly Campaign Committee (DACC). This unit is perhaps the most sophisticated, well-funded, state-level legislative campaign committee in the nation, and it was truly a thrill to be a part of it. During my stint I was in charge of, or directly involved in, scores of competitive state house races.

It did not take long, however, to discern an omnipotent strain between DACC and other Democratic party organizations. We rarely joined forces with county party committees, and while we were happy to use the State Committee's bulk rate account (the lowest by law), we hardly ever consulted with those folks about what we were doing. In fact, on numerous occasions hostilities broke out over strategy, tactics, and resources. They were certainly not the enemy—but neither were we on the same team.

Upon returning to graduate school, it was surprising to find a lack of scholarly work on state legislative campaign committees (LCCs). The scholarship that did exist often merged these organizations with traditional party units in a neat conceptual bundle. Could scholars simply be on the wrong track? Perhaps New York was the exception rather than the rule? In any event, the new, complex dynamic between state LCCs and traditional party organizations throughout

xiii

the United States remained unexplored in the literature on parties. This book represents several years and untold hours trying to sort out this issue.

I am indebted to the many state, county, and local party leaders who took time out of their busy schedules to discuss the workings of their organization and its relationship with the legislative campaign committees of their state. The Nelson A. Rockefeller Institute of Government, Center for Legislative Studies, at the State University of New York at Albany and the Ray C. Bliss Institute of Applied Politics at the University of Akron provided various forms of financial support. The Department of Political Science at the State University of New York at Albany also granted monetary assistance. Dr. Martin Edelman, Chair of the Department, was always willing to aid my cause and Eleanor Leggieri and Maxine Norman supplied considerable help with transcription and word processing.

Sally Friedman has not only been a consistent source of inspiration and counsel, but a good friend. Her "can do" attitude often rubbed off, making momentous obstacles appear less so. I am also grateful to Robert Nakamura, John Green, Ralph Goldman, Malcolm Jewell, and John White for their thoughtful comments and suggestions. At SUNY Press, Clay Morgan and Christine Lynch did a superb job of tightening the book and keeping me on schedule.

Several graduate students at the University of Albany had a hand in this project. Barbara Dinehart was a dependable sounding board, a tireless copy editor, and fine confidant. Christopher Grill, David Olson, and Martin Shaffer, for better or worse, each owns a piece of the book.

I certainly have a debt of gratitude to Michael Malbin. It was under his recommendation that the Rokefeller Institute provided resources to get the ball rolling. His comments and keen insight during each phase of the project were indispensable. Dr. Malbin wishes for his sutdents to do well and goes the extra step to see it happen. I am fortunate to have worked with such an accomplished scholar and teacher.

Finally, I shall always be indebted to Anne Hildreth. For over three years her knowledge, constructive criticism, and editing talents helped transform a diffuse set of ideas into a book. Perhaps more importantly, she has been a wonderful friend, always there to push me forward with kind encouragement. Few will have the opportunity to work with such an enthusiastic, insightful mentor.

As much as I might hope to repay these and the many others who have rendered their assistance over the past few years, such an effort is not only unexpected, but impossible—the debt is far too large. The most I might do is to try to repay their attention, encouragement, and kindness to future students, colleagues, and family.

Introduction

In November of 1985, New York State Assemblyman Andrew Ryan was elected Clinton County District Attorney—thereby vacating his state legislative post in midterm. Ryan had been a member of the Assembly for eighteen years and by all accounts served his constituents well. Although never rising to the higher ranks of the Republican Caucus, he was a competent legislator and a strong voice for the Adirondack North Country.

Ryan's district, the 110th, was located in the far northeast corner of the state. Bordered to the south by the Adirondack Park and to the north by Canada, the district included all of Clinton County and a small portion of Franklin County. While historically a Republican stronghold, voter registration in the 110th was roughly divided between the two major parties. There were even signs of growing Democratic strength. Ronald Reagan, for example, received only 51 percent of the vote in 1980 and 55 percent in 1984– modest figures in comparison to neighboring districts. The Clinton County Legislature was evenly split between Democrats and Republicans, and several of the larger towns were controlled by the Democrats, e.g., Plattsburgh and Messena. Moreover, both the Clinton and Franklin County Democratic party committees were active, often providing significant support to their candidates.

Ryan safely held his seat despite the mounting Democratic presence; in most elections, he faced little or no opposition. As long as he wished to remain, Ryan was perceived as a permanent fixture. His election to District Attorney, however, triggered considerable interest. In an open-seat contest the district was no longer a safe bet for the Republicans.

The special election that followed Ryan's retirement engaged a battle of wits, resources, and determination that extended far beyond the North Country. For local Democrats, it signified a rare opportunity to use their growing organization to secure a voice in the state legislature. For local Republicans, it represented a chance to stem the

1

Democratic tide and maintain a long-held seat. At the state level, the election was an opportunity for Speaker Stanley Fink to flex his political muscles by utilizing the Democratic Assembly Campaign Committee (DACC). Developed in the 1970s and run by Fink's right-hand lieutenant, Tony Genovesi, DACC was seen as a preeminent legislative campaign machine. While the Democrats held a solid majority in the Assembly, augmenting the Caucus is seen as an important goal for any good speaker. For State Republicans, the special election provided another opportunity to turn national Republican strides into state legislative victories. The state GOP could not afford to lose another member. They, too, would utilize a legislative campaign organization, the Republican Assembly Campaign Committee (RACC). Although the stakes were just one seat in a 150-member body, the people running these campaigns were also playing for power, reputation, momentum, and ego. During the winter of 1986, political eyes were turned toward Clinton County.

By the end of the campaign, the "Plattsburgh Special" would hold a unique place in the history of party politics in New York State. Perhaps more importantly, in many ways this election demonstrated the growing impact of state-level legislative campaign committees and the changing role of traditional party organizations. A profound transformation of state legislative politics and state party dynamics is underway throughout the nation. The special election in New York during the winter of 1986 heralded many of these changes, both positive and negative. The story is worth briefly repeating.

The Clash and Collapse of the Democrats

Friction between the local Democratic party organization (the "Locals") and the Democratic Assembly Campaign Committee began almost immediately after Ryan announced his retirement. New York State Election Law directs county party organizations within an assembly district, through a joint convention, to nominate candidates for special elections. A primary is not needed. The Franklin and Clinton County Democratic committees held a joint meeting and emerged with a candidate.

At the same time, DACC undertook an extensive benchmark survey. It tested issues, themes, and the appeal of numerous local personalities. The individual to emerge from the poll as the best candidate was *not* the candidate chosen by the local party organizations. As a result, the choice of the nominee marked the first in a series of disputes between the two camps. Perhaps as a sign of good faith, the

Locals yielded to the professionalism and sophistication of the legislative campaign committee. The candidate was to be Robert Garrow, a well-respected county legislator. "After all," noted a local party official several years later, "they were going to spend tons of money. What did we know; we were just country bumpkins."

Under strong advice from DACC, the Locals were asked to gather enough signatures to put Garrow on a newly created line. Unique to New York and Connecticut, cross-over party endorsements allow candidates to combine their vote totals from two or more ballot positions.[1] Although the effectiveness of such a move is questionable,[2] the traditional logic is "the more lines the better"—particularly in a close race. DACC pushed hard for the second ballot spot, but, because the requisite signatures could only be gathered by voters registered in the district, the legion of personnel sent from Albany could provide no help. The most they could do was prod the Locals—which they did frequently. The signature gathering process was slow, tedious work, especially in the harsh North Country winter. Anxiety and hostility between the camps grew.

The relationship worsened when, for whatever reason (there are several rival explanations), the leaders of the county party committees failed to submit to the local Boards of Election the necessary paperwork to list Garrow on the ballot as the Democratic candidate. A tremendous blunder had occurred, and Garrow's chance of victory was greatly damaged by the oversight. DACC turned up the heat on the Locals to gather four thousand signatures, well over twice the necessary amount, in order to secure the second line—now the only line. Without that ballot position, the election would be over before it began.

The residual effect of the gaffe was a new source of animosity between DACC and local party activists. DACC officials, now financially deep in the Garrow campaign, were furious. Without the Democratic line, the chances of success were slim, and they did not hide their disappointment and frustration. From the Locals' perspective, the omnipresent pressure of "Fink's Raiders" was an intrusion on their turf. Although DACC supplied dozens of workers and trunks of money, it was, after all, "run by New York City hacks who knew little of North Country life or politics."[3]

The growing hostility did not end there. Perhaps the greatest area of conflict centered around strategic decisions during the campaign. The two camps passionately disagreed over the appropriate way to reach voters. The Locals believed radio and television were the best way to disseminate Garrow's message (the Plattsburgh/Burlington area is a relatively cheap, inclusive media market). Genovesi, having been seasoned in New York City politics, chose to rely on direct mail. It was, he argued, the best way to ensure that the entire "target group" would be exposed to Garrow's name and message. The Locals argued forcefully that electronic media were less expensive and more effective, but because DACC held control of the purse strings they were never used.

By the end of the campaign nearly twenty *district wide* mailings were sent on Garrow's behalf. They were, by most counts, drab pieces of mail. According to Genovesi, the idea was to use black and white to suggest (on a subliminal level) newspapers, ergo, legitimacy and trustworthiness. Because they were all mailed over a short period of time, it was not uncommon for voters to receive several pieces each day. Genovesi argued that this type of saturation would increase the candidate's name recognition, but the Locals believed the technique would only feed the time-honored theme that all Democrats were "pawns of New York City interests."[4] This was not, they exclaimed, the way candidates ran for office in the North Country. If it did increase Garrow's name recognition, it would be in a negative direction.

As for the candidate, his loyalties were torn. He could side with the Locals at the risk of losing his entire campaign treasury, or he could play along with Genovesi and DACC, at the risk of alienating his friends and fellow party regulars—as well as losing the campaign.

By election day, hostilities had reached a boiling point. The Locals had renounced their association with DACC, and Genovesi had the windows of his headquarters covered; neither the media nor party volunteers were allowed to enter. DACC operatives worked on their own, often duplicating the work of the Locals. Although DACC made a tremendous last minute push—as many as forty people were sent from Albany during the last weekend of the campaign to "hit the streets," and literature was mailed by the truckload—Garrow lost the election 15,130 to 11,988.

Within hours of the polls closing, the DACC entourage departed Plattsburgh leaving behind a legacy of hostility that has lingered for years. As an interesting and perhaps relevant epilogue, six of the DACC operatives involved in the Plattsburgh Special were fired. Several claimed they were let go because they had criticized DACC policy. This type of divided loyalty was deemed intolerable. Although enrollment numbers remain roughly even, Albany Democrats have avoided involvement in the North Country.

The Republican Team

The story of Republican effort in the Plattsburgh Special, on the other hand, is one of teamwork. For starters, they had foreknowledge of Ryan's plan to run for District Attorney, which allowed them to begin assessing candidates and themes long before the Democrats. Shortly after the November election, both state and local Republicans agreed on Christopher Ortloff, a former local television news anchor, as their candidate. Two lines were quickly secured (Republican and Conservative), and the campaign was underway.

The Republican Assembly Campaign Committee also played a significant role. Unlike DACC, local party regulars were involved at every stage of the campaign, from the planning of the overall strategy to its implementation. There was a mutual agreement that Ortloff, being a familiar face on television, should rely on electronic media. The local party was called upon to conduct grassroots activities, such as literature drops and telephone banks, while RACC produced radio and television spots in Albany. The number of operatives sent to Plattsburgh was only a fraction of their Democratic counterparts.

Ortloff also played a larger role in the direction of the campaign. He felt strongly about a number of conservative issues and made sure his campaign focused on them.

In many ways, Republican efforts in the Plattsburgh Special represented a model of teamwork and interdependence. The campaign professionals from Albany were able to supplement local organization resources with state-of-the-art campaign technologies.

If the truth be told, however, much of the Republican success can be attributed to the conflict among the Democrats. The hostility between DACC and the Locals reinforced the Republican line that Albany Democrats were trying to "buy the seat" and Garrow, if elected, would be but another of Fink's pawns. Republican gains were thus closely linked to Democratic disunity.

The Melding of Legislative Campaign Committees
with Traditional Party Organizations

This short detour into the annals of New York State politics is illustrative of the overall thrust of this book. The research focuses on the emergence of state-level legislative campaign committees (LCCs) and their relationship with traditional geographic party organizations (state, county, and city committees). It examines the import of LCCs from a party perspective. That is, the focus is on where these new units fit in the party structure, their relationship with various elements of the organization, their activities in comparison to traditional party functions, and their impact on existing structures. Although recent studies are replete with approval for these new organizations—they are pointed to as a response to the changing political environment—their relationship with and bearing on state and grassroots party organizations has not been examined in any systematic way.

Over three hundred traditional party leaders (state and county chairs) were interviewed. The picture that emerged is one of dualism, not integration. Moreover, the scope of LCC activities and their perceived aversion to broad-based party projects suggest a reexamination of their partylike nature. Rather than being evidence of party adjustment or growth, LCCs are best viewed as independent, election-driven machines, little different than campaign consulting firms.

Prior to the late 1970s, few state legislative caucuses (or legislative leaders) had established centralized campaign units. Throughout the early 1980s they flourished, and today are found in forty states. In addition to providing financial assistance to incumbents, challengers, and open-seat candidates, state LCCs now furnish extensive high-tech campaign services such as polling, computer data base facilities, direct mail services, electronic media production, campaign consultants, and overall campaign strategies. Many now provide candidate services which far outweigh the assistance of traditional party units and political action committees. In many states they have become the dominant player in state legislative elections.

Perhaps eager to find evidence of renewal, most students of parties seem to welcome their arrival. John Bibby, a leading scholar in this field, notes: "State legislative campaign committees, composed of incumbent legislators, operate in both the upper and lower chambers of most state legislatures. These committees have become the principle party-support institutions for legislative campaigns in many states" (Bibby 1990, 31). Anthony Gierzynski, in the only other full length work on state-level LCCs to date, suggests they have "developed, or are developing into what are indisputably party organizations. . . . Adaptation [to the modern political environment] has spread to the state level" (Gierzynski 1992, 116–119).

Such salutations may be premature. Scholarly research on state LCCs has been limited to aggregate analysis of their resources and expenditures and a small set of interviews with LCC officials. An examination from the perspective of traditional party organizations (TPOs) has not, to date, been conducted.

If these new units are not coupled with traditional party organizations and, in fact, compete with them for influence and resources, they may represent a new challenge to parties. Throughout our nation's history, political parties have been important community organizations linking citizens to their government. They help coalesce an exceedingly complex system and give voters a choice—both in candidates and in policies. American parties encourage participation, mediate conflict, and empower the economically disadvantaged. If state LCCs are found to be autonomous, narrowly focused, office- and level-specific campaign machines, their collision with traditional parties may be no less, and perhaps more significant, than single-issue groups, candidate-centered campaigns or political action committees (PACs). At the very least their growth would not imply "party" maturation or adjustment.

By examining these new units from a traditional party vantage, this book speaks to how political organizations are formed. It is frequently and forcefully argued that state LCCs were created to fill a void left by the parties. Nevertheless, their goals, activities, and interactions with party committees may defy this functionalist view. Perhaps their development was (is) independent of party dynamics. And it is even possible, as will be argued in subsequent chapters, that their rapid growth is a reaction to *expanding* state party organizations.

This book also examines the transformation of political communications from a direct, personal means, to impersonal, high-technology techniques. Not long ago voters were solicited by local party volunteers on their door steps. This type of personal contact helps forge a link between citizens and elected officials. Political communication today is often remote and unidirectional—that is, voters *get* information but are unable to *give* information. While many see this change as troublesome (Polsby 1983, in particular), others seem to accept it as inevitable and not altogether disruptive (Kayden and Mahe 1985). This research looks at the role of LCCs in this transformation. It will be shown that these units rely on professional consultants with little or no ties to the communities where they are campaigning and find little value in grassroots activities. Even if we were to find room in our notion of party to include LCCs, how these units operate and what they seek to accomplish may imply that they are less beneficial than previously envisioned.

Traditional Parties, LCCs, and Popular Governance

Because they are new and have only recently caught the eye of scholars, little is known about where state-level legislative campaign committees fit in. We might speculate three possibilities; they represent a positive development, a harmful change, or will have little impact on existing structures and practices. To a large extent this depends on one's view of party.

With little conceptual precision, the intonation of recent LCC studies (as noted above) suggests that they signify a positive development. By coming to grips with new technologies, sophisticated methods of campaigning, and modern finance restraints, LCCs have helped parties become relevant, if not central players, in state legislative elections. Party organizations are better able to meet the challenge of PAC influence and candidate-centered campaigns.

From a Downsian (1957) vantage, LCCs may indirectly provide several systemic benefits. By using resources in open and challenge races, as well as reelection campaigns, they may foster a competitive electoral environment. Electorates have become increasingly unpredictable, and heavily financed challengers can now defeat incumbents in otherwise "safe" districts. Legislative campaign committees have been at the forefront of saturation campaigning—i.e., the shifting of campaign resources from noncompetitive races to a few targeted ones. One of their goals appears to be to acquire or maintain a majority of legislative seats. As such, interparty competition might also increase. Second, because state legislative candidates now require huge war chests and LCCs have been able to tap into a flood of special interest money, responsible party government may become a byproduct. In order for members to receive assistance, they may be called upon to toe the party line and support the caucus. This "team-centered" atmosphere in legislatures may lead to coherent policy development.

The flow of campaign contributions to legislative leaders may also break the link between special interests and rank and file members. (Loftus 1994, 39) "By collecting resources from PACs and legislators who receive contributions from PACs, legislative party caucus campaign committees [may be] placing an extra step or two between candidates and interest group influence" (Gierzynski 1992, 122).

Responsible party advocates, those who perceive a close link between popular governance and intermediary structures, might sense relief as well. Party organizations now appear to have sufficient institutional support resources—money, staff, and facilities—to better articulate, aggregate, and mobilize interest. The connection between people and government is enhanced in this "strong party" environment. Legislative responsibility will surely increase, as will the congruity of defined policy alternatives. The resolution and mediation of conflict will no longer fall to the haphazard whims of elite-based interest groups. At each level (individual, institutional, and systemic) it may be argued that the democratic process is strengthened by the development of LCCs.

These perspectives assume a close fit between traditional party organizations and LCCs: again, that LCCs are, in fact, an adjustment by *the parties*. If the link between LCC and traditional parties is much looser, however, several additional questions should be raised: To what extent are the activities performed by LCCs similar to traditional party activities? If the functional analogy is strained, to what degree do LCCs compete with TPOs? Finally, if they do, in fact, compete with TPOs, what impact will they have on party organizations and, in turn, our political system?

To understand why such a development may have serious implications, it may be helpful to examine briefly the central functions rendered by traditional parties.

One of the foremost roles performed by parties (and perhaps the most immediately apparent) is forging united action within an exceedingly complex, diffuse political system (the aggregation of interests). Separation of powers, bicameralism, federalism, layers of jurisdictions, regionalism, ethnic divisions, and many other forces drive our government in disparate directions. Students and practitioners of politics have acknowledged the instrumental role played by parties to overcome, in V. O. Key's (1964) terms, this "constitutional obstruction."

A theme emerging from LCC studies suggests that these organizations are, first and foremost, concerned with elections in their own house of the legislature. While each party caucus may be more unified and seemingly stronger, that is not to say policy development will be either coherent or timely. Without inclusive party structures linking the branches, a great advantage goes to those seeking obstruction and gridlock. This may be particularly acute in difficult times—such as budget politics—where painful, long-term solutions are necessary. Key notes: "The independence of candidacies in an atomized politic makes it possible to elect a fire-eating governor who promises great accomplishments and simultaneously to elect a legislature a majority of whose members are committed to inaction" (Key 1949, 308).

If LCCs are found to be myopic, office-specific campaign units, it is doubtful they can or will choose to fulfill any unifying role. From an election-centered guise there are few incentives to support a party ticket. Any such "added baggage" may only hinder efficacy. In fact, it may even suit their needs to distance members from unpopular candidates on the party ticket—including the gubernatorial candidate. The same might be said about the articulation and support of a set of policy alternatives, e.g., a party platform. Instead of joining with other components of the party to enact a platform, each LCC will pursue those issues that best aid their candidates.

Without party structures to bridge this constitutional obstruction, it becomes increasingly difficult for citizens to distinguish the "ins" from the "outs." Accountability judgments become impossible. When candidates in each house and each branch run independent of, and often at odds with, candidates under the same party banner, notions of policy responsibility are obscured. The electorate is left disheartened, confused, and apathetic. The voter knows neither whom to blame or praise.

The importance of nominating and supporting a full range of candidates ("slating") is apparent from yet another perspective. It has fallen exclusively upon party organizations to offer alternatives in noncompetitive areas and in districts with entrenched incumbents. Although basic to democracy and the concept of accountability, it is very doubtful that nonaligned, election-driven units would use resources for the sole purpose of providing voters a choice. Their functional mandate, as will be seen below, appears to be quite the opposite: to concentrate resources *only* on close races.

Traditional local parties organize and oversee elections, encourage political participation, and educate voters. The degree to which LCCs would be willing to perform these functions is again dependent upon each activity's electoral utility. LCCs are not community-based structures. The use of imported campaign professionals is evidence of their transient nature. Activities such as educating the public and encouraging civic participation will be conducted sporadically, if at all.

Local parties are often seen as channels through which demands of participation can be accommodated and new groups of citizens brought into the political system. Community-based parties (i.e., the Locals) in particular, provide an important outlet for the fulfillment of perceived civic duties. "They are communities in themselves, which function to promote broader involvement in the larger community"

(Pomper 1980, 9). For many Americans they are also important social institutions. Again, such functions cannot be afforded by ephemeral, transient campaign organizations. Additionally, a shift of political communication from personal to high technology may trigger declining governing legitimacy. Local party organizations reduce the distance between private feelings and public life by promoting civic virtue (McWilliams 1980, 53). If the revolt against the nationalization of government is prolonged, the import of grass-roots party structures may be heightened.

It may be argued that community-based party structures do a better job of selecting competent, qualified candidates than do organizations that endorse candidates based *solely* on their ability to win. (The same might be said regarding the disclosure of corruption.) By creating socialization mechanisms and incentive structures, grass-roots parties perform an important screening and promotion incentive function, perhaps not furnished by LCCs.

Finally, although the link between legislators and special interest money may be weakened by LCCs, the new relationship between contributors and legislative leaders may make it easier for the former to unduly influence policy. To be sure, the very fact that interest groups now direct contributions to the caucus leadership, rather than rank-and-file members, implies a centralization of power.

If, then, state LCCs are independent of traditional party organizations and only perform office-specific campaign activities, a logical query is whether the two can coexist. Perhaps. But the concerns of party scholars regarding the growth of candidate-centered campaigns, single issue groups, and PACs would seem equally relevant here. Nonaligned campaign organizations invariably compete for resources and influence. As support from one structure increases, dependency on the other decreases.

A State-Level Focus

While the Plattsburgh Special, as well as the remainder of this research, speaks to state-level LCCs, the complexity and importance of this new development can be seen at the national level as well. We are thankful to scholars such as David Adamany, Paul Herrnson, Diana Dwyre, and Gary Jacobson for their work on national-level LCCs. A considerable body of research has been accumulated on the four national committees: the Democratic Congressional Campaign Committee (DCCC), National Republican Campaign Committee (NRCC), the Democratic Senatorial Campaign Committee (DSCC), and the National Republican Senatorial Committee (NRSC). Blossoming in the early 1980s—perhaps due to the lack of national committee resources—these organizations are now viewed as integral parts of the national party organizations. Their base of resources and services provided to candidates seems to suggest the parties are again "making a difference" (Herrnson 1986).

Nevertheless, if these congressional organizations are truly integral parts of the national party committees, why would, for example, the Director of the National Republican Campaign Committee (then Ed Rollins) advise Republican House members "not [to] hesitate to oppose the President...."[5] Historically the President has been viewed as the head of the party. Is there now a division between executive and congressional parties? Perhaps a better understanding of the relationship between the Hill Committees and the national party organizations is also needed.

Resisting the above temptation, this study limits its focus to state-level organizations. State LCCs are a development of the last decade and only now gaining attention. The new relationship between these new units and local party committees, termed the *key cogs* in the party structure by a leading party scholar (Eldersveld 1982), is a timely, important topic of study.

Areas of Inquiry

The emerging relationship between LCCs and party organizations represents a complex development with a number of subtle nuances. Consequently, several approaches and areas of inquiry will be used. The core of the analysis consists of three sets of surveys: 1) a case study of New York State where leaders of both state party committees and seventy-eight county committee chairs were interviewed; 2) a survey of state party leaders throughout the nation, including those in states currently without LCCs; and 3) a survey of county party chairs in Ohio, Tennessee, Indiana, and Florida. In total, over three hundred traditional party leaders have provided their input regarding these new organizations.

The analysis looks first at formal and informal linkages, as well as the variables which may alter this relationship. An examination of the types of activities performed by both LCCs and TPOs will then be undertaken. Conceivably, they operate independently but conduct the same tasks. On the other hand, beyond supporting the same candidates for state legislative office, perhaps LCC activities are much narrower or unique. Are these new units, for example, concerned with general party building activities—such as voter registration drives and community service?

The more general perceptions of traditional party leaders will be another area of inquiry. How do state and local party leaders see legislative campaign committees? Are they as optimistic about LCCs as are most party scholars? Simply put, to objectively label these new organizations a boon for parties we might also ask the subjective views of those in the political vineyards.

Finally, with these steps taken we can begin to answer whether or not LCCs are truly appendages of traditional party committees, and how their activities and goals compare with traditional party activities and goals. We can then speculate how they might impact existing structures and popular governance.

At the outset, it is important to note the dearth of state-level LCC studies. Malcolm Jewell and David Olson's (1988) work on state party organizations presents a modest look at these new committees. This material is certainly helpful and no doubt has been the impetus for several recent works, yet it is limited by its cursory and somewhat outdated data. More recent studies are generally limited in their analysis to only one or a handful of states (Rose 1987; Johnson 1987; Jewell and Breaux 1989; Stonecash 1990, 1991; Salmore and Salmore 1989; Gierzynski and Breaux 1991; Dwyre and Stonecash 1992; Redfield 1992; Simon-Rosenthal 1993; Shea 1991). Unfortunately, many of these studies are unpublished (e.g., conference papers). Anthony Gierzynski (1992), in a work cited extensively throughout this book, can be credited with the most comprehensive analysis to date. Yet he examines only one-third of the LCCs and leaves a number of questions unanswered.

A second caveat is that the diversity of LCCs makes neat typologies difficult. The structure, function, and objectives of each LCC are somewhat unique. Variables contributing to this variety may include environmental constraints, each state's political history, the stage of development, personal dynamics, and many other nuances. Although generalizations are suggested, the numerous variety of these organizations should be kept in mind.

Blueprint of the Book

Chapter 1 presents a review of state legislative campaign committees; their distribution throughout the nation, their structure, modes of operation, and role in state legislative campaigns. Chapter 2 takes a close look at the reasons for their development. Were LCCs simply created as a response to waning party strength?

Chapter 3 looks at traditional geographic party organizations. Why study the relationship between two units if one is no longer relevant? Here the vitality of state and local party committees is assessed, and the tenets of both the rational-efficient and party-democracy models are outlined. The end of the chapter presents a hybrid view of American parties. With these steps taken, the remainder of the analysis can proceed from a theoretical grounding.

Chapter 4 sets out a list of expectations and hypotheses regarding this new relationship, as well as the impact of a number of control variables. On the whole, it is expected that few formal linkages and a limited range of project interdependence will be found. The services provided by the LCCs will be much more candidate specific than those activities performed by traditional party units, particularly local organizations, and the perceptions of party leaders will suggest a reexamination of the merging of the two. This chapter also outlines the data used to test these expectations.

Chapter 5 presents the case study of New York. This state was one of the first to develop LCCs and has historically maintained strong party organizations. A number of interesting findings are reviewed. Chapter 6 looks at the state-level relationship throughout the nation. This is followed in Chapter 7 by an analysis of county-level dynamics in four states. Chapter 8 synthesizes findings with the hybrid model of traditional party organizations, suggests how changes within state legislatures have driven LCCs from the party fold, and discusses the future of traditional parties in an era of rational-efficient legislative campaign organizations.

It is argued in the conclusion that numerous changes—foremost of which has been the legislative professionalization movement during the past two decades—have led to the growth of LCCs and that these new units are best viewed independent of traditional parties. As distinct organizations that perform a narrow range of activities, state-level LCCs may prove to be yet another challenge to traditional parties. Legislative campaign committees were created to endow legislators and caucus leadership with vast resources and centralized campaign services without the constraints of party labels, tickets, and platforms. Unlike party structures, there are few mechanisms or incentives to link branches of government or houses of the legislature. They may be thus fueling, in Walter Dean Burnham's terms, the "accelerated decomposition of nominally partisan coalitions across office specific and level specific lines" (1989, 20). Their use of transient campaign operatives and indirect modes of communication may be contributing to public alienation and apathy. Moreover, as the power and influence of these organizations grows, the powers and activities performed by traditional party organizations will decline. Rather than being evidence of party renewal, this book suggests LCCs are but another agent in the "radical recomposition of the American political system" (Burnham 1989, 20).

One

Some Background on State Legislative Campaign Committees

An appropriate place to begin the examination of the new relationship between state legislative campaign organizations and traditional party units is with a brief look at the former. What are legislative campaign committees (LCCs), and what do they do? What difference do they make in state politics? This chapter sketches the short history of these new organizations.

WHAT ARE STATE LEGISLATIVE CAMPAIGN COMMITTEES?

Legislative campaign committees are appendages of the legislative caucus, created to support and manage state legislative campaigns. Fashioned after the four national congressional campaign committees, they provide a centralized pool of resources and expertise for reelection, open-seat, and challenge candidates. They may be active during election periods or the entire legislative cycle. In some states—primarily ones with professional legislatures—LCCs provide extensive campaign services, such as candidate seminars, survey research, media production, direct mail, and computerized targeting. In these states they have become dominant players in legislative elections. In other states their services are more modest, generally limited to cash contributions.

State legislative campaign committees have been active since the late 1970s in New York, Illinois, Wisconsin, California, and Minnesota. They have recently (during the late 1980s) taken hold throughout the nation. Forty states now host LCCs. Figure 1.1 highlights where they are currently located. Factors contributing to their growth and dispersion will be discussed in detail.

In states which have LCCs, there are generally four units—one for each party in each house of the legislature. For example, in Illinois

17

Table 1.1
States with Legislative Campaign Committees

	Yes	No		Yes	No
Northeast					
Connecticut	X		Vermont	X	
New Hampshire	X		New Jersey	X	
Maine	X		New York	X	
Massachusetts	X		Pennsylvania	X	
Rhode Island	X				
Midwest					
Illinois	X		Kansas	X	
Indiana	X		Minnesota	X	
Michigan	X		Nebraska		X
Ohio	X		North Dakota		X
Wisconsin	X		South Dakota	X	
Iowa	X				
South					
Delaware	X		Kentucky		X
Florida	X		Mississippi		X
Georgia	NA		Tennessee	X	
Maryland	X		Arkansas	X	
North Carolina	X		Louisiana	NA	
South Carolina		X	Oklahoma	X	
Virginia	X			X	
West Virginia	X		Texas	X	
Alabama		X	Missouri		
West					
Arizona		X	Utah	X	
Colorado	X		Wyoming		X

	Yes	No		Yes	No
California	X		Alaska	X	
Idaho	X		Hawaii	X	
Montana	X		Oregon	X	
Nevada	X		Washington	X	
New Mexico	X				

Source: Gierzynski 1992 and Simon-Rosenthal 1993

there are the House Republican Campaign Committee, the Republican State Senate Campaign Committee, the Illinois Democratic Majority Committee, and the Committee to Reelect a Democratic Senate.[1] Legislative campaign committees of the same party (in the same state) generally operate independently of one another—thereby limiting their activities to campaigns in their branch of the legislature.[2] As such, when we speak of the LCCs in a given state, we are referring to four organizations operating in two election arenas.

In some states, LCCs are legal subdivisions of the state party committee. In Florida and New York they are formally linked with the state party committees. The distinction between legal edifice and practice, however, is often pronounced. Jewell and Olson note: "In New York the legislative campaign units are legal subdivisions of the state party committees but in practice are as autonomous as possible" (1986, 222). Gierzynski found *all* of the LCC officials in his study, noting "state party organization exercised no control over their activities" (1992, 49).[3]

Legislative campaign committees should be distinguished from leadership political action committees, which are used to transfer funds to state legislative candidates. Here caucus leadership collects and allocates money according to need, support for the leadership, or any other criteria (Gierzynski 1992, 101). There are no organizational structures or staff. Although leadership PACs are important financial variables in legislative campaigns, have implications for leadership and party discipline (Jewell and Olson 1988; Salmore and Salmore 1989), and are no doubt interesting, new players, the remainder of the work primarily centers on legislative campaign committees. The objective here is to uncover the linkages and interactions between the activities of the legislative campaign units and traditional parties. The latter plays no role in leadership PAC activities. As such, leadership PACs might be best viewed within the context of either party-in-government, election finance, or candidate-centered campaign studies.

HOW ARE LCCs ORGANIZED?

Thus far, LCCs are noted as appendages of the legislative caucus, organized to provide help during elections. Scholars of parties have, for some time, pointed to the importance of the structural dynamics of party organizations. By understanding how a unit is arranged, it is argued, insight is gained into its behavior and objectives. Speaking of traditional party organizations, Eldersveld writes:

> Parties came into existence to perform certain critical functions for the system, and derived their basic form in the process of implementing these functions. If one is interested in understanding the tasks presumably fulfilled by parties, it is necessary to analyze the party as a functional structural subsystem (1964, 164).

This is certainly no less true for state legislative campaign committees.

An important, yet rarely cited, distinction within LCCs is the difference between the "official committee" and the "operations unit." The *official committee* refers to the organization *within* the caucus that makes up the campaign committee. The variety of these structures is vast. In some states official committees are composed of the entire membership of the party caucus. Others have actual committees consisting of a chair and several members appointed by leadership. Various positions, such as finance director, distribution chair, or voter registration officer, may be divided among the committee members. A third type is where legislative leaders form the entire committee; examples are in Oregon and Wisconsin. Finally, a few official committees include individuals who are not members of the legislature. The House Democratic Campaign Committee in Maine includes the state treasurer and state auditor, in addition to the caucus leadership. Illinois and Indiana have similar arrangements (Gierzynski 1992, 46–47).

The exact locus of control within official committees is difficult to discern. Does it always follow that "committees" have dispersed oversight, and are therefore more democratic, than units with centralized decision-making structures? Do rank-and-file members have a greater say in committee-based LCCs? The answer to this query (more generally) has puzzled scholars for some time. Francis (1985), for example, found that, in roughly one-half of state chambers, party caucus leadership was the principal instrument for expressing control, regardless of structural dynamics.[4] We might suggest, at the very least, that official committee control would parallel other internal dynamics. That is, in those states with strong leadership structures or a tradition of aggressive caucus leaders, the LCCs will fall under the same rubric. The exact number of rank-and-file members seated on official committees will say little about who controls their activities.

Gierzynski (1992, 50) found it useful to place control of LCCs along a continuum—ranging from an inclusive arrangement where all members have input (far left) to an exclusive structure where only caucus leadership influence decisions (far right). This analysis, based solely on official committee structure, suggests that most of the LCCs lean toward the right side of the continuum. From his *interviews*, however, he finds nearly all of the respondents mentioned that party leadership controls the activities of these organizations. Although the wishes of members were considered, final decisions were made by legislative caucus leadership.

It is also perhaps no little matter that caucus leadership generally raises the lion's share of LCC resources. As argued in the next chapter, a core impetus behind the development of these new units has been the explosion of special interest money at the state level during the past decade. Rather than contributing to rank-and-file members, much of this money is channeled to caucus leadership because of its position of power. Rarely concerned with their own reelections, it is used by leadership to pursue other goals, including the augmentation of the size of the caucus. It stands to reason that if leadership raises most of LCC money, it will have control over that unit's activities.

When we speak of legislative campaign organizations, then, we are referring to the electoral strong-arms of the legislative caucus elite. To view these units as collectives, or aggregates, of member goals implies a decision-making process which may be inaccurate. Legislative leaders do pay attention to their members; few would remain so if they did not. But neither are LCCs simply democratic, committee-based organizations. They are structures used at the discretion of the caucus leadership, with input from the rank-and-file membership, to pursue their goals and objectives.

Operations units are the vehicles through which services are provided to state legislative candidates. Professional campaign staff generally form the core of these organizations, particularly those in states with full-time legislatures. They may be employed on a yearly basis or only during campaigns; most LCCs have both. Personnel hired only during campaigns are generally employed with the state legislature during the "off season." In New York, for example, Democratic operatives in the Assembly work either directly on the Speaker's staff or indirectly as part of "Communications Services," and Republican LCC staffers work for Minority Leadership or "Minority Research."

In many ways, operation units are similar to campaign consulting firms. Several have sophisticated computer and media resources at their disposal, run year-round direct mail programs, and have ongoing polling units. Paid operatives are not necessarily members of the party or even enrolled voters in that state. Many view themselves as campaign or marketing professionals rather than traditional party hacks.

These units are physically and structurally removed from the legislative caucus. In some states they are housed in the state party headquarters, but in most they are located elsewhere.

A rough abstract of the lines of authority in operation units consists of directors, regional coordinators, and foot soldiers. The directors oversee the entire workings of the units and report directly to the caucus leadership. Regional coordinators oversee several legislative districts or counties and make recommendations regarding LCC involvement, i.e., which races to target. During campaigns they either supervise one or a small set of races. In some instances they become the candidate's campaign manager, while in others they serve as persons who coordinate activities. Foot soldiers, as the name implies, remain either at the central headquarters helping to provide general services (such as running telephone banks or stuffing envelopes) or are sent to one of the targeted campaigns to do general scutt work, such as putting up posters and canvassing. In very few instances are they sent to work directly for the candidate or his/her campaign manager. During the final phases of campaigns, remaining foot soldiers are sent to close races to help with last minute projects—such as literature drops and get-out-the-vote (GOTV) drives.

The balance between legislative work (e.g., state business) and campaign activities has been a sticky issue for LCCs. As noted, the professionals who run the operations units are often also legislative employees. Gierzynski found it "frequently and strongly emphasized that, though the staff used for the operation of the campaign committees often came from regular legislative staff, they were hired separately on their own free time" (1992, 47). In Illinois, however, every professional legislative staff position is partisan, and most staffers are deployed by party leadership to work with the LCC during elections (Salmore and Salmore 1989, 198). This practice is by no means unique to Illinois.

Legislative campaign committee operatives in New York were accused of conducting their activities while on the state payroll. In the Fall of 1987 Manfred Ohrenstein, Minority Leader of the New York State Senate, was indicted on 564 counts of conspiracy, grand larceny, and related charges. The prosecution argued he had used state employees solely for the purpose of running campaigns.[5] One of the counts claimed operatives were paid up to $10,000 per month of state monies while conducting campaign activities. Ohrenstein argued that the indictment violated the line between legislative and executive affairs and that no law had been passed limiting such practices. Although this claim carried little weight in the lower courts, it was supported by the New York State Court of Appeals in the Fall of 1990. The Court said that, while hiring employees for campaign activities represented a gray area of ethics, there had been no laws forbidding it. Both houses of the New York State Legislature have since passed resolutions banning the hiring of operatives *solely* for campaign activities. Ohrenstein continued to serve as Minority Leader and oversee Senate Democratic election activities until 1993.

At the very least this arrangement, termed *tandem jobs* by *The New York Times* (September 19, 1990, 33), allows LCCs to contract the services of high-priced campaign professionals at a fraction of their salary. In most states these people are removed from the state payroll for the final month (or so) of the election and paid by the LCC. Whether they are involved prior to this point only on their own time is debatable. In any event, this practice affords candidates considerably more resources than mere disclosure information (the heart of recent LCC studies) would suggest. Even the most modestly funded LCC is able to utilize cutting-edge professionals. Without this arrangement, the impact of LCCs would clearly be less significant.

Beyond the scope of this work, the extent to which this type of cross-over activity occurs, its legality, legitimacy, and impact on campaigns is an important development in state politics. One perspective might hold that the parties have found a new way to provide patronage positions to loyal party workers. Those supportive of strong party organizations might find reason to condone, if not applaud, this practice. On the other hand, tandem jobs may be part of a centralizing, professional movement in party politics, and bode poorly for traditional local parties. Either way, this activity is yet another important dimension of LCCs which has not received close scholarly attention.

The relationship between the official committees and the operations units is another foggy area. Domineering legislative leaders may be directly involved in the oversight of their operations unit. They may provide instructions on every aspect: where, when, how, and on whom to spend resources. This appeared to be the case in Ohio, for example, where Democratic House Speaker Vern Rife had a strong hand in all his unit's activities. In other cases the committees may defer to the director of the unit. They may give broad directives, such as win more seats, but, on the whole, leave the operatives to choose which races to assist and distribute resources as they see fit. This type of arrangement exists for both majority party LCCs in New York.

Understanding these nuances and variations, along with other organizational factors such as legal restrictions and available resources, provides an important glimpse into LCC goals and activities. We might speculate, for instance, that LCCs with greater membership participation would focus more on reelection strategies than on open- and challenge-seat campaigns. These LCCs might be used as merely a caucus resource.[6] On the other hand, committees controlled by leadership might be more willing to concentrate on close elections—including open and challenge races. Other variations in strategies might be seen by looking at the difference between well-funded and less affluent organizations. Minority party LCCs, generally with less financial resources than majority party organizations, might spend more time on challenge- and open-seat races than on reelection campaigns.

Each of these subtleties may also provide telling information pertaining to the relationship between these new units and traditional party organizations. For instance, we might expect traditional party leaders to hold a closer, more positive working relationship with members of the official committee than with operation unit professionals. The latter's directives (to win legislative elections) are narrow and may not completely parallel party objectives—that is, support for a ticket or platform may be of little concern to LCC operatives. As such, LCCs with independent, aggressive operation

units (directors) may have sparse interactions with party committees. This appears to have been the case with the Democratic organization in the Plattsburgh Special. Official committee members (legislators), on the other hand, may hold an affinity for, or be the product
of, local party organizations. They may share the full range of concerns as party leaders. Nevertheless, as suggested above, their role
in LCC decisions and activities is generally limited.

In summary, the structural characteristics of state LCCs provide
important, yet limited, insight. Even Gierzynski's (1992) constrained
rationality model—where organizational forces are combined with an
individual rational choice perspective—may underplay the role of
caucus leaders and other actors. Studies which link the activities of
LCCs exclusively to either legislative leaders, the party caucus, nonlegislative officials, or party agents—rather than a complex interaction between these players—may be misguided. Just as scholars
eventually rejected the fixed, hierarchical model of American party
organizations in favor of stratarchy, more work needs to be done to
fully understand the structural nuances and interplay of forces within
LCCs.

Perhaps state LCCs are in a stage of development where structural typologies are premature. Each state's political history, environmental constraints, and individual influences will surely make organizational generalizations difficult.[7] Yet, as Eldersveld appropriately
notes: "Too much party research in America has had to settle for partial images of political reality" (1964, 2).

THE ROLE OF LCCs
IN STATE LEGISLATIVE ELECTIONS

The principal service performed by early state LCCs was to collect
money from political action committees (PACs) and channel it, on a
fairly equal basis, to all caucus members (Johnson 1987). They were
designed to protect incumbents and maintain the party's share of
seats in the legislature. Members were free to spend the money with
little interference from the committee. Thus, original state LCCs were
mere financial conduits—similar to leadership PACs today.

It soon became apparent that there were limits to this practice.
First, giving cash directly to members did not ensure its most effective use. There were few guarantees that the member would spend it
wisely (or at all), and a clash between old styles of campaigning and
new techniques emerged. Why would a LCC provide scarce resources

to a member, only to have it spent on bumper stickers and refrigerator magnets instead of more proven vote-getting tactics? Second, direct contributions are limited by statute in some states (Alexander 1992, 138). Even in the states which do not limit donations, reporting requirements often created problems; few candidates wish to be seen as a pawn of the party or the caucus leadership. In-kind contributions or services would better mask LCC support. Third, although cash contributions might help secure incumbent reelections, it did nothing to *expand* the seats held by the caucus. Finally, a vehicle was needed to establish priorities of resource allocation, e.g., safe seats versus marginal ones.

Over the past decade the services provided by LCCs and the types of candidates receiving this help have changed considerably. In addition to helping incumbents, they now assist challengers and open-seat candidates. There has also been a shift from direct contributions to support services; only a few still exclusively provide cash. Most LCCs now furnish extensive high-technology campaign assistance—such as survey research, computer data base facilities, direct mail services, electronic media production, candidate seminars, and the use of experienced campaign operatives. During the 1984 election the Republican House and Senate committees in Illinois, for example, raised about $1,027,000 and spent 90 percent of it on behalf of candidates; only 10 percent was contributed directly (Jewell 1986, 11).

By centralizing support services, LCCs have found a means to minimize per-candidate costs and provide help throughout the entire election cycle. Services also allow these committees to have more control over activities and, in turn, make campaigns more professional. Similar to their national level counterparts, they have adapted to modern campaigning by becoming brokerage organizations (Herrnson 1988).

Another new element of LCC activity involves fund-raising assistance. While few provide direct cash contributions, LCCs often help candidates solicit PAC and special interest monies. Individuals and groups anxious to gain favor with legislative leaders, or perhaps change the partisan makeup of the legislature, look for guidance. In order to make the best use of their contributions, one strategy is to use it where it will make a difference—in other words, on close races (Cassie, Thompson and Jewell 1992; Sorauf 1988, 307–317; Redfield and Van Der Slik 1992).[8] The Indiana House Democrats, for example, sit down with interest groups to discuss which races to target (Gierzynski 1992, 55). Willy Brown, Democratic Speaker in the California House, conducts similar meetings. This process is, of course, often a self-fulfilled prophecy; targeted races become close races. Simply put, PACs are guided as to where to spend their money, and candidates are instructed as to where they might find it.

It should be noted this matchmaking service does not mean candidates are given free reign over the use of the contributions. Targeted races are closely supervised, and new funds rarely escape the committee's notice. The money simply is combined with the larger pool of resources often under the purview of the LCC.

Closely targeting races suggests another important distinction between incumbent reelection committees (LCCs of the past) and modern LCCs. Although their first priority may be still to protect caucus members, growing resources and incumbent security have allowed LCCs to move beyond these races to challenge- and open-seat campaigns. In some instances incumbents receive no assistance whatsoever (Dwyer and Stonecash 1990, 26). Campaigns are targeted carefully; resources are provided to close races rather than sure winners or sure losers (Jones and Borris 1985; Stonecash 1988; Giles and Prichard 1985; Johnson 1987; Jewell and Olson 1988, 219–22; Gierzynski 1992, 71–92).

Focusing resources on close races allows LCCs to be key players in state legislative elections, while at the same time providing only a small percent of all campaign funds. By selecting as few as ten per election, they can infuse each with unprecedented resources. A few examples may give an idea of their impact: In 1986, the California Assembly Democratic Committee spent $725,000 on one Sacramento-area open seat (Salmore and Salmore 1989, 193); and during that same year the Illinois Republican Senate Campaign Committee doled out $100,000 in support of its candidates in *each* of five districts (Johnson 1987). In 1992, the Ohio House Democrats spent nearly $100,000 on just three campaigns during the final days of the election (Ohio Secretary of State 1993).

It might be argued that this practice—choosing candidates based on their ability to win rather than simply incumbency—suggests these organizations are partylike In fact, this is precisely what Gierzynski (1992) suggests. Several studies have found parties more likely than PACs or individual donors to contribute to close elections rather than to safe incumbents (Jones and Borris 1985; Gierzynski and Breaux 1991). Whether or not such a modest criteria can alone distinguish these units as party oriented is debatable. In any event, the days of block grants, equally distributing funds to all incumbents, are over. Members now must demonstrate their perceived vulnerability in order to get LCC help—often a difficult task.

This strategy appears to be shared by both Democrats and Republicans, and there is little variance between regions or levels of party competition. Recent works have shown there are, however, strategic differences between majority and minority party LCCs (Dwyre and Stonecash 1992). The former tend to support close incumbent races to a larger degree than minority LCCs. The logic seems to be that, if you already control a body, you need only secure the seats you have. On the other hand, minority LCCs spend a larger portion on competitive challenge- and open-seat races than majority party LCCs. The idea is similar, but in reverse; to control the perks of majority status, additional seats must be won.

Another important characteristic of LCC disbursements, and perhaps more directly related to our concerns, is their candidate-specific nature. The services provided by these new organizations can be extensive but are generally geared toward legislative candidates only. Little effort is made to support other candidates under the party banner. In their study of Illinois LCCs, Redfield and Van Der Slik (1992) found only two percent of expenditures going to nonlegislative candidates. The same can be said about broad-based party activities. Only four of the thirty-two LCCs in Gierzynski's sample noted they conducted party building projects, such as get-out-the-vote drives (Gierzynski 1992, 50–56).

Occasionally, LCCs at the national level have engaged in general party promotions—such as the National Republican Campaign Committee "stay the course" program in 1982 and their pro-Republican/anti-Tip O'Neill media campaign prior to the 1984 election.[9] But, as Gary Jacobson has noted, "Republicans were sufficiently disappointed with the results of their national effort in 1984 to redirect their efforts into strengthening local campaigns; in 1986, for the first time in a decade, Republicans had no common campaign theme" (1987, 85). What is more, Richard Fenno's (1978) notion that members of Congress run for Congress by running against Congress suggests broad, party-oriented expenditures may be ineffective and potentially harmful to candidates. Appeals, such as "stay the course," run the risk of binding candidates to adverse national trends and loathsome institutions (Herrnson 1992, 65). Broad-based programs run counter to the growing reliance upon local issues, a development highlighted by Fenno, Morris Fiorina (1977), and David Mayhew

(1974), among others. There is no reason to speculate why state LCC leaders would perceive their political environment differently.[10]

Do patterns of LCC expenditures imply anything about the objectives of these organizations? Perhaps. Gierzynski (1992) suggests that there are three sets of actors who may be involved in LCC decisions: individual legislators, legislative leaders, and the legislative party. Each has primary goals and pursues them rationally: legislators are concerned with reelection; legislative leaders with winning reelection, majority status, and party discipline; and the legislative party with maximizing the seats held, party cohesion, and the enactment of party policies. Allocation patterns, he argues, parallel the wishes of the legislative party. Resources are used to maximize their impact on close elections, the party's share of seats in the legislature, and legislative behavior. This explains their shift from incumbent-centered organizations to general campaign units. Again, seats are not added by the former. Candidate-specific activities underscore the objectives of the legislative party; promoting a full slate of candidates may not help, and may, at times, hurt the party's desire to gain more seats.

This perspective is, nevertheless, too broad and overly optimistic. If the legislative party is *also* concerned with policy, as Gierzynski suggests, the candidate-specific activities of the LCCs may be irrational. It requires consent from two branches of the legislature, as well as support from the executive, to enact policy. Do house committees assist senate races? Do senate campaign committees help gubernatorial candidates? Again there is little evidence that such cross-over support occurs. We may feel more confident arguing that the principal objective, and perhaps sole objective, of LCCs is to maximize the number of seats held. This limited goal concurs with patterns of LCC activities and the objectives of both legislative leaders and caucus members. Any notion of a policy-based motivation of LCC activity is questionable. A comment by former Wisconsin House Speaker, Tom Loftus, regarding the objectives of his LCC is illustrative: "Our only test is that the candidate is in a winnable seat and he or she is breathing, and those two requirements are in order of importance . . ." (Tom Loftus 1985, 109–110).

Along similar lines, there is little evidence to suggest LCC resources are used as a reward or punishment for legislative behavior. In fact, conflicts may arise between the wishes of LCC operatives and the party caucus regarding certain issues. If a legislator's vote is perceived by the operatives as potentially harmful, they may wish that member to vote against the caucus—or, at the very least, "take a walk." Recall LCC professionals are generally granted a narrow mission: to win elections.

Discord over policy stances occurs frequently in states such as New York and Illinois, where the caucus holds heterogeneous constituencies. One issues that often divides the Democratic caucuses in New York is gun control. Legislators from New York City seek stronger limits, while Upstate Democrats have a difficult time supporting such measures. In fact, the Democratic Assembly Campaign Committee has sought the support of the National Rifle Association for several of their Upstate candidates. Needless to say, this alliance was upsetting to many of the more liberal members from the City. They have also mailed letters to sportsmen throughout the state strongly criticizing the gun control policies of the governor (Cuomo, also a Democrat). The language of these mailings is surprisingly confrontational and aggressive. In a roundabout way, LCCs may be contributing to the *decline* of the party in government. For LCC operatives, maintaining/augmenting the caucus is an end in itself. Policy enactment or intracaucus harmony may be either irrelevant or antithetical to their mission.

If we are to draw an overarching conclusion from this review, it might be that these units are complex new organizations. Our knowledge of their internal dynamics, goals, objectives, and activities is limited. While several scholars have sought to answer these questions within a single state, comprehensive works are scant. Legislative campaign committees are effective, and similar organizations will undoubtedly arise at lower levels. Much more needs to be done to understand their place in the political process.

Two

Possible Explanantions for the Growth of State LCCs

Explanations for the emergence of new political organizations, such as legislative campaign committees, are often unclear. Several general perspectives are frequently used. The sociological view centers on the *functions* desired by politicians, business leaders, or formal governmental institutions. When there exists a gap between the functions performed by an existing organization and the needs of its members, the unit will innovate, or new structures may be created to supplement or replace the inadequate organization (Merton 1945). The economic approach holds that political organizations, similar to business firms, appear when conditions are favorable. They are then used to win power and disburse benefits. Urban party machines represent a case in point. Along the same lines, Weber (1967) would integrate the economic perspective with the political entrepreneurs who, on their own account and risk, create and maintain a political organization as a tool of power. The formal rules and regulations found in these structures serve to legitimize its authority. The urban party boss typifies such political capitalists. Finally, Lipset and Rokkan (1967), Mayhew (1986),. and others focus on the historical antecedents and patterns of political, economic, and cultural traditions. Certain subcultures are more agreeable to political organizations than others. To understand why political organizations prosper in one area and not another, they argue that a broader cultural perspective is needed.

The functionalist perspective has certainly dominated explanations of both national and state-level LCC development to date. Herrnson, commenting on the growing significance of the Hill Committees, suggests they "provide some preliminary support for the hypothesis that parties are capable of adapting to the changing political environment" (1986, 594). Writing over a decade ago on state party dynamics, Robert Huckshorn noted that state-level LCCs exist only in cases of "weakened party structures" (Dwyer and Stonecash 1992, 328, citing Huckshorn 1980, 101). Salmore and Salmore concur: "Observers of legislative caucuses' activities often note the extent to which they have taken over the electoral functions of what was conventionally thought of as party organization. This usually occurs because of the weakness of those organizations" (1989, 197). More recently, Gierzynski has argued "the widespread existence of legislative party campaign committees . . . is undoubtedly a result of the need to fill a void [left by the state party committees]" (1992, 12).

Nearly all interpretations of LCC development follow a similar logic: 1) the cost and technical component of presidential and gubernatorial elections has spilled into congressional and state legislative campaigns; 2) in order to respond to these changing conditions, candidates sought to band together in a larger organization with greater resources and expertise; 3) traditional party units lack these resources; and 4) legislative campaign committees were created to fill the void. From this perspective advocates of strong parties welcome these new units. Legislative campaign committees are seen as a check on the shift toward candidate-centered campaigns. Rather than conceiving the growth of LCCs as distinct from, and perhaps in competition with, traditional party organizations, most party scholars tie them neatly together in a functionalist bundle.

Nevertheless, three broad criticisms can be raised regarding this perspective: unexplained variance between states with similar party organizations; a mistaken assumption regarding the historic roles of parties in state legislative campaigns; and the surprising weakness of minority party LCCs. Each will be discussed below.

LCC Growth and Weak Parties

Viewing LCCs as a response to weak parties does not explain variations in LCC development. For example, some of the earliest, most active LCCs were found in New York and California. These states have very different party traditions. Mayhew's exhaustive study of state party organizations finds California to be "the last place anybody would look to find traditional party organizations, and in fact none turns up in records of the last half century" (1986, 185). New York, on the other hand, is noted as one of only seven strong party organization states (196). Legislative campaign committees in California were not created to bolster party organizations but to substitute for the party organizations that never were (Salmore and Salmore 1989, 197).

In New York, LCCs coexist with some of the most viable party structures in the nation (Jewell and Olson 1988, 66).

Table 2.1 notes the correlation between party organization strength and LCC resources. Party vitality is assessed with five measures. The first is extracted from Mayhew's (1986) work; the level of analysis is the state and the scale ranges from 1 (a weak party organization state) to 5 (a strong party organization state).[1] The next four measures are from Cotter et al. (1984). They rank party organization strength at both the state and local level—for both Democratic and Republican organizations (pages 28–29 and 52–53, respectively).[2] Unfortunately, a similar state-by-state breakdown of LCC strength has not been conducted. For present purposes, Gierzynski's (1992) data

Table 2.1
Correlation between Party Organization Strength
and Legislative Campaign Committee Strength

| | Party Organization Measures | | |
| | | Cotter's Measures | |
	Mayhew's Scale	Local Dems	State Dems
LCC Strength (contributions in dollars)			
Dem House LCCs	.02	.03	.19
Dem Senate LCCs	.59*	.71*	−.27
		Local Reps	State Reps
Rep House LCCs	.16	.44	−.20
Rep Senate LCCs	.55*	.65*	−.11

N = 18

*significant at > .05 level

Party organization strength is measured with two scales: 1) Mayhew's (1986) five–part measure, where 1 denotes a weak party state and 5 implies a strong party state; 2) Cotter et al.'s (1984) party organization index. It is compiled for both parties at the state and local level.

LCC strength is assessed with Gierzynski's (1992) data on expenditures in 1982, 1984, and 1986. This variable is measured in dollars.

is used. He aggregates the amount of funds contributed by LCCs to state legislative candidates in selected states.[3]

There certainly have been a number of forces that have transformed state legislative elections—several are discussed below. From the functionalist perspective we would expect that, in an era of dealignment and competitive/costly elections, states with weak central party committees would develop LCCs first and at a faster pace. Simon-Rosenthal (1993) is rather explicit about this: "In the absence of a state party apparatus raising money and providing campaign assistance to legislative candidates, legislative leaders stepped in to fill the void" (1993, 5). The converse would thus also appear to hold true—that is, a strong party state will have less significant LCCs, if any.

Although several of the correlations found in Table 2.1 suggest a relationship between LCC development and party strength, they are generally in the *opposite* direction. Those states with the most viable party committees also have the most extensive LCCs; the relationship is generally positive, *not* negative. This appears to be particularly true with regard to senate LCCs; over one-half of the coefficients are statistically significant and positive. The only negative relationship is for state-level Republicans, but these coefficients are modest. Overall, Table 2.1 provides little support for the "party decline leading to LCC growth" view of LCC development.

A parallel argument regarding the relationship between party vitality and LCC growth posits that the greater the variance between state party organizations in a given state, the more likely the weaker organization will develop LCCs. Gierzynski writes:

> The best developed caucus committees within each state tend to be Democratic committees—such as those in Wisconsin, Maine, Minnesota, and Indiana. This may have something to do with the fact that the Democratic state party organizations in those states tend to be weaker than the Republican state party organizations (1992, 13).

While this may appear straightforward, it is difficult to support empirically. Again using Cotter et al.'s rankings and Gierzynski's data, the correlation between Democratic state committees (in states where they are weaker than the Republicans) and Democratic LCCs is .30. This figure was not found to be statistically significant at the .95 level, due perhaps to the rather small sample (n = 18). A comparable analysis cannot be conducted for Republican organizations, as nearly every Republican LCC in Gierzynski's sample is found in a state with a strong Republican party organization. Thus, the modest finding for Democratic organizations and the exclusion of Republican units again do not buttress this "adaptation through need" perspective. At the very least, we might be hard pressed to explain why this dynamic might apply to Democratic organizations but is subordinate, if not irrelevant, to Republican LCCs.

Another criticism can be made by comparing house and senate LCCs in each state. If LCCs are simply a response to waning state party strength, we would expect house and senate units to develop at roughly the same pace. There is little evidence that this occurred(s). House Democrats in New Jersey established an aggressive campaign unit several years before the senate Democrats did the same. The California House Democrats, under the leadership of Jess Unruh, formed a legislative campaign organization some ten years before the senate Democrats joined the act. The Maine Republicans now have a Senate LCC, but no similar organization in the House. The same can be said for the Missouri Democrats. Moreover, while the Republicans in the Illinois Senate raised nearly one-quarter of a million dollars in 1981–1982, their colleagues in the House collected less than one-fifth that amount during the same period.

There is no evidence that house or senate candidates have historically received the lion's share of state committee assistance directed at state legislative races. Nor is there any indication that candidates running for either office have been (are) any more needy; both face the same political environment. Therefore, if party decline was the only explanation, or even the foremost explanation, the variance found in both the emergence and strength of LCCs within many states would appear contradictory.

The Assumption of Filling a Void

A second general critique of the functionalist view is that it assumes a much larger role is performed by parties than is historically accurate. We are led to believe these units were created by *legislators* to perform services once provided by traditional parties. Yet, it is debatable that state and local party committees were ever extensive players in state legislative campaigns. Although Cotter and his colleagues (1984) found state legislative campaigns to be an important piece of state and local party activity, and Frendries et. al have demonstrated similar findings (1994), it is much different to suggest that party committees were principal players in these campaigns. The aid of even the most aggressive party committees generally makes up only a fraction of the overall campaign effort. Party money does comprise the largest single source of money in state legislative races, but it is exceedingly rare that it amounts to more than one-fifth of the overall budget (Jones 1984; Sorauf 1988). In fact, during the 1960s—the period immediately prior to the germination of many LCCs—roughly one-half of the state party committees made no contribution to state legislative races whatsoever (Cotter, et al., 1984, 23). Jewell and Olson may have been correct to note that in the past "legislative candidates, whether incumbents or challengers, [were] on their own during a campaign, building their own organization, raising their own funds, and developing issues" (1988, 217).

A result of redistricting since the 1960s has been the creation of rural districts that include all or parts of several counties and urban districts that contain small parts of one county. In other words, today the boundaries of legislative districts rarely coincide with, or even approximate, county lines. As for party involvement in state legislative races, county organizations have historically been the base. This development makes it even less likely that party units are key elements in state legislative elections.

It is also not clear that LCCs were created by rank-and-file legislators to complement their electoral resources. As noted in the preceding chapter, these new units act as extensions of the caucus leadership and caucus members must often plead with them to receive any assistance. In some instances the incumbents get no help at all. In this light, it is tenuous that LCCs simply represent "a centralized source of campaign funds that candidates in need can go to for assistance" (Gierzynski 1992, 12).

Minority versus Majority Differences

Finally, Theodore Lowi's critique of functionalism (1963) holds that adaptation by parties is primarily a tendency of minority parties. He writes: "A stunning defeat at the polls is more likely to derange structure, prevailing interests and prevailing ideology" (582). The reorganization of the Democratic Caucus in the House following Reagan's early budgetary success and the creation of the Democratic Leadership Council in the mid-1980s are perhaps fitting illustrations.

There is little evidence to suggest that minority parties created state LCCs first or that these units are in a more advanced stage of development. In fact, the opposite appears to be the case. The earliest to develop and the most affluent units have been nearly universally in the majority.

All this is not to suggest that the sociological view is completely misguided; traditional parties may have been slow to respond to changing campaign technologies. Still, suggesting that these units were created to bolster outdated party units may be an overly simplistic explanation. Rather than take the functionalist argument at face value, a systematic analysis is in order. "Political scientists are not new to functionalism," writes Lowi, "but it seldom plays a sufficient part in their analysis. It is in the vocabulary but seldom in use" (1963, 582).

OTHER FACTORS CONTRIBUTING
TO LCC GROWTH

If party dynamics do not explain LCC development, what does? Several factors which may have led to LCC development and maturation are examined below. The first portion of the review looks at these changes more generally, and the second places them in relation to each other using multivariate techniques.

The Mushrooming Cost of Elections
and a New Competitive Environment

One decisive variable in the growth of state LCCs surely may have been the skyrocketing cost of state legislative campaigns during the last decade. Ruth Jones has noted "the cost of [state] legislative campaigns seems to have increased more rapidly and more sharply than most other campaigns" (1984, 175). A few illustrations may be helpful. The average contested lower house campaign in Oregon in 1980 was slightly under $50,000; in 1988 it was nearly $105,000. An average senate race in Washington State cost roughly $80,000 in 1980; in 1988 it was over $225,000. During this same period, the cost of Idaho state legislative races grew by 87 percent, and in Florida, 123 percent (Redfield and Van Der Slik 1992; Moncrief 1992; Gierzynski and Breaux 1991). These numbers are staggering, even when inflation is accounted for, and portray a pervasive trend.

Several explanations may account for this change. An increase in split-ticket voting over the last two decades has been well documented (Nie, Verba, and Petrocik 1976; Crotty 1984; Jacobson 1987; Wattenberg 1990). Voters increasingly cast ballots based on candidate evaluations and/or specific issue preferences instead of partisan loyalties. "Personalized incumbencies" and "particularized benefits" help ensure incumbent reelection in this environment, particularly at the state legislature level where less information on opposing candidates is available. In order for challengers to overcome this advantage, extensive campaigns are required. Challenger expenditures are effective in this environment—that is, the effects of expenditures are found to be greater for challengers than incumbents (Giles and Pritchard 1985, 72). Incumbents respond accordingly, thereby pushing up the cost for both.

Similarly, declining party loyalties suggest volatile electorates. Although studies pointing to a declining number of marginal state legislative elections may be telling (Weber, Tucker, and Brace 1991), incumbents are perhaps no safer today than in the past. This paradox is discussed by Garand (1991) at the state level and at the congressional level by Jacobson. Garand notes: "While incumbent vote proportions have increased, incumbent defeat rates have not declined appreciably, possibly because of the volatility of inter-election vote swings have increased" (1991, 9). In brief, partisan dealignment has increased the competitiveness of most open seats and altered the definition of marginal districts. Seats once considered safe or solidly Republican/Democratic are increasingly open to challenge. Campaigns which are targeted and infused with heavy resources are able to overcome what in the past may have been an overwhelming partisan disadvantage. In New York, the Democratic Assembly Campaign Committee was able to defeat three Republican incumbents in 1990 by saturating their campaigns with unprecedented resources. Each of the districts had an overwhelming Republican enrollment advantage, and may have been considered safe in years prior. Another timely illustration in that same election was the surprisingly strong challenge against New York State Senate Majority Leader Ralph Marino. Marino, a key player in Albany politics and in the Nassau County Republican machine, was barely able to hold on to his twenty-year seat.

It may be also that state legislative candidates—both incumbents and challengers—find it increasingly difficult to run effective grassroots, low-cost campaigns. Sociological changes over the last few decades, such as the decline in civic group membership and less discretionary time for nonfamily activities, make old-style campaigning difficult. Candidates are driven to media-centered campaigns to communicate with voters. The days of neighborhood networks and word-of-mouth campaigns are disappearing, even at the state house level.

It is not clear whether the rising cost of campaigns contributed to the growth of state-level political action committees (PACs), or heavy

PAC contributions during the 1970s increased the cost of elections; in other words which is the chicken and which is the egg? In any event, the role of PAC money at the state level is another important development. In many states, incumbents now receive over 50 percent of their campaign budgets from PACs. Political action committee money in Maryland, for example, doubled during the 1980s (Alexander 1992, 124, citing Common Cause, 1990). This trend does not appear limited to geography, demography, or political leanings.

Legislative campaign committees have joined the act. These new units have become major vehicles for PACs, as well as individuals, to gain influence with legislative leaders. In New York, 40 percent of all special interest money used in legislative elections in 1992 was contributed to the legislative campaign committees (Sack December 3, 1992). In tandem with special interest monies, an interesting role reversal has developed between state legislative leaders and members of Congress. Anxious to avoid redistricting problems, a tide of money recently drifted from Washington to state capitols. House members, particularly those from states with shrinking congressional delegations, contributed heavily to state LCCs during the last two elections (Gruson June 1, 1992).

Finally, the frequency of state legislative elections (many states hold both house and senate elections every two years) compounds the financial pressures of state legislative campaigns. Legislative campaign committees may have been developed to offset this omnipresent strain.

It is uncertain whether LCCs are simply a response to the rising cost of campaigns or are, in fact, a major part of this development. It might be argued that the reliance on nontraditional, expensive modes of campaigning—media-centered campaigns, extensive public opinion polling, and high-powered strategic counseling, etc.—was antecedent to the establishment of LCCs at the state level. Perhaps these changes compelled legislative leaders to create units capable of taking advantage of them. Centralized units help cut costs. Moreover, the growing volatility of state legislative electorates may have led legislators to seek refuge with one another. This line of reasoning parallels Schlesinger's notion of merging of candidate nuclei during competitive periods (1985, 1991).

Because state legislative elections are now exceedingly expensive and because legislators can no longer count on partisan electorates, it makes sense that LCCs have been developed as a byproduct. This might help explain why these new units have been created in both strong and weak party states. It would also explain why they are least pronounced in the South—the region where legislative competition has been low until quite recently.

Fragile Majorities

Another general trend which may have contributed to the growth of LCCs is the importance, yet growing uncertainty, of majority party control. Conceivably due to declining party loyalties among the electorate, there has been a sharp decline in the margin of seats held by majority parties in state legislatures (Gierzynski 1992, 11). This change has been dramatic in three of the four regions and is noticeable in the South. Much of the resources and perquisites now available to state legislators are most pronounced for the majority caucus—not to mention the ability to control committees and the flow of legislation. The growth of LCCs might be seen as a response to fragile majorities or as a mechanism to attain this important position.

A negative relationship emerges when the spread of seats between party caucuses (in each house) is correlated with LCC resources. This is particularly true during the mid-1980s, the precise time when many LCCs were developing. In 1986, for example, the correlation between the variation in senate caucuses and LCC resources was -.21. This suggests LCC resources are more extensive in states where the split between the majority and minority is slim, and it is consistent with Simon-Rosenthal's (1993) finding of a high correlation between partisan competition within legislatures and the mere existence of LCCs in that state.

A cursory review of 1992 also provides support for this conjecture. Legislative campaign committees from states with narrow majorities appear to have had disproportionately large war chests. In Ohio, for example, the House is controlled by only five seats. The Democratic House Campaign Committee—the majority unit—raised nearly $5 million in 1992. In the Senate, where the spread between the parties is much larger, the majority LCC (the Republicans) raised only $2 million during the same period. We might also compare the war chest of the Ohio House Democrats with the New York State Assembly Democrats. The latter also controlled the majority, but with a very large margin (nearly forty seats). In 1992 they raised less then one-half the funds of their Ohio counterparts.

While it is difficult to infer causation, it is at least logical to expect contributors to perceive the implications of majority party turnover.

Simply put, these new units may have been created and are maturing because of frail legislative majorities.

Aggressive Leaders

The import of legislative leaders, such as Michael Madigan in Illinois, Willie Brown in California, Tom Loftus in Wisconsin, Warren Anderson in New York, and Vern Riffe in Ohio, should not be dismissed. The exact role these and other leaders played in the creation of their respective LCCs is a bit unclear and is understudied. The ability to see favorable environmental conditions and create viable organizations would seem to require aggressive leadership. This effort may be aided in states with strong party-in-government structures; the perceived ability of the caucus leadership to control the flow of legislation certainly might help finance these new units. Former congressman Tony Coelho (D-Ca) has been often credited with transforming the Democratic Congressional Campaign Committee during the early 1980s. The role of state legislative leaders has certainly meant no less to their organizations.

Perhaps Weber's (1967) discussion of political entrepreneurs or the economic perspective is more to the point than the functionalist view. The rising cost of legislative campaigns coincided with, or was fueled by, the rapid increase of political action committees following the Federal Elections Campaign Act of 1974. From what we know about the strategies of PACs—their eagerness to secure access to decision-making structures—caucus leadership might have been the target of a flood of special interest monies. In Pennsylvania, for example, "a large number of PACs contribute disproportionately to the campaign committees of party leaders" (Jewell 1986, 12). Clever legislative leaders simply found the opportunity to turn PAC monies into leadership resources. This would help explain the variance between minority and majority party LCCs, the unexpected relationship between strong party states and LCC strength, and differences between houses within the same state. Willie Brown of California may have hinted at the true impetus behind his LCC when he noted: "I don't use [LCC resources] based on party participation or party loyalty; I use it based on speaker loyalty" (Salmore and Salmore 1988, 197).

Legislative Professionalism

A final general trend has been the professionalization of state legislatures during the 1970s, which may have heightened the appeal of state legislative office (Rosenthal 1990; Chubb 1988; Fowler and

McClure 1989). Over the last few decades there has been renewed interest in state and local institutions, i.e., Reagan's New Federalism and the decentralization, neighborhood movement beginning in the late 1960s. State legislatures responded to their increased responsibility by lengthening sessions, expanding office and staff resources, and increasing their own salaries. States holding annual legislative sessions grew from nineteen in 1962 to forty-three in 1986; legislative salaries in ten states reached the median family income by 1979 (Chubb 1988). Notions of a "citizen-legislature" are rapidly vanishing from state government.

The pace of professionalization, termed *congressionalization* by some (Alexander 1992), did not slow in the 1980s. In New York, legislative salaries during this decade climbed to $57,500. Extra remuneration for leadership posts and per-diem allocation provide upwards of an additional $45,000. Allocation for staff resources, both in state capitals and in district offices, have seen a similar increase. The average number of staff members per legislator in New York is only slightly lower than in the House of Representatives.

In their study of why people decide to run for Congress, Linda Fowler and Robert McClure find the growing financial benefits and personal prestige of state legislative office as a new force behind the declining number of state legislators willing to run for Congress. The amount of exposure given to state legislators, due both to the increased workload and promotion resources (franking, etc.), make these positions prized for young, ambitious pols. The growing tenure (declining turnover) of state legislators may be testimony to this perspective (Niemi and Winsky 1987).

Rather than focusing on changes in the electorate or the political environment, Alan Ehrenhalt (1992) suggests that the type of person willing to run for public office has changed. The modern pressures and strains of campaigning filter out certain would-be politicians and leave others—ones who actually enjoy the rigors. These young, aggressive people are more likely to see their job as a life-long profession, than a brief stepping stone to other career goals.

We might speculate, then, that LCCs were created as a means of protecting not only jobs but professions. This may increase employment opportunities for campaign professionals who relentlessly market their services to individuals—yielding a perpetuating cycle. It is telling to note that *every* state with what might be termed a professional legislature[4] now has a legislative campaign committee; only 50 percent of the states with part-time legislatures have these units.

A Multivariate Analysis

The relative import of each of the aforementioned changes in the development of state LCCs is difficult to assess—each has certainly played a role. Many of these new environmental conditions are tied to one another, such as the cost and competitiveness of elections. One attempt to sort out these nuances is to operationalize each dimension and to include them in a multivariate analysis.

The time frame used for this test is the mid-1980s. This is done for two reasons. First, we are interested in the conditions which led to the creation or development of LCCs, and most LCCs were formed during this period. Second, by selecting 1984-86 as the period of analysis, we are able to combine two sets of data on LCC resources, yielding a larger sample than if a more recent period was selected. (As noted above, there have been few comprehensive studies of LCC resources.)

The Variables: Two dependent variables are used. The first is whether or not the state hosts an LCC. Thirty LCC states were identified by 1986 (Jewell 1986). Being a dichotomous measure, a logistic analysis is used. The second dependent variable is a measure of LCC vitality. The resources and activities of these new units may be significantly greater in one state than in another, depending on a number of variables. In order to operationalize this dimension, Gierzynski's (1992) data on LCC budgets during the 1984 election cycle is combined with Jewell and Olson's (1986) survey of LCC resources, also from 1984. The total sample is seventeen, roughly one-half the LCC states.

Several independent variables are introduced. "Party Strength" is a measure of the state party committee vitality in each state. This is extracted from Cotter et al.'s analysis (1984, 28–29).[5] A measure of state-level partisan competition is Austin Ranney's often used index. Here the average of three indicators of Democratic strength are tallied from 1981 to 1988: the percentage of popular vote for gubernatorial candidates, the percentage of seats held by the Democrats in the legislature, and the percentage of time the Democrats held both the governorship and a majority in the state legislature (see Beck and Sorauf 1992, 38–40). The range of scores on this scale are from 1.00 (complete Democratic success) to .50 (truly competitive), through .00 (complete Republican success). Thus, the closer the score to .50, the more competitive that state. In order to make the interpretation of the regression coefficients easier, this scale is converted to suggest that the *higher* the ranking, the more competitive the state. Delaware, New York, Nevada, Michigan, and New Jersey are at the top, and nearly all the southern states are at the bottom of the scale.

"Marginal Seats" is the number of marginal state legislative districts. Weber, Tucker, and Brace (1991) examine election returns in twenty lower state houses from 1950 and 1986 and determine the average number of competitive districts. This figure is divided by the total number of lower house seats to create a measure of the relative marginality.

A measure of legislative professionalization is also included. Kurtz's (1992b) three-part scale—based on length of session, staffing levels, and member pay—is used. States at the bottom of the scale are the least professional or part-time bodies, and those at the top are believed to be full-time and professional.

Unfortunately, a reliable measure of the relative cost of state legislative elections is difficult to operationalize. While there have been studies of a small set of states (the largest being ten, conducted by Breaux and Gierzynski in 1992), comprehensive state finance works, particularly for this time period, are scant. Thankfully, a team of scholars is now in the process of collecting this information in twenty-five states.[6]

The reader will note modest variation in the time frame used to operationalize the measures. For example, Marginal Seats is calculated from 1950 to 1986, and Professionalization is based on data from the late 1980s. However, the concepts measured by these variables are fairly rigid. That is, states that had professional legislatures in 1988 are likely to be the very states foremost in that direction during the early 1980s. The same can be said about partisan competition. Moreover, the marginality of lower house seats is a good, albeit imperfect, indicator of the marginality of state senate seats.

Findings: Results of the logistic regression, using whether or not the state held a LCC in 1984 as the dependent variable, are found in Table 2.2. Although the levels of statistical significance are somewhat disappointing, legislative professionalization clearly emerges as the most likely variable to change the odds of a state's hosting one of these new units. Conversely, the strength of the state party organization appears to make little difference. The overall model predicts a modest 77 percent of the cases.

Table 2.3 notes the results of an ordinary least square (OLS) regression, using LCC resources as the dependent variable. By examining the standardized coefficients, we can again see that legislative

Table 2.2
Logistic Regression of Factors Leading to the Creation of State
Legislative Campaign Committees

Variable	Coefficient	Significance
Professionalization	11.3	.16
Marginal Seats	1.9	.52
Ranney Scale	.2	.45
St. Party Strength	.1	.49
Constant	−22.8	.16
Goodness of Fit	15.57	
Percent Predicted	77.78%	

Dependent Variable: The state did not host an LCC in 1986 (0); the state did host an LCC in 1986 (1).
N = All 50 States

Table 2.3
OLS Regression of Factors Contributing to the Strength of State LCCs

Variable	Slope	S.E.	Beta	T–Ratio
Professionalization	723.4	296.3	.46	2.44
Ranney Scale	55.1	28.5	.36	1.93
St. Party Strength	1.5	1.1	.32	1.44
Marginal Seats	−1456.5	1178.0	−.27	−1.24
Constant	−3167.8	1188.7		−2.67

R–Square = .51
Dependent Variable: Total LCC resources in 1984–1986 election cycle, measured in dollars (in thousands).
N = 17

professionalization is the strongest variable in the model. In fact, it is the only variable statistically significant at the 95 percent confidence interval, although with such a small sample this may be an overly rigorous criteria.

Other interesting findings emerge from this regression. The extent of statewide partisan competition (Ranney Scale) seems to play an important, positive role. Recall that the scale is inverted, suggesting that, as levels of competition increase, LCC resources also expand. The number of marginal seats also seems to be an important factor: as the number of marginal seats decline, so too, apparently, do LCC resources.[7]

It should be noted that it is possible that the causal arrow presented here is reversed. That is, perhaps growth of legislative resources leads to marginal seats. Yet because both the marginal seat measure and the statewide partisan competition variable seem to have roughly the same influence on the dependent variable, and it would be a stretch to reverse the causal arrow for the latter (Ranney Scale is a measure of statewide election returns), we might feel confident in the current model specification.

Once again, the strength of state party committees seems to have little bearing on LCCs. In fact, where a negative coefficient might be expected (party atrophy leading to LCC strength), the slope is again positive.

For both the logistic and OLS regression, a number of additional controls were introduced, including minority and majority differences, population and local party strength. None of these measures had any significant bearing.

This review has demonstrated that a mix of variables – many distinct from party activity—have contributed to LCC development. Increased costs of campaigns, declining majority party margins, and the professionalization movement have each pushed legislative leaders to forge distinct organizations. And they were able to do so because the state legislatures have grown vastly stronger, relative to governors, and PACs, accordingly, have been putting more money into state legislative races.

Three

The State of Party Organizations: Decay or Resurgence?

Frequent comments during the early phases of this project centered on the vitality of political parties in the United States. Why focus a research project on a relationship if one of the players is no longer relevant? How can there be measurable interactions between two organizations if one is inconsequential? Searching for linkages here may be akin to contemplating why American League pitchers cannot hit curve balls.

Scores of writings seemed to buttress these assertions. Decline, decomposition, atrophy, and demise perspectives can be grouped into several broad areas. Those addressing declining partisanship clearly led the way. Numerous works underscore a marked decline in the number of people affiliated with either of the two parties, as well as a lessening of intensity for those who remain party identifiers (Crotty 1984; Wattenberg 1984, 1990). The growing number of independents, the rise of split-ticket voting, divided government, and fragile majorities are pointed to as behavioral manifestations of a prolonged dealigning period (Nie, Verba, and Petrocik 1976; Jacobson and Kernell 1983; Burnham 1970, 1989). We might also include an overall drop in voting levels (Ladd and Hadley 1978) and lower confidence in parties as vehicles of change (Dennis 1976). The second area focuses on declining party-line voting in Congress and state legislatures, perhaps due to the democratic reform movement of the 1960s and 1970s (Burnham 1989; Brady, Cooper, and Hurley 1979). Although during the past decade there may have been a resurgence of party loyalty (Rohde 1991; Davidson 1992), this may simply be a response to budget politics and divided government, likely to evaporate when these conditions change (Malbin 1987, 104). A third area centers on the loss of control of party nominations—particularly presidential nominations (Polsby 1983; Kirkpatrick 1979). The vast body of literature on the growth of candidate-centered campaigns is also illustrative here (Agranoff 1976; Salmore

47

and Salmore 1989A, 1989B; Wattenberg 1991; Jacobson 1992). One might include the emergence of well-intentioned, yet damaging, party reform commissions, civil service reform, the establishment of the American welfare state, and an overall increase in education and affluence in the electorate as harmful changes for parties (Broder 1971; Ranney 1975). The proliferation of PACs, following the Federal Election Campaign Act of 1974, and public funding of presidential elections have allowed candidates to find help elsewhere (Sorauf 1988; Alexander 1992). What is more, for-hire professional consultants (pollsters, direct mail specialists, media advisors) provide services independent of the party (Blumenthal 1980). Even if it were suggested that party organizations, particularly national committees, are doing more than in the past, their *relative* strength may have declined.

If these studies merge to form a bleak picture of party vitality; that, in fact, they have withered to the point of irrelevance, why not center this study exclusively on LCCs? Again, perhaps they are simply filling a void left by the parties. The answer is that political parties in the United States continue to exist and, in many respects, are experiencing a resurgence. As noted below, party organizations in particular are as robust and active as they have been at any point during the past fifty years. The party is far from over.

Another set of issues focuses on the varying notions of "political party." How one defines party will surely guide evaluations of their vitality and relationship with other political actors. In a general sense, notions of party might be placed on a continuum ranging from a purely election-driven group, to a membership-based, responsible party model. From a Downsian perspective—where the sole impetus of party activity is to acquire control of government—organizations such as LCCs might appear partylike. Interaction between these units and traditional party committees might suggest the merging of "candidate-centered nuclei" brought on by the changing political environment, specifically the decline of party in the electorate (Schlesinger 1984, 1985, 1991). To argue that parties in the United States are infused with motivations beyond electoral concerns, many would argue, is to distort reality into a romantic vista—found only in the hearts and writings of certain academics.

On the other hand, if parties are thought of as mass-membership organizations, holding an ideological and policy component—as the responsible party model implies—LCCs could be seen in a very different light. Not only might they be defined as "nonparty" organizations, but antithetical to traditional party units. Platforms and policies are not simply the by-products of office-seeker coalitions, as suggested by the economic approach, but the catalyst for party membership and activity. Office-specific campaign organizations, such as candidate-centered campaigns (and perhaps LCCs), are not interested in party tickets and therefore care little about policy enactment. At the very least, although these groups may interact and assist one another as a means, their goals are very different.

This chapter first examines the vitality of parties. It takes a close look at recent party organization studies and then briefly outlines a few other resurgence perspectives. The contours of both the rational-efficient and party-democracy models are then reviewed, allowing an analysis of LCCs within a more theoretical framework. In the end, a hybrid view of traditional geographic party organization is suggested. With these steps taken, an assessment of the emerging relationship between LCCs and traditional party units and critique of the former's partylike nature follows in forthcoming chapters.

PARTY RESURGENCE PERSPECTIVES

Party as an Organization

Although many of the most influential early works on political parties centered on party organization (Michels 1962; Duverger 1954; Key 1956; Ostrogorski 1964; Eldersveld 1964), this area was, for the most part, neglected during the 1970s. It appears as though scholars concerned with party demise focused their attention on changes in behavior—the voter, the legislator, the candidate. They were confronted with the grim prospects of nonpartisan elections, party-less politics, interest group overload, and PAC power. Drawing a tight fit between the health of our political system and vitality of parties, scholars fixed their outlook on areas of behavioral decomposition, specifically, party-in-the-electorate and party-in-government. Party as an organization, viewed merely as an agent of those who control it rather than as a separate entity with a life of its own, was pushed aside.

Beginning around 1978, a small group of scholars, either through bits and pieces of prior research or personal experience, began to question the validity of party decay as a unidimensional phenomena. Because party-in-the-electorate has clearly withered, does it also imply that party organizations have declined?

Today, those who view the demise of political parties as premature often advance an organizational perspective. Over the last several years, scholars such as Paul Herrnson, Ruth Jones, David Adamany, Cornelius Cotter, James Gibson, John Bibby, Robert Huckshorn, and many others have sought to broaden the evaluation of party vitality to include a host of organizational variables; operating budgets, paid staff positions, full-time headquarters, and support services available to party candidates. One comprehensive, nationwide study conducted by Cotter, Gibson, Bibby, and Huckshorn (1984), termed the Party Transformation Study, for example, found state and local party organizations experiencing significant growth over the past two decades. Numerous similar works suggest growth and adaptation by the two national party committees (Herrnson 1986; Jacobson 1985; Adamany 1984).

In short, organizational perspectives point to mounting evidence of party resurgence at both the national and state levels. While these perspectives do not profess to refute decline theories completely, they draw attention to variables which may indicate traditional measures of party strength are perhaps shortsighted and underdeveloped. At a minimum, the picture is certainly more complicated.

The study conducted by Cotter et al. (1984) is impressive in its comprehensive sample (a nationwide analysis), the number of variables addressed, and a focus on *both* state and local committees. Many of their findings have implications relevant to our investigation, making a cursory review worthwhile.

Robust parties, they argue, are organizationally complex and have developed programmatic capacity. Organizational complexity requires an enduring headquarters, leadership, staff, and budget. Strong committees thus will have a bureaucratic organization in the Weberian sense. Programmatic capacity implies activities related to goals, that is, institutional support operations and assistance to candidates during elections. Virile party organizations will have ongoing institutional support activities and something to offer candidates.

Using a number of sources – interviews with a sample of state party chairs, a mail survey of other active chairs, and a poll of 560 former state chairs – the study looks at the changes in state party organizations along these two dimensions from 1960 to 1980. Overall, findings suggest "it is quite difficult to find much supporting data for the thesis that [state] party organizations have weakened. Indeed, on most indicators, the contrary conclusion is warranted" (Cotter et al. 1984, 30).

With regard to organizational complexity, nearly all of the evidence points to growth. The number of state committee staff more than tripled, the average operating budget grew from $180,000 to $341,000,[1] nearly all states had accessible headquarters, and the number with full-time staff and paid party chairs doubled. The picture is similar for programmatic activity. Nearly all the indicators of institutional support increased. Most committees published and distributed newsletters, conducted fund-raising operations, produced get-out-the-vote drives, and conducted opinion polling. There has been, however, a modest decline in issue development.

On the whole, the extent and types of services given to candidates had also spread. Candidate seminars, media assistance, public opinion polling, and literature production have all increased. Although direct cash contributions had similarly grown—both in the amount dispersed and the number of candidates receiving it—the type of candidates receiving it had somewhat shifted. Whereas gubernatorial candidates were the principal beneficiaries during the 1960s, U.S. House and state legislative candidates were the main recipients by the 1980s. One area of decline is candidate recruitment. Perhaps due to increased competitiveness, the rise of candidate-centered campaigns, or simply the decline in the need, fewer state committees recruited candidates for all offices.

Turning to the local party committees, findings were similar. They surveyed an impressive 7,300 county level party leaders. The number of paid staff was relatively small, but low turnover suggests stable structures. Nearly all had a complete set of officers, and more than half operated campaign headquarters. Over two-thirds distributed literature, organized fund-raising events, contributed money to candidates, and organized telephone campaigns—along with numerous other activities.

Another important finding pertains to the relationship between the county committees and other campaign organizations. The data suggested that the largest sphere of involvement, for both Democrats and Republicans, was state legislative campaigns (1984, Table 3.5). Although roughly 26 percent were often involved in congressional and gubernatorial campaigns, 43 percent were often involved in state legislative races. Since the study was conducted before most states had developed legislative campaign organizations, it will be interesting to see if there have been any changes along this dimension.

One of the unique facets of American parties is the diffuse pattern of relationships between layers. Legislative campaign committees have yet to be fit into this puzzle. Several of Cotter et al.'s findings point to interesting possibilities. For example, local committees appear to put more resources into state legislative races than in the past. At the same time, they continue to work independently of the state committee. Perhaps, then, the development of legislative campaign organizations during the 1980s has led to the unification of state and local forces on state legislative races. Local party organizations may interact little with the state committee but frequently with the legislative campaign committee. On the other hand, maybe a division of labor has emerged where the local committees conduct grassroots activities and the LCCs engage in more high-tech projects. Both spheres could be involved in these races without ever working together. A third possibility is that local committees are no longer involved in state legislative races and the Party Transformation Study is outdated. That is, local committees have been pushed aside and have retreated to local elections. Again, these questions lay at the heart of this project and will be addressed more fully in subsequent chapters.

Cotter et al.'s study was followed by several similar projects. The next year the very same group of scholars (Gibson et al., 1985) compared their findings on local committees with a survey conducted in 1964 by the Center for Political Studies (reported in Beck 1974). They concluded that local parties countrywide were substantially more active in the 1970s than in 1964. William Crotty edited a collection of case studies on urban party organizations in five cities, concluding that "local parties are active in critical areas of campaigning, that they appear to be principal actors in the electoral process, and that there is no evidence of an atrophying of party activity or organization (1986, 30)." The Advisory Committee on Intergovernmental Relations conducted its own research. Their findings paralleled Cotter, et al.'s, with nearly all indicators pointing to organizational augmentation. Numerous works have been directed towards sorting out government regulations of state and local parties (ACIR Report 1986); their financial condition (Jones 1984); and modes of collecting and disbursing resources (Alexander 1992; Gierzynski and Breaux 1991).

More recently, Gibson, Frendreis, and Vertz found county party organizations continue to be involved in numerous electorally relevant activities, "including candidate recruitment, joint planning with candidate organizations, and various independent campaign activities" (1991, 225). Much of this activity was directed at state legislative races. John Frendreis et. al. (1994) conducted a study of local party involvement in state legislative races in eight states during the 1992 election. Their overarching findings include: 1) county committees have become stronger with regard to organizational structures; 2) involvement in state legislative campaigns has increased; and 3) even state legislative candidates recognize the growing role of local parties in their campaigns.

The picture emerging from these studies is one of renewal, or at the very least stability, rather than decline. State and local party organizations have not withered away. In fact, many of these studies imply there may be a relationship between decline in other aspects of party (such as in-the-electorate) and organizational augmentation. Cotter and his colleagues note:

> The year in which *The American Voter* appeared (1960) marked the beginning of a decade or more of growth for party organizations. As subjective party attachments weakened in the 1960s and 1970s, the level of party organizational strength increased (1984, 33).

One explanation for this paradox is that party organizations have been so successful that they have pulled voters away from party attachments. Another, as will be examined in greater detail, reverses the causation—that is, party organizations have benefitted from declining party loyalties.

There is no clear answer as to which element of a party is most reflective of its overall health. Many would argue that levels of partisanship and straight-ticket voting are principal indicators, as they tie directly to popular governance (Burnham 1970, 1982, 1989; Coleman 1994). Without disputing this claim, party organization studies, at the very least, complicate the decay perspective. Unidimensional vistas are overly simplistic. Most importantly for this study, party organizations are exactly the component with which we are concerned. That is to say, how does the emergence of LCCs affect party functions, activities, and goals? While the arrival of these units may also affect party-in-government and levels of partisanship, such topics are beyond the scope of this project.

Other Renewal Perspectives

Although there is mounting evidence that state and local party organizations have not withered during the last several decades, few

scholars have developed integrative models linking organizational resilience with partisan atrophy. Joseph Schlesinger's (1965, 1984, 1985, 1991) work is an exception. Taking a page from Downs's view of parties as a "team seeking to control the governing apparatus by gaining office in a duly contested election" (Downs 1957, 25), Schlesinger conceives of party organization as candidate-centered aggregations. Each candidate has a group of supporters with a particular aim at winning office. The party is an ad hoc *set* of candidate-oriented "nuclei," transforming and recomposing each election. Voters are consumers investing in the marketplace by supporting one candidate or brand. The fate of a party organization is therefore modified by the structure of opportunities (rules) and level of competition.

Schlesinger argues that as the political market becomes increasingly uncertain (i.e., partisan dealignment, split-ticket voting, independents), candidates are driven to join forces. While party organizations may offer loyal workers side-payments for their participation, the demand for, and uncertainty of, winning office is the principal catalyst of party organization. In areas of weak electoral competition, such as southern states during much of this century, party organizations are empty vessels. Conversely, in areas of high competition party organizations are more active.

Simply put, changes in party-in-the-electorate over the last several decades help explain the growth of party organizations. Candidates face uncertain electorates and costly campaigns and come together to overcome these challenges. When the rules of elections and party competition change, so too will party organizations. Rather than being entities independent of candidates, party organizations are by-products of those conditions which shape the expectations and ambitions of candidates. "It is the very weakness of partisan identification among the voters which is a stimulus for the growth of partisan organizations" (Schlesinger 1985, 1167).

Even though candidate-centered campaigns have surely changed the landscape of electoral politics, and such rational choice perspectives may be a powerful tide in academic views of party, a few points concerning Schlesinger's model are worth noting—perhaps in retort. The first relates directly to legislative campaign organizations. If one views LCCs as elements of candidate-centered aggregations (the party), one might expect LCCs of the same party to work together as competition and uncertainty increase. That is, those of the same party (the house and senate units) will join forces as well as unite with nonlegislative candidate nuclei during periods of high electoral

competition (greater economies of scale, etc.). Again, there is considerable evidence of volatile electorates but little to suggest that LCCs join forces or work for nonlegislative candidates. Nor does there appear to be any significant variation based on levels of party competition.

Secondly, although ephemeral candidate-centered aggregations may appear realistic, party organizations often have a more durable character (see Mayhew 1986). Schlesinger not only suggests that party organizations rise and fall depending on environmental changes but fluctuate during stages of the election cycle. Party organizations are, for example, more active in the election period than in the nomination stage (1985, 1153). But are parties this malleable? Many would argue local party organizations have a much more enduring character and are involved in numerous nonelection activities. Political traditions and generational lags may too grant a party organization vigor unexplainable by Schlesinger's focus on nonorganization variables. As Cotter and his colleagues note:

> However fruitful Schlesinger's theory, and replete as it may be with useful implications for the traditional party organizations in the form of local, state, and national party committees, it is a theory of campaign organizations, not party organizations (1984, 4).

Finally, although the rational-choice approach to the study of parties provides an overarching theoretical perspective, as is often the case, analytic parsimony may be offered at the expense of reality. It is suggested, with some degree of caution, that parties in the United States hold a more consistent policy agenda than this perspective would imply. Although parties have lost some power over the control of nominations, they continue to screen and select candidates by offering significant shortcuts in the nomination process. There are differences between the party culture of the Democrats and Republicans, and these differences lead to distinct party behavior (Klinkner 1994), a condition inconsistent with rational-choice perspectives. Additionally, the degree to which parties operate in a market-type environment is questionable. "The dominance of the two parties has been written into law and tradition and they enjoy benefits in candidate recruitment, funding, and certification not available to potential competitors" (Crotty 1986, 10). Realistically speaking, the two major parties face little competition.

Another set of renewal perspectives presupposes there has been a shift in party organization activities—specifically, the movement from grass-roots groups to state and national organizations. Several recent works, and perhaps conventional wisdom, argue that there has been a centralization/nationalization movement brought about by reform statutes during the 1970s, changing demographics (mainly suburbanization), new communications technologies, and a sharp focus on national politics (Kayden and Mahe 1985; Epstein 1986, 200–238; Bibby 1990; Beck and Sorauf 1992). Here, atrophy of *local* party committees is viewed as inevitable. Few scholars appear willing to argue that urban machines, what few there are left, are not withering away.[2]

One powerful argument along these lines is presented by Kayden and Mahe (1985). They assert grass-roots parties simply no longer matter. Not to despair, the principal function preformed by parties—communication with the voter—is still being performed through high technology means, i.e., telephone banks and direct mail. The loss of local parties "may not be so catastrophic for the democracy as it seems because it does not affect the flow of information to the voters . . ." (121). Party activity has simply shifted to a different level; local parties have followed the fate of neighborhood civic organizations.

A few points can be made regarding this view. While it may be that campaign finance laws and changes in technologies have augmented state and national committees, such a transformation need not be inconsistent with local party resurgence. The days of the urban machine are clearly drawing to a close. Yet, numerous studies (several cited above) refute local committee decline. To suggest that grass-roots committees will inevitably decompose due to party centralization may be descriptively inaccurate. Merton (1945) contends organizations will continue to exist so long as they fulfill a need not otherwise afforded. Growth at the top need not lead to atrophy at the bottom—particularly when each level performs different functions.

During the last few decades, there has been renewed interest in local governance that is consistent with the pervasive localism in American politics. If the revolt against the nationalization of government is prolonged, the import of grass-roots party structures may be further heightened.

Kayden and Mahe's own definition of strong parties recognizes the importance of neighborhood organizations. They note: "strong parties are characterized by a meaningful organizational structure:

one that can make decisions and is relatively accessible to those seeking to participate in public events" (8). Their concern with accessibility, however, appears somewhat misplaced in their tranquil discussion of local party decomposition. If there indeed has been a shift from local party to state committees, what have been the causes, and what will be the consequences?

What role have LCCs played in this transformation? It has been suggested by Polsby (1983, ch. 4), among others, that the shift of political communication from personal to high technology will trigger declining governing legitimacy. Parties serve as intermediaries between governing institutions and the public. As communication becomes one way, this intermediary capacity is changed. Have LCCs been a catalyst in this process, or have they aided local party organizations in reversing this trend?

The alliance between the state and local party organizations also may be more meaningful than Kayden and Mahe suggest. Frendreis, Gibson, and Vertz (1990) examined the role of county party organizations on state party dynamics. By organizing and recruiting full slates of candidates for local offices, grass-roots units can have a positive impact on state party strength. They note: "the efforts of partisans to build and work through their county organizations appear to be part of the overall process of party competition and party system change" (232).

To many, community-based party organizations throughout our history have played a pivotal role in educating the electorate and encouraging average citizens to become involved. By running tickets of candidates, they help provide a choice, even in districts heavily dominated by the other party. They are vehicles for the fulfillment of perceived civic duty and, for many Americans, are important social institutions. Although there appears to be little evidence to date of extinction, their displacement surely may have a negative impact on popular governance.

Another resurgence perspective attempts to link growing ideological polarization between the parties with organizational vigor. By interviewing party activists (convention delegates) in 1980 and 1988, Stone, Rapoport, and Abramowitz (1989) find a growing divergence on policy stands between the two parties. This rift among party elite may either reflect or lead to similar differences among followers (voters). Their data imply an emerging realigning period where the parties readjust to attract followers. Partisanship is thus solidified and party-in-government strengthened. During these periods, party organizations may experience a resurgence. It should be noted that this line of reasoning—that party realignments imply a universal boost to parties—runs counter to Schlesinger's argument outlined above.[3]

As a final note, recent elections may prove to be a boost for the two major parties. For one thing, the bleak picture of declining partisanship may have bottomed out. A growing number of first-time voters seem to have found a home in one of the two parties, reversing a trend toward nonparty enrollments. The 1992 election had the highest turnout in thirty years and possibly an increase in straight-ticket voting[4] (See *The New York Times*, November 5, 1992; Section B). Rather than running from his party label, as many recent Democratic candidates have done, Bill Clinton spoke often of a "new" Democratic party. There seemed to be a sharp division between the parties' platforms—particularly on social issues—and both nomination conventions served as vivid showcases for these differences (Fine 1994). Bush campaigned hard for a Republican Congress, as did Reagan. The Democratic party, a unit often viewed as organizationally inept, appeared to unite in a team effort. Dissention and splintering, characteristic of recent elections, was noticeably absent. Moreover, since 1994, the Republican contract with America has not only solidified the caucuses within Congress, but provided voters with clear differences between the parties on core issues.

One inauspicious outcome was the surprisingly strong showing of Ross Perot. Whether or not he might be considered a third party candidate, or simply a candidate-centered phenomena, is unclear. Party scholars might argue the latter. Only time will tell if Perot turns his following in the direction of a party or allows it to dissipate; recent trends suggest the latter. If he is viewed as a non-party candidate, his 19 percent showing surely strikes a blow to champions of responsible party government and party resurgence scholars.

DEFINING PARTY:
GOALS, FUNCTIONS, AND STRUCTURE

How do you define a political party? What makes one organization more "partylike" than another? Are parties member-oriented or simply tools for the office-seeking elite? Is intra-organization democracy required, and what role do ideology and policy concerns play in party activities?

Scholars have wrestled with these and other questions for some time. To many, party is simply a "team of candidates seeking to gain office" (Downs 1957). Such a definition, they argue, is realistic, free of normative views implicit in the responsible-party model, and distinct from politics peripheral to parties such as public opinion and voting behavior (Schlesinger 1985, 1152). For others, however, parties are a complex structure linking members, organization, policy, and activities. Definitions of party are also often qualified by the political system and time period. The Greens Party in Europe is very much different than the Democratic Party in the United States, and the "amateur associations" in California during the 1960s are distinct from most party committees today. There is a continual struggle between theoretical parsimony and depictions of reality. Why do certain parties thrive in areas where they have little chance of controlling office? Others might argue the greatest challenge to party scholars is to provide a definition free of normative qualifications. How one defines party, they suggest, is too often dependent upon what one believes parties *should* look like. Needless to say, a neat paradigm of party structure, function, and goals—particularly for those in the United States—remains elusive.

In order to survey the impact of legislative campaign committees on traditional party units and to access the party-like character of the former, it is necessary to spell out what parties in the U.S. look like, what they do, and what they seek to accomplish. If, for example, to the Downsian view is favored, an assessment of LCCs may be much different than if parties are seen as having a more durable character and holding policy constraints. Evaluation of linkages between the units may be colored also by notions of appropriate party activities.

This section takes a brief look at the divergent views of "party" by breaking perspectives into two camps: the rational-efficient school and the party-democracy model. Referring to the discussion of LCCs in Chapter 1, they can now begin to be fit into these two perspectives. Finally, the focus is narrowed to "traditional geographic party organizations," and their structure, functions, and goals. A hybrid model is suggested.

Models of Political Parties

To structure the diverse, often contradictory, views of party, William Wright (1971) neatly framed scholarly perspectives along a continuum. At the polar ends are the rational-efficient and party-democracy models. As noted above, the rational-efficient perspective holds that parties are organized and function to win elections and gain elected office. Systemic benefits within this model, such as linkage, representation, and conflict resolution, are derived as by-products of party competition. Old-style urban machines are characteristic of this perspective. The party-democracy model sees party activity from a purposive vantage. Policy outcomes and legislative responsibility are critical. So too is intra-party democracy. Traditional European socialist parties are examples here. Table 3.1 highlights some of the differences in the objectives, functions, and structure of parties within the two models.

From the rational-efficient guise, parties are only one of a variety of competing political actors in the pluralist system. Relying on an economic analogy, emphasis is on the competitive struggle to gain office in the free market (fair and open elections). Party platforms are continually shifted to solicit the support of consumers (voters). The representative function performed by parties parallels other groups; interest groups articulate interests, and parties aggregate them. Conflict is seen as disruptive and plays no role in governing.

Although many in the party-democracy camp would concede that the economic perspective may, at times, appear more realistic (particularly in the United States), "it suffers from a blind spot in the extreme pragmatic view that whatever works is good, that the ends justify the means" (Wright 1971, 23). Rather than view party as one of many actors in a pluralist system, party-democracy advocates see them as goal definers. Parties develop platforms based on purposive criteria related to activists' values and policy preferences, often advocating change. The party seeks to win elections only as a means to implement its policies. It is the primary link between the citizens and government and plays a dominant role in government. In a slightly narrower focus, parties provide the opportunity to control elites by structuring competition, selecting and supporting office-seeking individuals, and using actual and perceived threats of electoral retribution. Finally parties are said to articulate and mediate conflict peacefully, as well as make agreement and consensus possible.

Rational-efficient parties emphasize only electoral activities; all other functions are subordinate. Activities are limited to election periods, and party worker incentives are material (patronage). Responsible parties, on the other hand, have ideological, electoral,

Table 3.1
Contrasting Attributes of Rational-Efficient and Party-Democracy
Models of Party

Attribute	Rational-Efficient	Party-Democracy
View of Democracy:	Pluralist View Conflict Avoided	Party Goal Definers Conflict Part of Change
Functions:	Election Activities	Linkage Aggregation Articulation Participation Community Service
Objectives:	Win Elections/ Control Office Efficiency	Policy Ideological Unity
Structure:	Cadre/Professional	Mass Membership Amateur
Role in Government:	None—Members Granted Autonomy	Interdependence Between Member-Party Organization
View of Intraparty Democracy:	Hinders Efficiency	Essential
Incentives for Participation:	Material	Mix of Purposive, Social, and Material

* Portions of this table were extracted from Wright (1971, 17–54).

and governing functions. They operate throughout the calendar year and conduct many activities unrelated to winning the next election.

According to the responsible school, all modern political systems are highly complex, the American system particularly so. The magnitude of our governing institutions, as well as their diffuse structure (separation of powers, bicameralism, and federalism), make coordinated government action extremely difficult, e.g., V.O. Key's (1964) "constitutional obstruction." In order for such a system to survive, a mechanism to bind government spheres, leaders, citizens, and groups in united action must be developed. What emerges in this complex system are linkage structures which yield positive action in the face of fragmentation, conflict, and mass involvement (Eldersveld 1982). The primary structure is political parties.

The responsible-party model further holds that these organizations serve to promote compromise among interest groups, and to form a medium by which voters express their interests to government officials. In short, parties organize participation, aggregate interests, channel conflict, and link social forces to government institutions.

The organizational structure of rational-efficient parties consists of a cadre of political entrepreneurs. There is a large degree of centralization and no formal party membership. The organizational style is professional, where workers, leaders, and candidates are often recruited from outside the organization or self-recruited. Efficiency is stressed over all else (Wright 1971, 40). There is little, if any, organizational continuity after the election.

Responsible parties maintain a highly integrated structure. Formal membership is critical, therefore grass-roots committees play an important role. The style is amateur-based and leaders rise through the ranks as loyal, hardworking activists. Candidates who receive support from the organization are recruited from within and must be programmatically and ideologically in tune. One's ability to win an election is subordinate to ideological purity.

Finally the two models are at odds regarding their role in government. There is an interdependence between the party and elected officials in the responsible model; autonomy of elected officials is not only allowed in the latter but stressed.

Where do traditional American-style parties fit into these perspectives? Most scholars place parties in the U.S. toward the rational-efficient end of the spectrum. They argue party membership is certainly questionable (particularly in light of dealignment), as is the extent of intraparty democracy; generally speaking, a small set of party elites makes decisions for the entire organization. Ideological diversity and constituent imperatives are tolerated, and party-line voting in government is far from unified. Moreover, there are numerous linkage structures, such as special interest groups, which may play an equal or greater role in the democratic process than do parties. The rise of candidate-centered campaigns is seen as a further push in this direction.

One must be cautious, however, not to fit American parties too close to the economic model; a number of points can be raised from the opposite perspective. Reforms of the early 1970s opened up the Democratic and Republican Parties towards intraparty democracy. Although ideological diversity is generally tolerated, this is not always the case. Party remains the best predictor of a legislator's vote (Clausen 1973; Kingdon 1989), and party organizations perform activities in nonelection periods—including those not directly related to winning office. Both party leaders and candidates are often recruited from within. On the whole, party activities are conducted by amateurs—they do so on their own time for purposive and social incentives; economic (patronage) rewards are infrequent.

Fitting LCCs into Models of Party

An observant reader will have, by now, noticed a close fit between the rational-efficient model and legislative campaign organizations. The central (perhaps sole) end for LCCs is to reelect caucus members and secure more seats. Their range of functions is accordingly limited. Notions of party platforms or tickets appear extraneous to their central mission, and their activities are generally limited to election cycles. They hold little concern for intra-organizational democracy; such a process would be viewed as an impediment to efficiency. They seem to be highly centralized, nonparticipatory groups.

The similarities with the rational approach model continue. They are generally run by professionals, where incentives for participation are material; purposive rewards are irrelevant and social incentives, if any, mere by-products of long hours and close working conditions. Both LCC strategists and foot soldiers may be recruited from outside the party, and candidate support is generally based on ability to win. Policy making may be an ancillary concern. To the contrary, members are often encouraged to support those issues which aid their election chances, even at the expense of policy solidarity (recall Rollins' letter to Republican House members).

Where LCCs may depart from the rational-efficient model is their role in government. Although it has been argued LCCs focus little attention on policy concerns (Dwyre 1994), they may have an impact on party-line voting (Herrnson 1988). Legislators may be called upon to support the party leadership or risk losing reelection support. It should be emphasized that "support for party leadership" does not necessarily imply programmatic support, but perhaps simply organizational coherence such as voting for the caucus leadership.

With this one minor exception, the fit between the rational-efficient model and LCCs is close. These new organizations are designed to win elections and provide candidate support services. Those scholars who view them as partylike must surely ground their argument from a rational choice vantage.

Conversely, those who view parties with a policy focus, playing a role in government, having a civic role, and granting benefits to members as well as office seekers, might view these new organizations as non-party groups. They may be seen in the same light as candidate-centered organizations, campaign consulting firms, or PACs.

A third conjecture, however, is that LCCs should *not* be viewed as separate entities but as part of a diverse party organization. Their activities might be only a portion of overall party functions. In this light they would simply be used at the discretion of party leaders as service agencies. Rather than viewing party in the traditional tripod perspective, we might introduce a fourth sphere, somewhere between party-in-government and party-as-an-organization. Intra-party democracy, policy concerns, and nonelection activities might be addressed in one of the *other* spheres. If little else, perhaps they are appendages of the party organization. This seems to be an implicit assumption found in most recent party organization studies.

But if one is to accept this line of reasoning—that LCCs are a new component within the overall party organization and not simply campaign machines working independently—it is imperative that we closely examine the pattern and extent of linkages. If they are found to be structurally and functionally autonomous, their goals and activities must be evaluated in relation to traditional party goals and activities.

DEFINING TRADITIONAL GEOGRAPHIC PARTY ORGANIZATION

The following chapters examine the relationship between legislative campaign organizations and traditional geographic party organizations. The objective of the discussion at hand is to clarify and define what is meant by the latter. By carefully distinguishing traditional parties from other groups, more precision with regard to their similarities and differences with LCCs can be achieved.

Structure[5]

Traditional geographic party organizations (TPOs) are based around legally defined divisions: ward, town, city, county, or state. They are frequently termed *town, city, county, and state committees*. Within each committee there exists a hierarchy of leadership. Party leaders, in particular, are central figures. The chair is usually the heart of the organization, but other officials and active members play important roles.

Declaring allegiance to a party—such as legal enrollment—does *not* enlist an individual into the organization as a member. Membership implies an active association with the organization. There are few official dues or duties, but rank-and-file members may be called upon from time to time to contribute financially to the organization by attending events—such as dinners and socials. Some TPOs may have official rules regulating which members shall serve on the committee while, in others, this determination is less formal. Committee members may be elected in party primaries, appointed by party officials, or be seated through a local caucus.

Not to discount a trend toward centralization over the past two decades, Eldersveld's stratarchy continues to describe the relationship *between* the committees within the overall structure. Each unit is allowed to conduct its own activities—particularly those within its own electoral sphere. There are few commands from the state level down to the base of the organization. At the same time, however, each committee is aware of its place in the overall structure, and there are a number of formal and informal ties. Interactions between layers is generally reciprocal; assistance flows in both directions.

The principal impetus bringing the different party strata together is election activities. Various layers of the party will often work together on the same election or general activity. For example, a city committee may work with a county committee on a congressional race, or a county organization may help the state committee get out the vote.

Finally, traditional party organizations are fairly permanent, ongoing structures. They are not dependent on transient issues or personalities. In this regard, local political mores and style are an important part of their activities.

Functions and Activities[6]

The principal functions performed by traditional geographic party organizations center around winning elections and controlling government offices. Nevertheless, in noncompetitive areas—where the minority party has little or no chance of success—party organizations exist and perform activities. The same can be said about districts with entrenched incumbents. One of these activities is to secure a full slate of candidates, thereby offering the voters a choice. As such, winning elections is clearly not the sole purpose for their being.

Election activities are often directed toward particular candidates. Examples here might include granting the party's nomination to a candidate or providing direct assistance during the general election, such as a monetary contribution. Special emphasis is placed on reelection campaigns. To a large extent, then, traditional party organizations are geared toward winning elections and therefore target resources to candidates with the best chances of winning. This would lead, for example, to more energy and resources given to Bill Clinton than to a local candidate not likely to win.

Many activities are *also* designed to support the full breadth of candidates running under the party banner. Support for the ticket, or slating, guides such activities. TPOs clearly do not provide all candidates with the same resources, yet each candidate is considered part of the overall, enduring team. The strategy of running away from one of the party's candidates in order to help secure the election of another is antithetical to their mission.

Along similar lines, TPOs are concerned with long-range party development. An example would be voter registration drives and cosponsoring community events, such as food bank drives during the holidays. They also seek to identify and clarify policy positions. This is not to suggest that their ideological and policy concerns take precedent over winning elections, or that all candidates fit neatly under the party's ideological contours. But rather, core differences, customs, traditions, and a desire to aid helpful groups, highlight an enduring policy framework. Ideological concerns are neither central nor irrelevant. Here too, parties serve an educational function by informing voters and the media of these differences.

Party activities tend to be dominated by the dictates of the election calendar; most activities occur during election periods. Nonelection activities, nonetheless, are conducted throughout the year, such as organizational maintenance functions or social activities.

Traditional geographic party committees, by state statute, oversee and carry out elections, i.e., provide election inspectors, staff boards of elections, and so on. They are also often important social institutions.

There exists a separatism or dualism between party organizations and party structures in government (Eldersveld 1982, 136). This is not to say elected public officials cannot also be party officials. In fact, many hold both roles. The important point is that they are separate structures, and any linkage is incidental.

Goals and Incentives

The primary goal of traditional geographic party organizations is to win elections and control governmental office. They do so for material benefits (patronage, government contracts, etc.), to implement certain policies, and to make organizational maintenance and growth easier.

The incentives for individuals are also mixed. They are material, purposive, and social. No one motivation guides all party activists. A general pattern might be tentatively suggested: incentives at the leadership level tend to be a mix of material and purposive. Some, but not all, traditional party organizations provide material reimbursements to its leaders. On the whole, leaders/activists tend to be more ideological than rank-and-file members. At the grass-roots membership level, social incentives may be more important. For those people interested in becoming "involved," parties often provide this opportunity.

Four

Theory, Data, and Method

Although the import of state LCCs has gained the attention of most party scholars, as well as students of politics in general, for the most part analysis has proceeded in a nontheoretical fashion. A leading scholar of parties in the United States, for example, suggests these new units are "increasingly important elements of the state organizational structure" (Bibby 1990, 31), but such assertions have not been evaluated in any orderly way.[1] It appears taken for granted that LCCs merge nicely into the traditional structure, perform partylike functions, and have become an integral element of party resurgence.

Several factors may suggest that integration perspectives are indeed appropriate. For one, as noted, there can be formal/legal linkages between LCCs and the state party organization. In some states they emerged as legal appendages of the party committees. At the very least, this relationship may be financially beneficial for both the parties and the LCCs. During the past decade, party committees have received help from numerous reform statutes—such as higher contribution limits and the lowest possible rate on postage. Some LCCs also may be physically housed in the state party committee headquarters. Third, there appears to be a degree, albeit infrequent, of strategic harmony between units at the national level, and they have occasionally engaged in general party promotions.[2] It may also be the case that legislators who serve on legislative campaign committees are state party officials. (The same may be said about paid staff.) Finally, there is a longstanding belief, especially among realignment theorists, that party organizations are tied closely with other elements of the party—specifically party-in-government (Beck and Sorauf 1992, 10–11). In his oft-cited case study of New York State politics, for example, Warren Moscow found a close fit between the wishes of county party leaders and the voting behavior of state legislators (1948, ch. 10).

Perhaps these variables (either independently or combined) buttress an integration perspective. That is, for these reasons and others, LCCs are best viewed as elements of the overall party structure, and their services should be seen as partylike. On the other hand, these pieces may tell only part of the story. From the earlier review of LCCs and the critique of traditional parties in Chapter 3, a very different picture seems to emerge—one of dualism rather than integration. Perhaps a systematic, theory-based analysis should precede wanton categorizations.

> [I]n the study of political parties, as in many other areas of political research, classification too often becomes an end in itself. Typologies may be useful in early exploratory stages of research, but the analysis of the determinants and consequences of various types of party organization requires more rigorous measures of relevant organizational dimensions (Gibson, Cotter, Bibby, and Huckshorn 1985, 195).

At its core, this project focuses on two related issues: are LCCs part of, and do they act like, traditional party organizations? The former addresses the type and extent of linkages, while the second compares objectives and activities. If LCCs are indeed part of a *party* resurgence/adaptation movement, a close fit and/or similar behavior might be expected. That is to say, LCCs would be in some way tied to traditional party organizations, and, even if they are not formally coupled, their activities and goals would roughly parallel party activities and goals. Their systemic functions would coincide with, and even complement, TPO functions. One might then feel confident that "parties" have adapted to a new political environment.

It is by now clear this is *not* likely to be the case. The development of legislative campaign committees appears unrelated to traditional party vitality. At the heart of this research is a basic supposition that LCCs are autonomous, rational-efficient organizations. They exist and act independent of party committees and are concerned with a narrower set of goals and activities. Legislative campaign committees might be best viewed as transient, electoral-based units, rather than party appendages.

As argued in the previous chapter, TPOs are stable organizations that hold a broad set of objectives. They are certainly not exemplary party-democracy units, but neither are they election-driven machines. At the very least, traditional parties conduct projects and perform functions that extend beyond winning elections. If, then, LCCs are found to be distinct units that conduct a limited number of activities, their growth does not imply "party" adjustment. Only by understanding *where* they fit and *what* they do can one begin to speculate how LCCs might impact existing party structures.

To closely examine these suppositions, four areas of inquiry will be pursued. First, given the posited definition, where do LCCs fit in the traditional party structure? Simply put, are they formally tied to the overall party organization or do they exist independent of it? Second, what are the programmatic linkages, such as the level of strategic and activity-based interdependence? Third, regardless of linkages, how do the activities and objectives of LCCs differ from party organizations? Finally, from the perspective of traditional party leaders, should these new units be considered "partylike" or something altogether different?

This chapter lays the conjected groundwork for answering these questions. After presenting expectations, they are tested empirically in chapters 5, 6, and 7.

A crystal clear picture is not anticipated. A complex relationship dependent on a number of forces is likely to emerge. A list of a priori expectations and hypotheses are offered as *controls*. Each supposition is based on the notion that LCCs are independent, election-driven organizations, and that TPOs hold a broader set of concerns. For example, *level of interparty competition* may be an important variable in this new relationship. High electoral competition might lower strategic cooperation. As autonomous, rational-efficient units, LCCs would appear not to share decision-making control with party leaders—particularly in highly competitive areas. Several other variables are introduced but, again, should be only considered ancillary to the principal foci on the extent of LCC independence and a comparison of goals and activities.

Two additional points should be noted at the outset. First, the data used to test many of the controls come from either the state or county level. Certain variables will apply to one sphere and not the other. For example, the degree of legislative professionalization is an important control but can only be used in cross-state comparisons. Second, in some instances respondents are asked to be informants (to provide factual information) and at other times are called upon to provide perceptual accounts. While the validity and reliability of the former may be questioned because they are (to a degree) subjective measures, there are also limits to less qualitative sources.[3]

The final portion of the chapter reviews the data used to determine whether or not these suppositions can be supported.

AREAS OF INQUIRY AND CONTROL HYPOTHESES

Formal Linkages

One of the first steps in looking at the relationship between two groups is to assess the formal linkages. For some, such as Duverger (1954), the prescribed "articulation" between the various subunits is a critical ingredient defining that organization. With regard to LCCs and traditional party organizations, such linkages refer to party bylaws or state statutes. Simply put, are LCCs formally connected with party organizations, as an appendage, branch, service agent, or are they independent?

While it has already been noted that certain LCCs are legally connected to the party organization, on the whole one might expect to find few formal linkages. As the critique of the functionalist perspective in Chapter 2 suggests, it is not clear whether these units were created as a mechanism of the party or as a response to waning party assistance. Rather, it is argued that they were created by legislative leaders (or groups of legislators) to meet *their* needs: support for the caucus leadership, reelection assistance, a vehicle to augment the size of the caucus, or a combination of such factors.

If, then, LCCs were created by legislative leaders to suit their needs, why would they choose to be linked to another organization? Would this not create added constraints, a diffusion of resources, and bring into play additional actors? One reason for such linkage might be the financial advantages granted party organizations, as noted above. It is suggested that this concern will be offset by the desire for exclusive control of resources and strategic decisions.

An example may help illustrate this point: In state X, the House is firmly controlled by the Republicans, while the Senate is narrowly held by the Democrats. The X Republican State Party Committee believes it would be beneficial to control both chambers. It calls upon the House Republican LCC to contribute heavily to Republican state senate candidates. After all, losing a few seats in the House might well be worth controlling both chambers. It may even be a goal of the House Republican LCC to have its party control the Senate—particularly if one of its objectives is to enact policy—yet it may have more pressing needs, primarily the reelection of caucus members. In short, the objectives of the state party committee may be much broader than the concerns of the LCC. Further, states with high levels of interparty competition might be expected to hold structurally independent LCCs.

Project Interdependence

Formal linkages tell only part of the story. A functional interdependence may develop, where the two organizations come to rely upon one another for assistance. Because certain activities and goals of both LCCs and TPOs are shared (winning elections),[4] one might expect this type of relationship to exist. Although few ties will be found on paper, a very real relationship, or interdependence, may be established.

One must be cautious when assessing this dimension. Speaking of party subunit interaction, Cotter and his colleagues point out:

> Interdependence . . . implies joint activity toward common goals, or it implies a process of reciprocity in which the party organizations at different levels assist each other in achieving their goals. When one level of the organization consistently exploits another for its own purposes, such an asymmetrical relationship cannot be considered interdependent (1984, 72).

Additionally, cooperation along a very narrow range of activities does not imply organizational interdependence. For instance, in many areas party organizations rely upon labor unions for the use of their offices during campaign periods (telephone lines, conference rooms, etc.). Union members may even assist on certain projects. Because the cooperation is limited, both in scope of activities and duration of time, and is unidirectional, it could not be concluded that the two are interdependent.

In order to be even more precise, interdependence can be divided into three clusters: 1) institutional support activities; 2) candidate-directed services; and 3) material interdependence.

Institutional support activities are those projects aimed at sustaining an organization. For both LCCs and traditional party organizations, fund-raising and services to subunits are examples. They may also include those projects that enhance the capacity of the organization to perform services to candidates and other political actors. Here voter registration, electoral mobilization programs, and the acquisition of equipment and facilities apply. In order to provide services, the organization must stand on firm ground and acquire the necessary resources.

On the whole, *few* institutional support linkages are expected. Money is the mother's milk of politics. The ability of the LCC to achieve its goals is directly tied to available resources. Many, but not all, of the goals of traditional party organizations are also dependent on resources. Certain institutional support activities (and general party building activities) such as get-out-the-vote and voter registration drives, may not coincide with, or even run counter to, LCCs objectives. It seems reasonable, then, to expect each unit to focus on its own support activities. What is more, Cotter and his colleagues found very low levels of institutional support interdependence between units structurally linked, such as county and state committees (1984, 73). There is no reason to suggest that this condition would be enhanced for organizations *not* formally connected.

This relationship may be modified in those states where the legislative committees are relatively new or have limited resources. If LCCs provide only modest services, such as distributing funds to incumbents, their institutional support needs will be small. In such cases, LCCs may work with traditional party organizations on fundraising or voter mobilization programs. Conversely, more extensive LCCs will be less likely to become interdependent with state or local party committees. With the ability to stand on their own, they will do so.

Party status may also alter this relationship; minority party organizations may be more likely to interact along this dimension than will majority units. Those out of power will have greater impetus to innovate and interact with one another. This may be especially true for rational-efficient organizations, where some control over resources may be sacrificed in the name of efficiency and greater chance for electoral success.

Finally, and related to the above, the level of party competition will impact upon institutional support coordination. Institutional support interdependence in competitive two-party states will be *less* frequent than in states dominated by one party. Along the same lines, those states with close majority/minority divisions in the legislature may see less interaction. Simply put, as the stakes increase, each unit will focus on maintaining its own organizational imperatives.

The second area of possible interdependence is *candidate-directed activities.* This refers to the services provided candidates—such as financial support, media assistance, survey research, direct mail, telephone canvassing, and so on. By pooling resources and expertise, each can benefit from greater economies of scale. Why should both units conduct a telephone canvass and produce a brochure for the same candidate when they can combine resources and cut costs?

Schlesinger's argument regarding level of party competition leading to increased coordination between campaign nuclei, discussed at length above, should apply to the relationship between LCCs and traditional party organizations. In other words, candidate-directed interdependence should be greater in competitive, two-party areas than in noncompetitive areas. Again, the same will hold in states with closely divided legislatures.

Candidate-directed interdependence can be further divided into two areas: *strategic considerations* and *tangible services*. The former relates to behind-the-scene judgments which determine the direction of a campaign and the appropriate mix of activities. Which candidates to support and how much to spend would be examples. Tangible services refer to specific activities, that is, the implementation of strategic decisions.

We would expect interdependence to be greater for tangible services than for strategic considerations. These new units will frequently call upon party committees, particularly at the local level, to assist with labor-intensive projects. The use of Locals to collect nominating petitions in the Plattsburgh Special is an illustration. Cooperation on strategic decisions, however, will be scant. Many LCCs are highly technical units, staffed by professionals. Although all politics may be local, it is doubtful LCCs will call upon party activists (generally amateurs) for strategic advice. A division of labor is thus conjectured, where LCC operatives control campaign strategy and traditional party committees implement grass-roots projects.

The contrast between strategic decisions and tangible services should be less pronounced in those states where the LCCs are modestly funded. These units will have had little chance to develop the technical competence and facilities necessary to conduct activities independent of the party committees—such as polling operations and media production studios. On the other hand, advanced LCCs only require the assistance of party activists for labor intensive projects and therefore will be less inclined to share strategic control.

Material interdependence means the sharing of facilities, equipment, and personnel. Do LCCs use the same headquarters as the state party organization? Do they share computers, cameras, printers, or telephone banks? Does the staff—paid and volunteer—work for both organizations?

Economies of scale would once more suggest that the two develop some level of material interdependence. Why should both purchase a computer system, for example, when the cost could be divided without significantly limiting either's use? The same might be said about headquarters or support staff.

The larger, more extensive the LCC, the less material interdependence will be found. Better funded LCCs will have the resources to control their own equipment and pay their own staff. These units will find it efficient and practical to break from, or never be formally affiliated with, the state committee, and they will have the resources to do so.

A physical division between the state committee and the LCCs will surely create additional costs for both. One advantage of this dualism might be full control over decisions and resources. Another very important consideration relates to fund-raising. A pronounced distinction between traditional party organizations and LCCs is the ability for donors (PACs, large individual contributors) to funnel contributions directly to legislative leaders through the latter. By doing so, contributors feel as though they get a bigger bang for the buck—greater access to the influential. The appearance of being merged with the state committee may reduce this advantage. They may lose in the short run by departing from the state committee but in the long term LCCs may gain from their independence.

Activities: Similarities and Differences

By understanding what legislative campaign committees do, and comparing these activities with those of traditional party organizations, one gains a better understanding of what these new organizations mean and where they fit in the political process. Setting aside institutional support (discussed above), activities can be divided into those broad-based or targetable. As the name implies, *broad-based activities* are those projects which help an array of candidates running under the party banner, often referred to as general party building projects. A partial list includes:

1. Voter Registration Drives
2. Get Out The Vote Activities
3. Party-based Media Advertisements

4. Grass-roots Training Programs

5. Social Activities to Reinforce the Faithful and Attract New Activists

6. Support for Community Oriented Events to Build and Maintain Favorable Image

7. Development and Articulation of a Party Platform

Similar to broad-based projects, *targetable activities* can be applied to a range of candidates. An important difference, nevertheless, is that they might *also* be directed to a specific candidate. For example, an organization may choose to use its polling service to aid a group of candidates or only one. This determination *cannot* be made for broad-based activities like voter registration drives. A partial list of targetable activities includes:

1. Polling

2. Financial Contributions

3. Candidate Seminars

4. Media Assistance

5. Direct Mail

6. List Development

7. Candidate Recruitment

Cotter et al. (1984), as well as several other recent studies (Frendreis et. al. 1994), suggest traditional party organizations conduct *both* broad-based and targetable activities, which is consistent with the view of traditional party organizations outlined in Chapter 3. Although state party organizations may focus on targetable projects and local committees spend most of their time on party building activities, both sets of projects receive some attention at each level.

This is not expected to be the case with LCCs. Broad-based activities would be deemed inefficient and often counterproductive. It even might be helpful to run away from other candidates of the same party, or simply ignore them. Their goals may reach beyond member reelection to caucus augmentation and support for the caucus leadership, yet each of these objectives is best satisfied with a narrow set of activities and by limiting the number of candidates supported.

The professionals who run LCC operations units are generally not recruited from within the party organization. Similar to marketing specialists, they bring skills and talents centered around the promotion of individual candidacies. As suggested in Chapter 2, LCCs now select a limited number of races and infuse each with unprecedented resources. Due to the effectiveness of this targeting strategy, combined with the narrow set of objectives of LCC leaders, broad-range activities will be rarely conducted.

Legislative campaign committees will focus on projects such as direct mail, polling, media assistance, and monetary contributions. Little effort will be spent on voter registration drives, broad-based get-out-the-vote programs, or community issues, and they will aid only their state legislative candidate. It would be rare to find LCCs supporting local, gubernatorial, or federal office candidates. It would also be unusual to find an LCC in one house assisting candidates (of the same party) in the other.

The level of party competition will modify this relationship. Specifically, states with high party competition will hold LCCs even *less* likely to conduct broad-based activities. Conversely, LCCs in states with low levels of party competition might be expected to conduct a somewhat wider set of activities. We might also speculate that LCCs formally tied will be perceived to engage in broad-based activities more often than those structurally autonomuus. This may be the case either because the state committee coerces them to do so or because legal ties simply pull perceptions in a more optimistic direction. In other words, if TPO leaders see these units as formally tied to their own organization, they might perceive them as concerned with party-building activities.

Are LCCs Partylike? The View of Party Leaders

Among the few scholars who have sought to systematically analyze the impact of these new organizations, the key query appears to be, are they partylike? On the first page of his book, Gierzynski asks: "What type of organizations are legislative party campaign committees? Can they be considered party organizations or are they merely political action committees" (1992, 1). Surprisingly, he never addresses the extent of linkages with traditional party organizations or the perspectives of traditional party leaders; his list of "relevant actors" (17–21) refers only to those in the legislature and no mention is made of either state or local traditional party officials.

For the present purpose, the view of traditional party leaders has been sought: that is, state and county chairs. They were asked to evaluate LCCs in four general ways: 1) the relationship between these units and their organization; 2) the willingness of LCCs to assist the state/county party committee; 3) the "partylikeness" of LCCs; and 4) the overall impact of LCCs on their party organization. Combined, these measures should provide a rough guideline as to whether party elites view LCCs as party units or as entirely different organizations.

It is expected on the whole, that TPO leaders will see LCCs as distinct from the party and unwilling to lend assistance. In brief, they will be seen as nonparty organizations. This may be especially true for local party leaders. Legislative campaign committees target races, which means providing little or no support to challengers who have little chance of winning. The state party committee may understand this as a reasonable strategy. But the local parties in districts where the legislative candidate is neglected might disagree passionately. Often, county party committees work hard for their state legislative candidates and find it difficult to see why higher up organizations—particularly those with "money coming out their ears"—would not lend a hand. The LCC operative who must explain to a county chair why her candidate will not receive assistance faces a difficult chore to be sure.

Along similar lines, in many states the state committee is controlled by the governor, usually through the hand-picked party chair. Here the governor's goals may parallel LCC objectives and see the need for targeting marginal districts. Or he may want some priority given to legislators loyal to the program. Again, local party leaders may not agree with these decisions.

The greater the disparity of resources between the LCCs and party organizations, the more party officials are expected to see them in a positive light. This conjecture may, at first, appear counterintuitive. It might be expected, that as the resources become equal and neither has the ability to dominate the other, interactions would increase and the relationships improve. The opposite is suggested. When both units are roughly parallel in strength, a struggle for control over the other's sphere leads to hostilities. Animosity may develop over strategic control, as well as influence with the candidate. When one unit dominates the other due to superior resources, the smaller generally follows the wishes of the larger and may be grateful for *any* help rendered. In many instances the weaker unit is so pleased with the help, because they could not do these things independently, that control is deferred freely. It is only when each group has the ability to grapple for control and demand things from the other that strained relations develop. Friction between the Clinton County Democratic Committee and DACC (the Plattsburgh Special) arose because the former had ideas as to how campaigns should be conducted and considerable resources to implement them.

The optimal situation, from the standpoint of the LCC, is for the local organization to take on those chores that LCC operatives view as important but labor intensive. Often these projects include literature drops, putting up lawn signs, and telephone canvassing. Control of strategy, message, theme, and resource allocation remains firmly within their grip. If the local committee is weak and unfamiliar with more complex campaign techniques, this arrangement would be acceptable. When the party committee is strong and also adept at using modern campaign techniques, it will demand to play a larger role and direct involvement in strategy. When this happens, there will be ongoing conflict, particularly when opinions over strategy differ— as they usually do. It is doubtful that the traditional party leaders will perceive these "intruders" as part of their organization.

An illustration may further clarify this supposition: a Democratic LCC is targeting a race in X County. The operations unit puts together an extensive campaign plan—focusing on polling, direct mail, and a thin range of issues. They begin implementing the plan in a wave of activity. The X County Democratic Committee, having considerable resources and expertise, also puts together a plan which focuses on television, grass-roots activities, and a different set of issues. Each group is well funded and staffed by professionals. Each will seek to control the direction of the campaign and develop a relationship with the candidate, her family, and her staff. Animosity will germinate, and members of the county party committee will invariably feel as though the LCC is more akin to a candidate-centered consulting firm, than a party organization.

This is not to say thematic and strategic choices will always differ. Yet, in most cases, one group (the party committee) will be Locals, and the other "outside hired hands." The former will always believe as though they know what is best in their district, while the latter will rely upon professionals and see the Locals as amateurs. The important point is that the likelihood of the two units conflicting will increase as the variance of resources and campaign sophistication narrows.

Similar to perceptions of broad-based activities, where LCCs are legally tied to the state party committee, perceptions of their party-likeness may be more positive. State committees may have *some* control over LCC activities in these states. More likely, formal bonds will simply pull perceptions toward a positive light. This may be especially true for TPO leaders who have had little exposure to LCCs.

Finally, the extent to which the LCCs interact with party committees and conduct broad-based party activities will have a strong bearing on perceptions. The less independent and rational-efficient that LCCs appear, the more partylike they will be perceived by the party leaders.

DATA AND METHODS

Several sources of data will be used to test these suppositions. The first is a case study of New York State, one of the earliest states to develop legislative campaign organizations. Each of the four LCCs in New York is significant—both in resources and services provided candidates—and has become a key player in state legislative elections. It is also an important state in measuring the relationship between LCCs and party organizations because of its long history of viable state and local party committees (Mayhew 1986, 32–46; Cotter et al. 1984). Personal interviews with state party leaders and a telephone canvass of seventy-eight county party chairs were conducted in the Spring of 1991.

Moving beyond New York State, the second set of data focuses on the state-level interactions. Here a survey of state party chairs and executive directors was conducted in December 1992. The population of state party committees (one survey per committee) was mailed a questionnaire. Fifty (50 percent) of the committees completed and returned the instrument, thirty-two of which have LCCs in their state.

A third data set consists of the population of county party chairs in four states. Excluding New York, the other thirty-nine LCC states were divided along two dimensions: party organization strength and LCC vitality. The states were then grouped into four clusters. One state from each quadrant was randomly selected; they are Ohio, Indiana, Florida, and Tennessee. Approximately forty county chairs from *each* state returned the survey, yielding a total sample of 169. The survey was conducted through the mail between February 20 and March 15, 1993.

The analysis will proceed in that order. Chapter 5 presents the case study of New York, Chapter 6 the state-level analysis, and Chapter 7 the county-level examination. One final piece of data consists of aggregate information on campaign finance, voter registration, demographics, election returns, state legislatures, state campaign statutes, and legislative campaign committees. A variety of sources was used to compile this information, and it will be used to augment the analysis of each data set and introduce further controls.[5]

Five

New York State: A Case Study

There are a number of important features, and perhaps advantages, to using New York State as a case study to begin examining the complex relationship between legislative campaign committees and traditional party organizations. Many of the concepts thought to be inherent in this new dynamic can be found here. New York was one of the first states to develop LCCs. These organizations—particularly those of the majority party—are today viewed as preeminent state-level campaign machines. In fact, their 1992 expenditures were significantly larger than their respective state party organization's. Each use state-of-the-art technologies and provide a variety of campaign services. A small body of literature has begun to emerge on these organizations, aiding our analysis (Dwyre and Stonecash 1992; Stonecash 1991; Shea 1991).

New York State also maintains one of the most highly paid, well-staffed legislatures in the nation. During the 1970s, changes in the length of sessions, the size of operating budgets, and staffing levels drastically transformed the role of the legislature; in many ways, it now stands on an equal footing with the executive branch. The power, prestige, and perks accompanying these changes have made service in the New York State Legislature a valued prize. Most legislators view their jobs as full-time professions and use the extensive resources at their disposal to ensure reelection. New York is certainly not alone in the movement toward professionalization, but it may be the most advanced in this direction.

New York is considered a strong party state. This can be seen from an organizational perspective, where local committees are particularly active (Cotter, et. al., 1984; Mayhew 1986), as well as a party competition vista (Bibby 1990). In races where LCCs target assistance, strong, aggressive party organizations are often present. As noted in the previous chapter, TPO strength may have a strong bearing on the type and extent of interactions between the two units.

83

An interesting structural relationship exists between the state party organizations and the LCCs in New York. Each of the LCCs is formally linked with the state committee through party bylaws. Yet, at the same time, scholars have noted their functional independence (recall Chapter 2). Along similar lines, New York is somewhat distinguished by its divided legislature. Since 1967, the Senate has been controlled by the Republicans and the Assembly by the Democrats. Any variation between majority and minority LCCs can be distinguished from party differences.

Finally, parties in New York State are perhaps the most heavily regulated in the nation. They are viewed as legitimate institutions participating in the process of government, constrained by government regulation (Scarrow 1983, 1). Party organizations in New York, according to Joseph Zimmerman, are "extraconstitutional institutions" (1983, 72). Everything from the selection of state committee delegates, to internal rules governing local party committees, to the staffing of boards of elections is regulated by statute. So, too, is the role of parties in the electoral process. Most of these laws are supportive of traditional party organizations and, at the same time, discourage the development of rival third parties.

This chapter takes a brief look at each of these features. More time is spent setting the context here than in subsequent chapters. These variables encourage an understanding of why state LCCs have developed, what their goals are, the scope of their activities, how these new units interact with traditional party organizations, and how party leaders perceive their activities and objectives. By detailing what legislative institutionalization has meant in New York, for example, we might better appreciate why LCCs target resources and are more advanced in some states than in others. The same might be said about the legal context, the shifting locus of party organizations from urban machines to county committees, and the growing volatility of the electorate.

The core of the chapter is an analysis of a survey conducted in the Spring of 1991. Leaders of both the state party committees and seventy-eight (of 124) county party chairs were interviewed. A host of questions was asked regarding their workings with and perceptions of LCCs. The empirical analysis is supplemented with a qualitative component. From 1986 to 1989, this author served as Regional Coordinator for the Democratic Assembly Campaign Committee. Where helpful, illustrations (anecdotes) based on personal experience with this organization are provided.

Overall, the merging of LCCs with traditional party organizations appears to be an imprecise conjecture in New York State. Although there is some variation—primarily a somewhat closer relationship among Republicans—the picture is of distinct organizations conducting different tasks. There appears to be a growing division of labor, where local committees are excluded from strategic decisions, and there is even some indication of growing hostilities—particularly among the Democrats.

THE NEW YORK CONTEXT

The Professionalization of the Legislature

One of the most pervasive trends in American politics over the last two decades has been the institutionalization of state legislatures. In the past, the archetypical state legislature consisted of amateur members, few resources and staff, and little ancillary support. The frequency and length of legislative session was short, and the average state legislator held his/her seat for just two or three terms. Members conducted policy research and constituent services personally. They generally held other jobs; legislative salaries—if there were any—were meager.

With the growth of state government during the 1960s and 1970s, and the New Federalism movement of the 1980s, came the professionalization of many state legislatures. "Like members of the House of Representatives, state legislators now preside over hundreds of programs and have leverage, however limited, over an enormous bureaucracy" (Chubb 1988, 143). The length of legislative tenure has also grown, suggesting an emerging full-time, long-term profession (Ehrenhalt 1992).

Benjamin and Nakamura (1991) separate changes in the New York State Legislature over the past two decades into three areas: the style and organization of legislative life; the locus of power; and the instruments of power. The principal change in legislative style has been the growing perception that legislative service is a career, rather than a temporary interlude. Whereas the average tenure for members in the 1960s was ten years, today the average stint is fifteen years. The percentage of members noting their occupations as legislator went from zero in 1964, to over 65 percent in 1988 (Benjamin and Nakamura 1991, xiv–xx).

Another change in style has been the growing length of sessions. Prior to the 1970s, it was rare that session extend beyond March.

Recent sessions generally run from January to July. During most of this time, members are required to be in Albany two or three days per week. Along with extended sessions, the amount of legislation passed has mushroomed. Over nine thousand bills are introduced each session, with roughly sixteen hundred being passed in each house (State of New York Management Resources Project 1988, 103). The Legislature is quickly becoming a full-time, year-round institution.

Each member now receives a base salary of $57,500. This, however, is only the beginning; extra stipends for committee assignments and party leadership positions are widely distributed. These lulus[1] range form $30,000 for top leadership positions, to $6,500 for ranking minority spots on committees. There are more committee and leadership posts in the Senate than there are members. As such, very few senators, if any, receive only the base salary. The picture is much the same in the Assembly, where there are thirty-six committees, fifty subcommittees, and over ten leadership positions. Members of both houses also receive approximately $125 per diem for travel and lodging when the Legislature is in session. All told, it is likely that the average New York State legislator makes over $75,000 per six-month session.

Staff within the legislature is extensive and also well paid. Each member is granted a lump-sum for personal staff—for both Albany and district offices. Although dependent on a number of variables—including the member's tenure, committee/leadership posts, and the size of the district—most members have about ten employees. The average salary for full-time professional staff is roughly $25,000. Nonmember personnel, such as staff on commissions and in-house service agencies, can also make considerable money. Counsel to committees and leadership often make upwards of $80,000; for many, their work with the legislature is considered part-time.

Each house now maintains extensive, state-of-the-art television, radio, and photography studios. When in session, members frequently use these services, particularly those from marginal districts, to reach voters back home. Party caucuses (in each house) support a unit specifically geared toward improving and expanding each member's public relations. At the very least, this service includes an ambitious franking program. Perhaps not coincidentally, the very same people who staff these units are often employed as operatives by the LCCs during election periods. The degree to which the two jobs overlap is, of course, debatable (see Chapter 1).

The second cluster of changes relates to the control of the legislative body. Throughout much of this century, the state legislature was generally overshadowed by external forces, usually the executive. Governor Rockefeller's strong hand during the 1960s is a prime illustration. The influence of several state and local party chairs was also heavy. Joe Crangle of Erie County, Erastus Corning of Albany, and Joseph Margiotta of Nassau County are examples. At roughly the same time many of the urban machines declined, resources and staff within the legislature expanded. The locus of power slowly shifted from outside forces to legislative leaders.

Finally, the instruments of power available to legislative leaders have changed. With regard to policy, the creation of in-house research units and legislative commissions has allowed the body to reduce its dependency on administrative agencies. One outcome of this independence has been a growing number of modifications to the governor's budget each year. Additionally, certain state court rulings[2] have held that Federal grants to state agencies must be channeled through the legislature, providing another boost to caucus leaders (State of New York Management Resources Project 1988, 117).

New York has had, formally and traditionally, intense party discipline and loyalty in the legislature. It is one of the most partisan, if not the most partisan, legislative bodies in the country (Hevesi 1985, 166; Scarrow 1983, 18–23; Moscow 1948, 170).[3] This strong leadership structure is not only central to policy initiatives but to perquisites— a system of rewards and punishment. Committee assignments, staff allotments, office resources, and franking privileges are all doled out at the leadership's discretion.

So, too, are the sacred "member items", i.e., pork barrel projects, which can run as high as $1.8 million per member (Kolbert and Uhlig, July 14, 1987). Legislators who support the party caucus, or are in marginal districts, may be graciously endowed. In 1987, one Assembly district in central New York received over $550,000, while a neighboring district received none. The latter was held by a Republican who faced a stiff challenge by the DACC in three previous races. This type of disparity between majority and minority districts is common and the ability (or inability) to bring home pork often surfaces during campaigns.

Members who unsuccessfully challenge caucus leadership can suffer harsh consequences. When Stanley Fink retired as Speaker in 1986 there ensued a scramble to fill his post. Arthur Kremer (D–Nassau County), then Chair of the prestigious Ways and Means Committee, entered the contest. Upon losing to Mel Miller (D-Brooklyn), Kremer was stripped of his Ways and Means job and given control of the Committee on Committees, perhaps the least prestigious of assignments. After two years, he retired from the Assembly altogether. Other examples of such hard-ball politics in Albany are common.

One additional tool of the centralized leadership is reelection resources: the LCCs. Prior to each election, members make a case to the leadership as to why they need (deserve) LCC support. The primary criteria used to make these decisions is the member's reelection chances, but sometimes other considerations, such as support for the leadership, are used. One member in Central New York has continued to receive significant help from the DACC even though he faces little opposition. He is considered a strong player in the speaker's coalition—loyal Upstate Democrats are somewhat hard to find—and is rewarded accordingly. Campaign resources have become leadership resources.

As members increasingly view their jobs as full-time professions, the stakes of majority party control and party solidarity escalate. According to Alan Hevesi, a student of New York politics and former Assemblyman, "in the New York State Legislature, to a degree surpassing that of any other legislature in America, the elected heads of the majority parties hold enormous power to control the destiny of legislative decisions made in their respective houses" (1985, 170).[4] Holding the majority matters for policy, perks, and reelection finances and is critically important for reapportionment decisions. With regard to campaign fund-raising, in 1992, the Senate Republicans raised five times the amount gathered by the minority Democrats, and, in the Assembly, the majority Democrats raised 28 percent more than the Republicans (Citizen Action of New York, 1992).[5] "Both houses are acutely conscious of their party situations and are continually using leadership resources to seek to improve their party's situation in each house" (Dwyer and Stonecash 1990, 12).

In summary, over the past two decades the New York State Legislature has moved quickly toward professionalization. Directly related to our concerns, New York's professional legislature provides tremendous incentives for reelection and for legislative leaders to augment their caucus. This too suggests, more generally, the important role context may play in LCC development and party–LCC relations.

LCCs in New York State

Legislative campaign committees in New York State were created during the mid-1970s. Formally, each was established as an appendage of its respective state party committee. The current committees are: the Democratic Assembly Campaign Committee (DACC), the Democratic Senate Committee, the Republican Assembly Campaign Committee (RACC), and the Senate Republican Campaign Committee. Both the Republican committees have divided their units into organizations that collect funds (the New York Senate Republican Committee, the Committee for a Republican Assembly), and another that allocates funds (the Republican Senate Direct Mail Account, Republican Assembly Campaign Committee).

Republican State Party bylaws note both an "Assembly Campaign Committee" and a "Senate Campaign Committee" within its list of "Other" state party committees. These units are to be "coterminous with the State Committee and to function as an integral part thereof." Little mention is made of their activities, relationship to other elements of the party structure, or control over them (Rules of the New York Republican State Committee 1993, 3).

In 1988, the newly elected State GOP Chair, Anthony Colavita, sought to amend the state party rules explicitly to place LCC funds under state party control. The idea was quickly rejected by Republican legislative leaders. Their concern was that "such a rule could mean the money raised by the legislative campaign committees would be used by the state Republican Committee for such things as gubernatorial campaigns" (Associated Press, September 20, 1988). The amendment never got off the ground.

As for the Democrats, LCCs are listed in the bylaws along with eight additional committees. The party leader in each house is given control over his/her respective LCC and has the power to appoint a treasurer and other members. The relationship between these units and other elements of the state party, or between one another, is left unstated (Rules of the Democratic Party of the State of New York 1994, Section 6).

With minor exceptions (the Senate Democrats, see Chapter 1), the amount of money gathered by each has grown appreciably. It has been demonstrated elsewhere (Dwyer and Stonecash 1992) that the percentage of candidate spending coming from these units has also steadily grown. The Senate Republicans, for example, contributed 34 percent of all candidate expenditures in 1984. In 1988 that figure had risen to 53 percent. Each of the other committees parallel this trend. By combining committees of the same party, it becomes clear that the LCCs now hold budgets larger than each of their respective state party committees.

Dwyer and Stonecash (1992) find LCCs in New York State prefer coordinated (on-behalf-of) spending over direct cash contributions. Housekeeping expenditures—such as payments for polling consultants, computers, overhead for facilities, and printers—imply that these units are more than mere financial distribution vehicles.

Disclosure information suggests that each of the LCCs uses a majority of its nonhousekeeping resources on a limited number of close state legislative races. In the 1992 general election, DACC vested most of its money on twenty-three races (out of 150), with three candidates receiving over $100,000. The Republican Assembly Campaign Committee was slightly more focused, targeting approximately seventeen races. Two of these races received over $150,000; both were unsuccessful challengers. The Senate Democrats limited most of their involvement to twelve races (out of sixty-one), eight of which were challenges. Senate Republicans used their money in a slightly broader fashion, infusing seventeen campaigns with heavy resources, mostly on incumbents (New York State Board of Elections, 1993).

These data appear consistent with Gierzynski's general finding that LCC resources are largely focused on competitive races (1992, 71–92). The 1992 data may also suggest a distinction, albeit modest, between majority and minority spending patterns. Consistent with information for the 1988 general election (Dwyer and Stonecash 1992, 337–340), majority party LCCs appear to have concentrated their resources on reelection campaigns more so than minority LCCs. This is true for both houses, but particularly so in the Senate where the split between the two parties is much closer.

An underexamined, yet important component of LCCs is in-kind assistance. Campaign organizations in New York are required by law to disclose all expenditures. This includes direct contributions (transfers out), in-kind expenditures, and non-allocable expenditures.[6] Unlike individuals and PACs, by holding the status of a party committee, LCCs are not subject to contribution limits.

Candidates and LCCs wish to steer clear of perceptions that they are "buying the district" with excessive resources. Several techniques are used to keep reported LCC expenditures as low as possible. Massive in-house volunteer activities are often utilized, thereby reducing or eliminating individual candidate expenditures. Each committee recruits dozens of volunteers, generally from rank-and-file membership or service agency office each night during the final months of the campaign. In June before an election, for example, the Senate Republicans send out a mailing to Senate Majority employees, inviting them to lend a hand. Rather than paying a mailing house to affix address labels, the Democratic Assembly Campaign Committee uses volunteers. Several hundred thousand pieces of mail are handled each night during the final weeks of the campaign. The same level of attention is sometimes given to telephoning; there are considerable savings on surveys, for example, if unpaid workers are used to make calls. Volunteer projects such as these are not only cost saving, but exceedingly difficult to divide into contributions to specific candidates.

Another technique is for legislative leaders to call upon caucus members and PACs to make financial contributions *directly* to targeted candidates, rather than contributing to the LCC. Candidates then turn over control of this money to LCC operatives.

Third, many of the people sent into districts during the final days of the campaign do so on their own time (i.e., vacation, personal time, etc.) and are thus unpaid. During the last weekend of the campaign, each LCC sends no fewer than twenty people out to races perceived to be especially close. For those accustomed to New York State politics, this sort of activity should come as no surprise. As Warren Moscow noted some time ago: "As long as one can remember, state and city employees who might be of value to their parties in a campaign have taken 'leaves of absence' or 'vacations' during campaign time to work for their party's ticket" (1948, 68).

Finally, the salaries for many of the operatives working on campaigns (or sets of campaigns) for an extended period are not disclosed as contributions to specific candidates, but rather as non-allocable expenses. Although an operative may spend weeks or months developing direct mail and radio advertisements for the same candidate, if s/he remains in Albany (the LCC central headquarters), s/he is not listed on the candidate's disclosure forms.

These techniques and many others suggest LCC assistance is much greater than Board of Elections data would indicate. And that a large portion of their targeted activity goes unnoticed to the public and scholars.

Party Organizations in New York State

The picture of traditional party organizations in New York State is somewhat muddled. Urban organizations, found in New York City, Buffalo, Albany, Utica, and many other cities, were frequently pointed to as illustrations of partisan machines. Many of these organizations have attracted a good deal of scholarly interest; so much so that Mayhew ranks New York a 5, i.e., a "party organization state" (Mayhew 1986, 32–46). Recently, the Nassau Republican Organization, under Joseph Margiotta, and the Monroe County Democratic Committee, lead by Fran Weisberg and Robert Brown, have emerged as powerful urban/suburban campaign forces.

The general pattern, however, is one of urban party decline. Few of the old-style machines remain virile. The once powerful Manhattan Democratic organization, for example, has decayed to but a shell of its former self. The Albany Democrats, for over a century a unified force, recently lost control of the county executive to a Republican and the mayor's office to an insurgent, reform Democrat—both unheard of in prior years. The Utica Democratic Club, once under the powerful auspices of Rufus ("Ruffy") Elefante, has not elected a mayor in over eighteen years and has struggled to keep a full slate of committeepersons. The Onondaga County Republican Committee, once boasting perhaps the strongest GOP organization Upstate, has seen its state legislative delegation dwindle from four to two (out of a total of six). If one is to find robust party organizations in New York State, the search must extend beyond traditional urban machines.[7]

The portrait of local party committees presents a somewhat different picture. During the 1960s, Stuart Witt (1967) found traditional local committees regularly supporting full slates of candidates everywhere in the state. During the 1970s and early 1980s, Cotter and his colleagues (1984) also found very strong local party committees. They ranked New York third among Democrats and second among Republicans in local party organization vitality throughout the nation (Cotter, et. al., 1984, 52–53).[8] County level committees, in particular, are well funded and staffed.[9] Where large urban machines may have withered, many local party organizations remain robust.

As suggested in Chapter 4, an important variable in the relationship between LCCs and traditional party organizations may be the relative strength of each. Although it would be a mistake to imply that all of the TPOs in New York are strong, the state does, at the very least, provide a broad range of traditional party organizations.

Electoral Competition

In the aggregate, New York is best viewed as a two-party state. Using Ranney's Index from 1981 to 1988, only North Dakota and Delaware are more competitive (see Beck and Sorauf 1992, 38–40). Although enrolled Democrats outnumber Republicans by a three to two margin, this advantage is generally negated by higher turnout among the latter. Along with a divided state legislature, the even balance between the parties can be seen in statewide elections. Mario Cuomo's first race, then an open seat, was exceedingly close, as was his loss to George Pataki in 1994. The U.S. Senate delegation is divided between Alfonse D'Amato (R) and Patrick Moynihan (D). Other state offices are also split; for over a decade, the Comptroller was a Republican (Edward Regan) and the Attorney General a Democrat (Robert Abrams). When viewed from the state level, New York appears to be a competitive two-party state.

Aggregate figures are somewhat misleading. Many areas throughout the state are noncompetitive. The clearest example is the near total domination of the Democrats in New York City—especially Brooklyn and Manhattan. Republican strength is equally potent in many rural counties. Suburban areas of the state are often considered the true battleground for most statewide elections.

During the past few decades there may have been a declining number of marginal state legislative districts. Weber, Tucker, and Brace look at the marginality of lower house districts from 1950 to 1986 in twenty states. Their overall finding is the near universal decline of competitive seats. Using a multivariate regression, they single out the institutionalization of state legislatures as the foremost variable causing this change. In New York, they find evidence of lowering marginality, but at a slower rate than other states (Weber, Tucker, and Brace 1991, 33–34).

It should be noted that the limits of vanishing marginals studies, cited in Chapter 2, might also apply in New York. Margins of victory appear to be rising, but defeat rates have not declined appreciably. This is due to the increasingly volatile and unpredictable nature of the electorate. In fact, there has even been a slight increase in the number of incumbent defeats in New York. Eight state legislators lost reelection in 1992—twice the number in the prior election and, excluding 1974, more than any election since 1968.[10] Many of the districts throughout the state, once considered safe, are today seen as marginal when infused with heavy resources. Members of the state legislature may also see their seats as "unsafe at any margin" (Mann 1977; Fenno 1978).

THE RELATIONSHIP BETWEEN LCCs AND TPOs IN NEW YORK STATE

To this point the stage has been set in New York by outlining changes in the legislature, the growth of the LCCs, the strength of traditional party organizations, and the degree of electoral competition. Having done so, one is better able to investigate and understand the relationship between these new units and traditional party organizations.

At the very least, this review has also shown that LCCs in New York are dominant players—both as tools of caucus leadership and within the larger electoral arena. Rather than a vehicle to supplement waning party organizations, it is conceivable that they were created as byproducts of the legislative institutionalization movement, as a piece of a strong leadership structure in that body, and/or as a response to growing electoral competition—likely a combination of all three. Each of these ingredients may speak to LCCs goals, activities, and interactions with traditional parties. In other words, by understanding *why* they were created, one may better understand *where* they fit and *what* impact they may have on traditional parties. The remainder of this chapter seeks to examine this dynamic in greater detail.

Four areas of inquiry will be used to do so. As noted above, each of the LCCs in New York is legally connected to the state party organization. One part of the analysis will discern the weight of this formal relationship. Are the legal bonds merely a facade, as suggest by Jewell and Olson (1988), or do they denote real constraints, as implied by Dwyre and Stonecash (1992)? Perhaps this formal connection helps pull the LCCs under the fold of the state committee and steers their activities in a partylike direction. A second focus will be a look at the functional interdependence between the LCCs and the traditional party committees. Conceivably, LCCs work together with the party organizations on a number of projects. If so, are these projects candidate services, or do they also assist one another with institutional support activities, such as fund-raising? A third area will be the perceived activities and goals preformed by the LCCs. Do party leaders see the enterprise of these new units similar to their own organization's? A final area of inquiry is whether party leaders view LCCs, on the whole, as partylike or something altogether different.

Interviews were conducted with both leaders from the state party committees and seventy-eight county party chairs in the winter and spring of 1991. The questionnaire of the county-level study is found in Appendix A.[11]

THE STATE-LEVEL RELATIONSHIP

The Republicans

The author's interview with William Powers, Chair of the New York State Republican Committee, took place in April of 1991.* Powers had just taken over the Committee from Patrick Barrett. Barrett had risen quickly to the state-level post by promising to find a viable guberna-torial candidate and to augment the party's coffers. He was unsuc-cessful on both counts—the two are, of course, closely linked—and he was replaced by Powers in December of 1990. Powers had previ-ously served as Vice-Chair of the State Committee and as Rensselaer County Chair.

As Powers took the helm, the State Committee was in a lapse. Recent efforts in gubernatorial elections were dismal. Pierre Rinfret, Republican candidate in 1990, came perilously close (less than one percent) to running third behind Conservative candidate Herb Lon-don. Such an outcome would have had profound consequences for the Republican organization. Party ballot positions for all elections in New York State are fixed by the previous gubernatorial election returns, and a third-place finish for the Republicans would have meant a shift from second to third slot. In New York, as in many states, control of the board of election offices (county and state level) is divided between the two parties with the highest vote-getting gubernatorial candidates. This change alone could mean the loss of thousands of jobs. The embarrassment of coming in third place would have seriously jeopardized lower-level candidates for years to come, as well as hamstring future state-level fund-raising.

Fund-raising during the 1990 election year had also reached a new low. The party appeared to be in the thralls of a post-Rockefeller, post-Anderson doldrums.[12] Recall that Cotter and his colleagues (1984) had once ranked New York State's Republican Committee moderately strong.

---

*Quotes by William Powers in this section are taken from the author's notes.

Bringing the Parts Together

A persistent theme during the interview with Powers was his desire to transform the Committee, to bring it back. In order to meet the challenges which lay ahead, the party must, he argued, "look forward rather than backward." The cornerstone of his plan would be to bring each of the components of the organization—the county committees, the two LCCs, and the state organization—into unified action.

According to Powers, the legislative campaign committees had moved in separate directions. The Senate Republicans had used their resources to secure their frail majority, while the Assembly Republicans had little reason to bestow their relatively finite capital on the ailing state committee and their statewide elections.

As Powers saw it, one of his first tasks would be to remind legislative leaders that the state committee was the center of the party organization. That is, in order for Republicans at all levels to be successful, there must be coherence and cooperation at the state level. "Many of the candidates for the Senate and Assembly begin their careers running for lower-level offices. [LCC leaders] should see these people as part of their 'farm team,' and begin working with them now."

What else Powers meant by coherence and cooperation is difficult to say. Did he wish to go as far as Colavita in trying to place LCC resources under the state Chair's control; or would coordinated campaign strategy be enough? His response: "What we need to do is to know exactly what each of the committees are doing and, when possible, work together. Does that mean sharing resources? Why not, were all in the same boat."

Party bylaws did not appear to be an important part of Powers's line of reasoning. According to these rules, each of the LCCs falls under the jurisdiction of the central party committee, e.g., Powers. As noted above, they are to be "coterminous with the State Committee and to function as an integral part thereof." Powers's logic, nevertheless, was based solely from an instrumental vantage; the units would be better off working together. He seemed reluctant to flex his bylaw muscles, perhaps not wanting to ruffle feathers or expose the weakness of the state committee. Another possibility is that LCC autonomy is now a strong norm.

This is not to say that Powers believed the State Committee had no recourse against LCC autonomy. The committee did possess, he believed, a very potent tool at its disposal—control of party nominations. Asked *how* he might compel the LCCs to work with the State Committee, Powers responded, "We control party nominations and it's that simple. Who do they think will carry petitions if we don't? They need us, so they've got to work with us."

Unlike many states, the nomination process in New York can be tedious. In order to be placed on the ballot under a party banner, either in a primary or general election, five hundred *valid* signatures are needed for Assembly candidates and one thousand for State Senate candidates. The details and technicalities of petition gathering in New York are no less than daunting (Moscow 1948, ch. IV). To be safe, candidates usually collect two or three times the necessary number. If a local party committee decides to undertake this task, as they have traditionally done, the process is timely and easy for the candidate. If the candidate's organization must gather the signatures, it becomes an expense, both in time and resources.

Powers's comment is most telling. Theoretically there are a number of ways to oblige a candidate or campaign organization to cooperate with a party organization. The party might withhold resources, services, or information. It might also use powerful elected officials to apply pressure. The Republican State Committee in New York has a sizeable portion of each—but so do the Republican LCCs. Perhaps the Chair retreated to a last bastion of exclusive party control: nominations. But is even this a viable threat?

Historically, good relations with local party leaders have been an important element of a state legislator's job. Moscow notes:

> In order to understand the relationship between legislator and legislative leader, between legislator and party policy, one simply has to remember that the Assemblyman is elected from a district, usually small in area and never larger than one county, that he must run for nominations as well as election, and therefore he must be on good terms with his county chairman [sic] and his district boss. This is also true of the State Senator, except that the area he runs in is larger (1948, 174).

This notion, however, may no longer hold water. For one, legislative districts were once apportioned on the basis of an 1894 constitutional amendment which made the sixty-two counties the core unit of representation. County borders, instead of population, were used for apportionment. With a total of 150 legislators, no county was to have less than one assemblyman. In a series of Supreme Court cases beginning with *Baker v. Carr* (1962)[13] and extending to the states in *Reynolds v. Sims* (1964),[14] the "one person, one vote" principle struck down this scheme (Lee 1967). Today both the Senate and Assembly are apportioned based on population and often include several counties, portions of counties, or both.

Second, and perhaps more to the point, as candidates have moved away from party assistance during general elections, i.e., candidate-centered campaigns, they have also developed personal organizations for nomination efforts. While gathering nomination signatures is difficult, it is certainly possible, particularly if the candidate has enough money to pay workers. Tight party control over state legislative nominations is today a rarity.

Project Interdependence[15]

Beyond the limited strategic cooperation, Powers was asked how often and in what types of activities the legislative committees and the state party committee interacted. The greatest area of cooperation appeared to be fund-raising. Along with running their own events, the three units work together on a large fund-raising gala each year.[16] As for other institutional support activities—such as broadbased media programs, voter registration drives, and grass-roots training programs, Powers conceded that neither of the legislative units was likely to provide more than cursory assistance. "That's not their job. Their expertise and money are used to win elections."

Interactions on candidate-specific activities were also scarce; few joint projects were conducted. To Powers, this was disturbing when, during the final weeks of the Rinfret gubernatorial campaign, the State GOP ran out of money. They realized the race was not winnable but were worried about being surpassed by the Conservative candidate. Calls for assistance were unheeded by the LCCs. The Senate operation was particularly flush. Again Powers reiterated his vow to use nominations as an instrument of LCC control; "That will not happen again, period."

The Democrats

In the spring of 1991 the New York State Democratic Committee was under the leadership of John Marino. Unfortunately, Marino was unavailable during the research for this project. A discussion was held with William Cunningham, the party's Political Director.*

---

*Quotes by William Cunningham in this section are taken from the author's notes.

One of the first themes to develop during the conversation with Cunningham was the distant relationship between the State Committee and the LCCs. "There is no question, each of the units operates independently of one another." Unlike Powers, Cunningham saw this relationship as generally a good thing. "By each LCC focusing on its own races, expertise and resources are available for gubernatorial campaigns and other races."

Cunningham did suggest that state committee coffers may have been hurt by the LCCs. "Campaign contributions are, more or less, limited and many would-be party contributors are now giving directly to [the LCCs]—primarily the Speaker's organization." DACC's annual Spring Fling, an event held in Albany toward the end of each legislative session, was cited as an example.

Like the Republicans, there appeared to be little project interdependence at the state level. Both of the LCCs occasionally used state committee telephone lines during the final stages of campaigns and during special elections. There is also some coordination on get-out-the-vote drives in certain districts, as well as cooperation on legal matters such as postage and disclosure regulations. Yet, on the whole, neither of the LCCs regularly seek the advice of, or work with the State Committee. Both the LCCs have headquarters separate from the State Committee, and the direction of assistance was nearly always in one direction, from the state committee to the LCCs. This was true for both financial interactions and candidate activities. Finally, according to Cunningham, it was almost inconceivable that either of the LCCs would help a nonstate legislative candidate.

A Peaceful Coexistence?

Controlling the Governor's Mansion is certainly at the forefront of the Democratic State Committee's concerns. In fact, the party was criticized during the 1986 and 1990 elections for concentrating resources on the gubernatorial campaign while neglecting state-legislative elections, even though Cuomo faced little real opposition. This was seen as particularly troublesome in 1990 when many Democrats believed the Senate was within their grasp; only three seats separated the parties.[17]

It is tempting to speculate that the neat division between each of the units best suits their needs. DACC has become the electoral arm of the Speaker (now the most powerful Democrat in Albany), who is free to use its resources as he sees fit. The State Committee, on the other hand, might be used simply as a gubernatorial campaign organization. Neither unit would wish to have the other control its resources and dictate its activities. Many of Cunningham's comments echoed this sentiment.

The only players out in the cold are the Senate Democrats. From a traditional party perspective, this might appear somewhat surprising. The division between the parties in the Senate is relatively narrow (about five seats), while the other house is easily controlled by the Democrats. Why not pool resources in an effort *also* to control the Senate? This line of reasoning assumes the LCCs and traditional party organization share identical goals. Little of my interview with Bill Cunningham or Bill Powers would support such a conjecture.

FINDINGS AT THE
COUNTY PARTY COMMITTEE LEVEL

The county is the most basic political unit in New York State. This is true for a number of reasons. As noted above, from 1894 until the 1970s, apportionment in the state legislature was based on county boarders. Current election law specifies the structure of party organizations, requiring each party to have a county committee. The law dictates how these committees are formed and manage their affairs, when officers are to be elected, and even specifies the dates of meetings (Zimmerman 1981, 73–75). Members of the state committee are chosen from the sixty-two county committees, and county chairs are periodically called upon to perform specific tasks, such as candidate designations for statewide office, cross-endorsement agreements, and special election nominations. The state's election machinery (boards of election, polling places on election day, and so on) are overseen by county parties. Moreover, the names of state and county party chairs are listed in the state's official publication, the *Legislative Manual* (Scarrow 1983, 4–8).

Beyond the legal context, the tradition of party politics in New York is county politics. Even the most legendary bosses (Tweed, Plunkitt, Murphy, DeSapio) have headed the New York County (Manhattan) Democratic organization, not a citywide structure (Costikyan 1966). This is also the basic pattern Upstate; Dan O'Connell was *not* the leader of the City of Albany organization, but the Albany County Democratic machine. Patronage always has been an important piece of party activity in New York, and it continues to be left to county party leaders to distribute.

In order to fully understand the connection between traditional party organizations and LCCs in New York, then, a county-level focus is warranted. Telephone interviews were conducted with forty-two Republican and thirty-six Democratic county party chairs. The sample represents 63 percent of the population. Four separate attempts were made to contact each chair; grounds for omission appear random—vacation, illness, too busy, refused.[18] All of the quotations in this chapter not otherwise cited are taken from responses to the questions in Appendix A.

An early section of the survey sought to measure the county committee's relationship with the state party organization. If LCCs are truly appendages of the state party, as bylaws suggest, the level of interaction between the county committees and the state party committees may be telling. Linkages with, and attitudes toward, this unit may guide linkages and evaluations of LCCs. Several indicators were used to measure the state–county committee relationship, including the frequency of communications, a seven-point scale, and an open-ended query.

Overall, relations with the state committee appear frequent and positive. Roughly 14 percent of the respondents noted they talked with members of the state committee at least once per week, 41 percent several times a month, and 73 percent at least once per month. The mean score on the seven-point, distant/close scale (1 very distant, 7 very close) was 4.2. Furthermore, 76 percent indicated a "friendly," "good," or "close" relationship to the open-ended question. Party differences appear minimal, with a slightly higher degree of interaction for Republicans. The correlation between county committee size and attitudes toward the state committee was also insignificant.[19]

Exposure to LCCs

The level of the exposure to the LCCs may be a strong determinant of attitudes and perceptions toward these new units. If the county party leader has had limited contact with these organizations (perhaps they either reside in a noncompetitive county or one where an incumbent runs unopposed), their view of LCCs will be much different than those who have had frequent contact. Chairs with limited exposure are expected to hold a more positive, or at the very least benign, view.

Table 5.1 divides the sample into three groups: "High" signifies the portion of chairs who reported at least one of the LCCs was involved in a campaign in their county; "Moderate" denotes chairs who have had other workings, contacts, or communications with at least one of the LCCs; and "None" indicates the portion of chairs who have had no workings or communications with them.[20]

As we can see, roughly one-half of the chairs in the sample have had a good deal of interactions with these new units. The portion of chairs in the Moderate category is somewhat larger for Republicans, as is the None group for Democrats. An additional question concerning the types of "contacts or workings" helps uncover the root of this variation between parties. Sixty-seven percent of the Republicans in the Moderate group said their relationship with the LCCs centered exclusively on LCC fund-raisers. GOP county party chairs were apparently listed on Republican LCC mailing lists. Democrats, on the other hand, did not have a similar link.

The number of Democrats and Republicans in the None category is somewhat revealing. Although LCCs have been around since the 1970s, are key players in state legislative elections, are structurally linked to the state committees, and have budgets that now surpass each of the state committee's, a sizeable portion of county party chairs have had no interaction with them. This is especially telling with regard to Republicans, where each county chair serves on the state party's executive committee. A number of chairs seemed utterly unaware of LCCs activities. As one upstate Republican noted: "I've never had any workings with either one. . . . I couldn't begin to tell you what they do."

Table 5.1
Level of Interaction with LCCs by Party of Chair
(In Percentages)

	Democrats	Republicans	Total
High	49	56	52 (N = 39)
Moderate	25	29	29 (N = 24)
None	26	15	19 (N = 15)
Total	(N = 36)	(N = 42)	100 (N = 78)

Respondents were asked if either a Senate or Assembly LCC was involved in a campaign in their county while they were chair. The High group denotes those in the affirmative. Those who said "no" were asked a follow-up query. The Moderate group are those with "other" contacts or workings, and the None group had no contact at all.

There appears to be no difference in the frequency of contacts with the state committee, attitudes regarding the state committee, or average tenure of chairs in the None group and those in the Moderate and High categories. In other words, these are not isolated, disgruntled, new party leaders.

Legislative campaign committees target resources on close races. No doubt strategic decisions limit their exposure in noncompetitive areas. It is thus understandable why some county chairs have had little direct interactions with them. Nevertheless, if LCCs are state party units, and if the legal/structural arrangements between LCCs and the state committees are more than superficial, one might expect each of the county chairs—a central component of the traditional party structure—to have a basic understanding of LCC activities. A minimal level of communication might be expected. While this appears to be the case most of the time, it is far from universal.

Even those chairs familiar with the existence of the LCCs were often unclear as to who controls them and what they do. As a field operative, it was part of the author's job to meet with county party leaders and explain, in a general sense, what the Democratic Assembly Campaign Committee (DACC) was going to do (or not do) in that district during the coming election. Most chairs expected "block grants" of money and vast input in strategic decisions. When they received little of either, they would often threaten to call the state party chair. These threats, in all frankness, were seen by DACC staff as empty.

Project Interdependence[21]

Nonstructural linkages are divided into three broad areas: 1) institutional support activities; 2) candidate-directed activities; and 3) material interdependence.

There appear to be few coordinated activities with regard to institutional support. Asked whether county committees "worked with [the LCC] to raise money," only 8 percent of the chairs answered in the affirmative. Moreover, just 11 percent said their committee "pooled resources with [the LCC] to fund projects during campaigns."

Candidate-directed interactions were also limited. Recall that this concept can be divided into strategic considerations and tangible services. Respondents were asked "how often during the campaign [s/he], or other members of the county committee, talked with staff members of the LCC." Fifteen percent said they never had contact, 44 percent said their communications were less than a few times per month, 22 percent said about once per week, and 19 percent said they talked on a daily basis. Respondents were then asked to use a seven-point scale to measure "how much they think [the LCC] listened to the county committee's input during the campaign (1 being the lowest and 7 the highest)." The mode response to this question was 3, with 65 percent noting 4 or less. Only 16 percent of the chairs stated their county committee worked with the LCC to develop a strategic plan for the campaign.

The modest level of strategic decision-making linkages also can be seen in the divergent types of activities conducted by the LCCs and the county committees. Over 80 percent of the chairs mentioned the LCCs were primarily responsible for activities requiring strategic choices—such as targeting mailings, media development, and issue formation—but only 19 percent suggested the county committees were also involved in such activities. Two-thirds said the activities of the county committee were nonstrategic, traditional grass-roots projects, such as door-to-door canvassing, stamping envelopes, and making telephone calls. Of the respondents who noted working with these units, many said their county committees simply followed the directions of the LCC. "They told us who to call, when to do it, and what to say," noted a Republican chair.

Several of the respondents expressed resentment over this division of labor. "We felt shut-out," said one chair, "[t]hey come here from Albany and do things that might work in New York City, but not here. . . . They never listen to what we have to say. If you ask me, that's why we lost [the] race." Other comments were similar: "We never know what kind of crap is going to hit the [voter's] mailboxes next." Also, "I'd get calls from people—and for that matter the media—and they'd ask me about what the campaign was doing. To tell the truth, I really didn't know what was going on. . . . It made me look stupid."

This feeling of frustration over the lack of strategic coordination appeared to be most acute during special elections. "The entire race took less than three weeks. There were so many people here from Albany, and so many things happening at once that even I was confused—and I was [the candidate's] campaign manager. I asked to be kept abreast, but all I got was a bunch of hot air."

It should be noted that several chairs expressed satisfaction with the level of cooperation with the LCCs. A Democrat from the western part of the state noted: "They sent over a lot of good people who really knew what they were doing. Other than a few minor skirmishes, we worked together fine." A Republican from the Hudson Valley

Region added: "We got along okay. They did their thing, and we did ours. It was a one-two punch."

The level of tangible-service interdependence was somewhat higher; 34 percent stated their committee "worked together with [the LCC] on projects during campaigns." Although this finding is more encouraging than for strategic and financial interactions, two points should be noted: First, the level of project coordination showed considerable variance. Whereas several chairs noted their committee's interactions with the LCCs centered exclusively on one or two short-term projects, such as looking up telephone numbers for a poll, others stated they worked together on several ongoing activities.[22] Second, chairs may be defensive about their committee's lack of involvement in races where LCCs were extensively involved and may have overestimated their committee's role. This bias may be particularly acute for recall questions, such as these.

A second measure of tangible interdependence was whether the chair had *sought* help on a project during the campaign. Forty-one percent stated they had requested assistance. Of those who did ask for help, 58 percent indicated they received the aid they needed. Again, if LCCs are financially and technically blossoming, and are elements of the state party, it seems odd that less than one-half of the county chairs would ask for assistance, with only one-half of these getting the help.

It was speculated earlier (Chapter 4) that interactions between TPOs and LCCs would be greater for tangible services than for strategic interactions. Overall, findings appear to support this conjecture. Legislative campaign committees in New York, for the most part, appear to oversee the direction and theme of the campaign—while traditional party units conduct labor intensive activities.

A note of caution should be made. Although TPOs appear occasionally to assist the LCCs, it is far less common to find the LCCs helping the county committees on nonstate legislative campaign projects.

Asked if the chair believed the LCC would "help on a local party project . . . such as putting together a voter registration drive," only eight percent said it would be "very likely" and 19 percent "somewhat likely." Conversely, 28 percent believed it would be "somewhat *un*likely," and 45 percent "very *un*likely." Responses concerning financial help for a similar project were even more pessimistic: a full 76 percent noted it would be "very unlikely" that their committees would receive financial help on a voter registration drive. Perceived assistance from Republican LCCs appears to be a bit higher than from Democratic LCCs, but it is also low. Table 5.2 highlights this finding, controled by party.

This finding is consistent with the author's experiences. The DACC was very reluctant to become involved in projects unrelated to the task at hand or to aid nonlegislative candidates. A few vivid illustrations may be helpful. While conducting an Upstate race, DACC arranged for the Governor to pay its candidate a visit and hold a rally and press conference on his behalf. Soon after this announcement, candidates for local posts (also Democrats) approached DACC and asked if they too could appear on the podium with Governor Cuomo. It was determined, however, that these candidates would defray the focus of the event and perhaps even hurt the Assembly candidate; in the DACC's view, many were "sacrificial lambs." In the end we suggested they not appear on the podium or at the press conference. They could, of course, attend the rally as part of the audience.

During another race, DACC was asked by the county chair to distribute pamphlets for local office candidates while it was distributing material for the Assembly candidate. It seemed simple enough; drop three or four pieces of literature instead of one. DACC politely took the material, placed it in the corner of the headquarters, and never distributed it. Again, we did not wish to dilute the voter's attention from our candidate, nor link him to sure losers.

Table 5.2
Perceived Likelihood of Assistance From LCCs, Controlled by Party*
(In Percentages)

	Very Likely		Somewhat Likely		Somewhat Unlikely		Very Unlikely	
	D	R	D	R	D	R	D	R
Help on Project, Such as GOTV Drive?	7	10	15	30	32	25	56	35
Financial Help for Local Party Activity?**	—	—	—	5	6	19	88	67

*Only those respondents in the High Exposure Group were asked these questions.

N = 39 (18 Democrat, 21 Republican)

**Unsure = 6% for Democrats and 10% for Republicans

Probability using chi-square is .28 and .42, respectively.

As a final illustration, during the heat of a campaign a DACC local headquarters received a telephone call from the Campaign Manager for the Democratic candidate for State Attorney General. Apparently, the candidate was coming the next day for a debate, and he wished to fax a list of questions people in the audience might ask. Facsimile transmission, many readers will recall, was considerably slower in 1986; one page over the Telex took seven minutes. The campaign manager had six pages of questions. The DACC refused the transmission stating that it simply could not tie up a telephone line for that much time. The campaign manager was livid: "You're a Democratic headquarters, how can you not help a Democratic candidate at the top of the ticket?" The caller was instructed that is was *not* a Democratic headquarters, but a headquarters for a Democratic candidate for Assembly. No transmission was sent.

The lack of strategic linkages and limited cooperation on tangible projects is certainly disquieting, at least from a party vantage. Throughout much of New York's history, local parties have played an important role in state legislative elections. Their withdrawal from the hub of these campaigns and relegation to only labor intensive projects may hold long-term implications. How long will they be willing to conduct mere scutt work? An important organizational incentive behind local party activity is a perceived meaningful role in elections. Perhaps, optimistically, they will find their limited role in state legislative elections satisfactory, or their campaign activities will simply be redirected to lower-level offices. From another vantage, this finding is illustrative of a centralization and professionalization movement in campaign communications. Legislative campaign committees target districts based upon their competitiveness, infuse these races with tremendous resources, and depart after election day. They do not maintain, nor are they concerned with, community ties. Voters are reached by the most cost-efficient means available, often by electronic media and direct mail. This is very different than what we are accustomed to, where a significant portion of state and local campaigning is conducted face-to-face. The impact of the loss of direct intermediaries, both on party organizations and popular governance, will be discussed in the final chapter.

Overall Perceptions of LCCs

One of the most revealing findings centers on perceptions regarding the coupling of LCCs in the party structure, the party-oriented inclinations of these units, and their overall objectives.[23]

Two measures were used to determine the perceived relationship between the state party organization and the LCCs. The first concerned their overall involvement in the campaigns. That is, did the activities of the LCCs represent the wishes of the state party organization, state party leaders, or were they acting as independent units? Table 5.3 notes the results, controlled by party. Few chairs perceive LCC actions as controlled either by the state party committee or state party leaders.

The second measure was an open-ended query: "In your own words, please tell me how you see legislative campaign committees fitting into the state party organization." Responses were coded into four groups: closely aligned, moderately aligned, moderately independent, and independent. Table 5.4 presents the results of this question, controlled by party and level of exposure. There appears to be support for the hypothesis that exposure to LCCs has a strong bearing on perceptions. Thirty percent of respondents in the Moderate exposure group view LCCs as either "closely aligned" or "moderately aligned"; as opposed to just 9 percent in the High exposure group. It seems that the more the county leaders know of the LCCs, the less they are to see them as an element of the party.

Table 5.3
"Whose Wishes Do the LCCs' Actions Represent?"
Controlled by Party
(In Percentages)

	Democrats	Republicans	Total
State Party Organization	12	11	11 (N = 4)
State Party Leaders	6	11	8 (N = 3)
Independent Units	82	78	81 (N = 29)
Total	(N = 17)	(N = 19)	(N = 36)

Only those respondents in the High Exposure Group were asked these questions (3 respondents are missing).

This was a closed-ended query: "Thinking back upon the legislative committee's overall involvement in the race, would you say their actions represented the wishes of the state party organization, state party leaders, or were they acting as independent units?"

Kendall's Tau = .17

Table 5.4
"How Do You See LCCs in State Party Structure?"
Controlled by Level of Exposure and Party
(In Percentages)

	High			Moderate		
	Dem	Rep	T	Dem	Rep	T
Closely Aligned	7%	0%	3%	13%	6%	8%
Moderately Aligned	0	11	6	25	18	22
Moderately Independent	20	11	15	25	38	33
Independent	73	78	76	37	37	38
Total	N = 15	N = 19		N = 8	N = 16	

Respondents were asked: "In your own words, please tell me how you see legislative campaign committees fitting into the state party organizations."
Those in the "None" category were excluded from the analysis because they were unable to form an opinion regarding this question.
Kendall's Tau = .20

Both measures strongly suggest the county chairs reject the conceptual merging of the state party organization and legislative campaign committees. Although Republican chairs may see a greater degree of harmony/coordination, overall they too appear to view LCCs as autonomous—beyond the reach of the state party organization. Control variables such as length of tenure, size of the county committee, and attitudes toward the state committee appear to have little effect on this perception.

This is certainly consistent with the view of LCC operatives in the DACC. Some may have considered themselves partisans, while others merely campaign professionals. None of the operatives, however, believed the organization was linked to the state party committee. The operatives did not know who the State Committee Members were or what they did—that was the Governor's organization. Occasionally, operatives would use party committee telephone bank during special elections, but interactions were generally meager. The DACC staff realized their status as "party committee" was helpful only in that it provided the lowest possible postage rates and a few other benefits accorded party units.

With regard to LCC objectives, chairs were asked whether they believed the new units were "only geared towards winning elections" or are "also concerned about other party activities." Results are noted in Table 5.5. Republicans clearly have a more optimistic view of LCC activities. Again, the level of exposure colors perceptions. County committee chairs who have worked closely with LCCs are much more likely to see the objectives of the LCC narrowly defined.

Although the finding that LCCs are generally seen as only geared toward winning elections is consistent with the author's overarching hypothesis, it should be noted that it challenges previous conjecture. Dwyer and Stonecash write: "These legislative committees engage in general party promotion (e.g., Republican and Democratic fund-raising, voter registration, pro-party media, etc.) . . . [they] take care of general party concerns in which individual legislators would not be inclined to invest" (1992, 333). While the data does not altogether refute such a claim, it does suggest *if* LCCs carry out these functions very few county chairs are aware of it.

Table 5.5
Perceived Objectives of LCCs, Controlled
by Level of Exposure and Party
(In Percentages)

	High			Moderate		
	Dem	Rep	Tot	Dem	Rep	Tot
Only Winning Elections	82%	47%	63%	78%	43%	56%
Also Party Activities	6	33	21	22	19	20
Both Equally	12	20	16	0	31	20
Other	N = 17	N = 21		N = 9	N = 15	

Respondents were asked: "A number of county chairs have felt legislative campaign organizations are only geared toward winning elections and, in general, do not care about party activities, while others have said that, although they concentrate on state legislative elections, they are concerned about party activities. Which is closest to your impression?" Choices were alternated each time. Again, those in the "None" category are dropped from the analysis.

Kendall's Tau = .19

4 percent missing

Perhaps because many LCCs are legally linked with state party committees, as in New York, scholars have been quick to draw a close fit between the two. Much of their research has been based on interviews with LCC officials or on aggregate data. What this finding suggests is that those in the political vineyards see things differently. According to traditional party leaders in New York, these units should not be seen as part of their organization.

TPO Strength

There was little support for the expectation that levels of party organization strength would modify the relationship between the TPOs and LCCs. A number of indicators of party strength (annual operating budget, number of members, number of active members, and number of paid staff positions) were correlated with sets of both linkage and perceptual measures. None of the coefficients were significant at the .05 level. In fact, many were in a positive direction, contradicting prior conjecture. The correlation between the operating budgets of the county committees and the level of input county chairs believed they had in LCC decisions, for example, was .27. This tentatively suggests larger party organizations have more input into LCC affairs than do smaller ones.

Party differences along this dimension are a bit more telling. Chairs of larger Republican committees worked more regularly with the LCC than chairs from larger Democratic committees. By introducing party as a control,[24] the regression coefficient between the county committees strength (their operating budget) and the chair's perceived level of input switches from a positive to a negative slope: from .04 to .02.[25] This suggests, again tentatively, that chairs of affluent Democratic committees are less likely to believe they have any real input into LCC decisions than are chairs of affluent Republican county committees.

For rank-and-file members, the institutionalization of the New York State Legislature has meant increased pay, perks, and prestige. Most state legislators now see their posts as occupations and use all of the resources at their disposal to hold on to them. Institutional changes have also caused important reverberations for legislative leaders. The shifting locus of power for external forces (party bosses, the executive) to their body has meant the ability to contest policy and budget decisions and to control resources.

For both sets of actors (members and leaders), then, the profes-sionalization movement has placed an intense institutional emphasis on winning elections. Elections have shifted from an external busi-ness—that is, the concern of party organizations, interest groups, and individual candidates—to an institutional imperative. At the same time, the volatility of electorates has added an unpredictable element. The outcome has been the emergence of legislative cam-paign committees.

Traditional party leaders perceive these new units to be uncon-cerned with augmenting party membership, supporting the ticket, or aiding institutional support activities. The two camps do share a con-cern for winning state legislative elections and controlling a majority caucus, but that is about all. We may be hard pressed to distinguish LCCs in New York as little more than independent consulting firms working for the benefit of the legislative caucus and its leadership.

Six

The State-Level Relationship

Ever since V. O. Key (1950, 1956) focused our attention, scholars have recognized state party organizations as an indispensable component of the overall party system. State committees, the most purely organizational and strategic level of the party stratarchy, help bridge the gap between local organizations and the national party committees. They serve to aggregate the diverse interests of numerous communities into a coherent party structure and, in government, help link governors to state legislators, house members to senators. Over the past few decades, they have also played an important role in presidential nominations (Beck, et. al., 1994; Biersack 1994). Recent studies suggest state parties are generally robust and professional, providing extensive services to candidates (Frendreis, et. al., 1994).

This chapter looks at the relationship between legislative campaign committees and state party organizations throughout the nation. Legislative campaign committees are state-level units. Studies which presume that these units are adaptations by parties refer to their place in the state structure; local party committees are rarely discussed. Are legal linkages, however, their only connection with state party committees? Perhaps there are also activity-centered ties. The question as to how state party leaders conceive of the LCCs in their state is also raised. If these units are to be envisioned as party-like, it might certainly be from a state-level vantage.

In December of 1993, surveys were mailed to the leaders of each Democratic and Republican state party committee in the fifty states. After three weeks a second, identical instrument was sent to those having not completed the questionnaire. In total, fifty of the one hundred organizations returned the survey. Figure 6.1 highlights the state committee that returned the instrument. There are thirty-one Republican and nineteen Democratic organizations included in the sample; twenty-seven of the Republicans and fifteen of the Democrats are from states which host at least one LCC.[1] The geographic distribution

113

of the sample appears random. It is also evenly divided between party chairs and executive officers, with a majority of the latter being Republican. As with the New York study, respondents were assured of the confidentiality of their answers.

The survey is supplemented with aggregate data, including demographics, LCC disclosure information, state committee data, the degree of interparty competition, and numerous other state-level measures. In a few instances, follow-up telephone calls were made to clarify responses.

The chapter begins with a look at the structural ties between LCCs and state committees, followed by an examination of their functional interdependence. Next is a look at the perceived objectives and activities of these new units and a comparison with state committee objectives and activities. Finally, time is spent reviewing how state party leaders generally think of LCCs—that is, whether they view them as party units or something else.

Figure 6.1
State Party Committees Included in the Sample

	Dems	Reps		Dems	Reps
Northeast					
*Connecticut			*Vermont	X	X
*New Hampshire	X		*New Jersey		
*Maine	X		*New York	X	
*Massachusetts	X		*Pennsylvania	X	
*Rhode Island					
Midwest					
*Illinois	X		*Kansas		X
*Indiana		X	*Minnesota		
*Michigan		X	Nebraska	X	X
*Ohio		X	North Dakota		X
*Wisconsin			*South Dakota	X	X
*Iowa					

Figure 6.1 (Continued)

	Dems	Reps		Dems	Reps
South					
*Delaware	X		Kentucky		
*Florida		X	Mississippi	X	X
Georgia	X		*Tennessee		X
*Maryland		X	*Arkansas	X	
*North Carolina		X	*Louisiana	X	X
South Carolina			*Oklahoma		X
*Virginia		X	*Missouri	X	
*West Virginia	X	X	*Texas		X
Alabama	X				
West					
Arizona		X	*Utah	X	X
*Colorado	X	X	Wyoming		
*California	X		*Alaska	X	X
*Idaho			*Hawaii		
*Montana	X	X	*Oregon		X
*Nevada		X	*Washington		X
*New Mexico	X	X			

Total Number of Democratic State Committee Respondents = 19
Total Number of Republican State Committee Respondents = 31
* States that host at least one LCC.

THE FORMAL RELATIONSHIP BETWEEN STATE PARTIES AND LEGISLATIVE CAMPAIGN COMMITTEES

The first step in assessing the relationship between two units is to examine their formal or structural linkages. Party bylaws may guide LCC activities, suggest a set of real or perceived constraints, and/or provide each unit with resources possessed by the other. The legal articulation between layers of the traditional party stratarchy guides a portion of each unit's behavior and relationship with other elements of the strata. In New York, on the other hand, the formal relationship between the state parties and the LCCs has been shown to have little practical import.

While it was suggested that certain LCCs developed as legal appendages of state party committees, on the whole, it was expected that most would be without formal linkages. The desire to be free of external constraints will lead to structurally autonomous units, regardless of the statutory benefits granted "party" organizations (primarily financial).

Table 6.1 notes the extent of structural ties, controlled by party. The stated expectation is only moderately supported; 56 percent suggested there were no formal linkages.[2] A slightly larger share of Republican organizations are nonaligned, but the differences between the parties appears minimal.

The levels of legislative professionalization appear to be an important factor.[3] Seventy percent of the respondents from states with full-time legislatures noted *no* formal relationship, compared with 28 percent in "hybrid" states and 36 percent in part-time states.

Table 6.1
Formal Linkages between LCCs and State Party Committees
Controlled by Party of Respondent

	Legal Relationship	No Legal Relationship	Total
Republicans	8	13	21 (65.6%)
Democrats	6	5	11 (34.4%)
Total	14 (43.8%)	18 (56.2%)	N = 33 (100%)

The question read: "Do you know if there is any *formal* or legal relationship between these organizations and the party state committee? If so, what is this relationship?"

Missing (17) is due either because the respondent is from a state without an LCC or he/she refused to answer the question.

Even though 44 percent did suggest a formal bond, few respondents (16 percent) said the LCCs in their state were under the direct control of the state committee. The most frequent comment concerning the type of legal arrangement between the units was that the LCCs are auxiliary organizations. These arrangements appear similar to that in New York, where the LCCs are "branch committees." A few others noted legal ties relating to finances. One Republican suggested that "bank accounts for both units are set up under the auspices of the [state committee] and all checks are signed by the [state committee] treasurer." Another noted that "members of the LCCs are also on the party's executive board." These and following quotes not otherwise cited are responses to Appendix B or to follow-up telephone conversations.

Beyond a fixed, legal arrangement, it was asked how the state party leaders thought LCCs in their state fit into the overall party structure. Sixty-six percent said they were *not* part of the party organization. Surprisingly, several of the respondents (30 percent) who noted a legal relationship between LCCs and the state committee, also suggested the former was not part of the state party.

Regarding another question,[4] only *one* respondent in the entire data set suggested the state party committee controlled the activities of the LCCs. This was very telling in that the sample is, after all, composed of party leaders. If we were to find any bias—a tendency for respondents to inflate their organization's importance—it would have pulled our findings in the direction of greater state committee oversight. Apparently, LCCs are perceived as autonomous regardless of explicit legal ties. This finding holds true for both parties and is consistent with that found in New York.

If the state party committee does not control the activities of the LCCs, who does? It was interesting to find just 12 percent of the party leaders indicating that a legislative caucus was responsible for LCC activities. Rather, roughly one-half said legislative leaders, and another 26 percent said a small group of legislators[5] ran the show. This is consistent with the contention in Chapter 1 that LCCs should not be conceived as caucus units, but as tools of the legislative elite. They are not member-based organizations.

It was speculated that the formal dualism would be most acute in states where LCCs are fully developed and have bountiful resources. Well-funded organizations have the luxury of being autonomous. A cross-tabulation was conducted between legal linkages and LCC resources,[6] and this conjecture appears to be supported. Although the small sample makes generalizations difficult, 75 percent of the well-funded LCCs are autonomous units, as compared to 50 percent in the middle-range group and 66 percent in the low category.

The relationship between formal ties and state laws supportive of parties was examined as an additional control.[7] A relationship does appear to exist; states with laws sympathetic to parties are more likely to find LCCs formally linked with state committees than are states without such laws. This would bolster the utilitarian view of LCC development and goals. That is to say, where it is helpful to formally link with state party committees, they do so. One respondent was rather frank about this: "They are adjuncts of the party so that they can raise and contribute unlimited funds to candidates, and that's the only connection."

PROJECT INTERDEPENDENCE

Informal linkages, or programmatic interdependence, may prove another telling piece of this new relationship. How often, and on what types of activities, do state committees interact with LCCs? Even though each unit may be formally independent of one another, by working together and sharing facilities/staff, they might be part of the same "team." The opposite also could be true. In Chapter 4 programmatic linkages were divided into three clusters: institutional support activities; candidate directed activities; and material interdependence. Each will be examined below.

Institutional Support Activities

Institutional support activities are projects designed to sustain the organization, such as fund-raising, service to subunits, member recruitment (voter registration drives), and recruiting candidates. Table 6.2 suggests the importance placed on these projects by the state party committees. Fund-raising, for example, was found to be a cornerstone of their activities. On a similar open-ended question, over one-half of the respondents noted some type of institutional support activity as their organization's principal activity. To what degree, then, do LCCs work with the state party (and vice versa) on such projects?

Few institutional support linkages were expected. The ability for LCCs to win state legislative elections is tied to available resources. Expending energy and capital to help sustain another organization may yield little direct benefit. If anything, the flow of assistance will be from the state committees to the LCCs. Table 6.3 highlights the

Table 6.2
Amount of Effort Expended on Certain Activities
by the State Committees

Activity	Mean Response
Fund–raising	8.46
Running Telephone Banks	7.29
Voter Mobilization Programs	7.04
Recruiting Candidates	6.90
Distributing Mailing Lists	6.85
Producing D. Mail for Candidates	6.52
Candidate Seminars	6.10
Contributing $ to Candidates	6.08
Helping Candidates with Advertising	5.40
Polling Operations	4.27
Issue Development	4.46
State Committee Newsletters	4.46
	N = 49

The question read: "Using a scale of 1 to 10—where 1 means very little and 10 means a great deal—note how much effort your committee spent on the following activities during the past year."

results of two questions regarding financial interdependence. The first is whether the state committee contributes funds to the LCCs, and the second asks whether the LCCs help fund state party activities.

Again, the sample appears to be divided. Approximately 40 percent of the state committees give financial help to the LCCs, and roughly one-half suggested LCCs help fund party activities. "Sometimes we pool resources for special projects, particularly when there's not a gubernatorial election," noted a Republican. "Other than that, [the LCCs] give directly to candidates." A few party leaders were more direct. "No! Absolutely not," stated a Democrat.

A cross-tabulation between these questions suggests, generally speaking, that financial interdependence either flows in both directions or not at all. Only two of the respondents who answered "no" to

Table 6.3
Financial Interdependence between LCCs and State Party
Committees

Does State Committee Give To LCCs?	Frequency	Percent
Yes	11	36%
1	3	10
No	16	53
	N = 30	
Do LCCs Give to State Committee?		
Yes	8	28%
Yes, but very little	8	28
No	13	45
	N = 29	

The two questions read: "What is the financial relationship between the state committee and these organizations? That is, does the state committee contribute money to these organizations? Do these organizations contribute funds to the state party committee?"

the first question answered "yes" to the second. Conversely, nearly all of the respondents that mentioned LCCs in their state do not give money to the state committee also said their state committee does not give to the LCCs. Interestingly enough, legal linkages do not seem to be an important part of this determination; LCCs legally tied to state committees are no more likely to pool resources than are formally autonomous ones.

With regard to fund-raising projects, findings are less ambiguous. Only 24 percent noted the state committee worked regularly with LCCs to raise money (for either organization). "They raise it from the lobbyist—sort of 'behind the scenes.' We use public fund-raisers such as events and direct mail," noted a Republican chair. Another Republican suggested, "they tap contributors the state committee couldn't." But a Democrat believed, "we are all after the same money," and yet another that, "there is some inevitable tension over fund-raising, and who should speak for the Democrats." A similar query asked the chairs to rank the level of coordination between the state committee and the LCCs on fund-raising projects, using a ten-point scale (1 being "very little" and 10 being "a great deal"). The mean response was a 4.9. Forty-three percent noted a value of 3 or less.[8]

There did appear to be a degree of cooperation on other institutional support activities. The average level of cooperation on get-out-the-vote drives and recruiting candidates, using that same ten-point scale, was 6.5 each. For voter registration drives it was 5.1. One caveat should be noted: These questions applied only to those respondents who believed the LCCs in their state engaged in these activities—which is rather few, as will be seen below. Obviously, if an LCC does not conduct get-out-the-vote drives, linkage questions along this dimension are moot. In a way, then, this measure is a rather soft test of interdependence.

It was hypothesized that three controls would effect the level of institutional support interdependence: the level of resources held by the LCCs, the extent of interparty competition, and the respondent's party status. To test the first, three bi-variate ordinary least square (OLS) regressions were introduced, using LCC resources (measured in dollars) as an independent variable. The dependent variables, were the ten-point scales measuring cooperation on fund-raising, GOTV drives, and candidate recruitment. A negative relationship was expected: that is, the more resources held by the LCCs, the lower the level of cooperation with the state party committee. Results are found in Table 6.4.

Only one of the regression coefficients (Recruiting Candidates) is in the expected direction. Better-funded LCCs appear more likely to cooperate with state committees on voter mobilization programs and

Table 6.4
Bivariate OLS Regression with LCC Resources ($) as Independent Variable and Ten-Point Cooperation Scales as Dependent Variables

	Beta	*S.E.*	*R-Square*	*N**
Voter Mobilization	.001	.001	.38	10
Fund-raising	.0006	.001	.17	30
Recruit Candidates	-.0004	.001	.01	27

*The N fluctuates due to the varying number of respondents who suggested the LCCs in their state engage in each activity.

None of the coefficients are statistically significant at the .05 confidence level.

fund-raising activities. The regression coefficients are, nonetheless, modest. The model with the largest slope increases the dependent variable (Voter Mobilization) from 3.8 (the constant) to 7.5 for the most affluent LCC. The r-squares also suggest these findings are far from descriptively complete.

A similar analysis was conducted for level of party competition. This measure is based upon Austin Ranney's Scale, recalculated for 1988 (Bibby 1990).[9] First, the range of scores was divided into three groups (Low, Moderate, High) and cross-tabulated with the financial interdependence queries. Second, another set of regressions was employed using the competition scale as the independent variable and the ten-point cooperation scales as dependent variables. Overall, the author's conjecture is moderately supported; increased party competition seems to *lower* institutional support interdependence. Each of the regression coefficients are in the negative direction. Unfortunately, the slopes are again modest, and the proportion of variation explained are each less than 10 percent.

It should be noted that, while the findings regarding level of party competition and institutional support interdependence are tentative, they certainly do not support the belief that high competition leads to the unification of candidate committees, at least along this dimension. If state party committees and LCCs choose to cooperate on helping to sustain each other's organization, as roughly one-half appear that they do, levels of interparty competition do not seem to play a role in the decision.

A final control was whether the respondent's organization held a majority or minority position in the state. More specifically, we might expect minority units to interact with one another more frequently than those already in power.[10] Findings reveal that majority units are just as likely to work together as are minority ones.

In states with a mixed party status (one house controlled by the Democrats and the other by the Republicans), LCCs were *less* likely to interact with the party. One supposition, based on a responsible party perspective, would be that the majority unit would work with the state party and help its minority counterpart—to spread the wealth. Without the support of the governor and the other house, policy enactment is much harder, if not impossible. In a sense, responsible parties either control both branches and the executive, or they are simply "out of power."

From an LCC vantage, the ends for a caucus leader may not be the control of government but the control of that house. It makes little difference if one's party oversees both branches or the executive; all the powers and perquisites accompanying majority control are inclusive to each house. This is particularly true in states with professional legislatures. It may even be beneficial for the caucus to have the minority party control the other branch of the legislature. In states where the executive and one branch of the are controlled by the same party, the leader of the other house wields considerable power. He/she becomes the sole spokesperson for the opposition party and is acknowledged as such by interest groups, the media, and the governor. At the very least, discovering that institutional support interactions are less frequent in states with mixed party control than in states with unified control may be yet another hint at what LCCs are all about.

Candidate-Directed Activities

Institutional support activities are only one way a party or campaign organization can spend its time. A second area of possible interdependence is candidate-directed activities. By pooling resources, each might benefit from greater economies of scale and undertake a broader range of projects. Interdependence may thus be greater in this dimension than for institutional support activities.

It was conjectured that interdependence would be greater for services than for strategic considerations. As in New York, LCCs will frequently call upon party committees to assist with labor intensive projects but will be reluctant to open their decision-making process to outsiders. It was also assumed that candidate-directed interdependence would be greater in competitive, two-party states than in noncompetitive states; running scared makes strange bedfellows.

Respondents were asked to use a ten-point scale to assess their organization's input in LCC resource allocation decisions. A significant portion indicated they had very little say; 44 percent answered with 4 or less. Although the mean response was 5.0, the distribution was clearly bimodal. In other words, as a group, respondents either marked the low end of the scale or the high end.

A follow-up telephone interview with one Democratic chair suggested nearly every aspect of LCC activity was overseen by the state Party committee. "For starters, members of these organizations are on the state party's executive board, so naturally there's close coordination. You also have to remember their operating budget comes from state party coffers. We have all the input we want." Interesting enough, the LCCs were not housed in the same building as the state committee. Another Republican leader noted: "The state party entered into an agreement with [the LCC] to hire and supervise a coordinator. So we have a good deal of input." A few others were less sanguine: "The legislative committee is subordinate to the state party. However, depending on the chair of the legislative committee, they do act alone. Often we have little say over what they do."

Introducing the respondent's party as a control produced an interesting finding. Democrats were less likely to believe they had a say on strategic decisions than were Republicans. In fact, 66 percent of the Democrats noted a score of 4 or less.

A second set of queries referred to a list of tangible services. The expectation that interdependence would be greater here than for strategic decisions appears to be supported. As Table 6.5 notes, the average for each item is higher than for the strategic cooperation mean. Candidate seminars and direct mail assistance stand out as cooperative efforts. In addition to having the largest standard deviation, the survey research question produced a bimodal response. It appears as though either the two units work together extensively on polling, or not at all. This may be one of the labor-intensive projects LCCs need and party committees can help with. One party leader boasted that his organization "made over 5,000 phone calls for legislative candidate [surveys]."

To test the interparty competition hypothesis, Ranney's scale was again introduced as an independent variable. Each of the candidate-directed cooperation scales was used as a dependent variable. Results are found in Table 6.6.

The coefficients again suggest that interparty competition has little to do with LCCs/state party interdependence. From the least to most competitive state, the model with the largest slope increases the dependent variable (Contributions to Candidates) by only 2.9 units. None of the r-squares is of consequence; the largest explaining just 6 percent of the variance.

Do poorly funded LCCs cooperate with state committees on candidate assistance more often than well-funded ones? In another OLS regression, using LCC resources as the independent variable, the only negative coefficient found is for candidate seminars. Most of the slopes are modestly positive, as are the r-squares. One clear exception is for direct contributions to candidates. Thirty-eight percent of the variance is explained by this one variable. Simply put, in states with better funded LCCs there is a higher level of interdependence, at

Table 6.5
Cooperation between LCCs and State Committees on Tangible
Candidate-Directed Activities

Activity	Mean Response	S.D.
Campaign Seminars	7.1	3.4
Direct Mail Assistance	6.8	3.0
Media Assistance	5.9	3.4
Survey Research	5.8	3.9
Contributing $ to Candidates	5.5	3.1

S.D. = Standard Deviation
N = > 22 for each item.
The cooperation scale query read: "Please use the ten-point scale to describe
the degree of cooperation between the state committee and the legislative
campaign committee for each project. In other words, do you work together
on the activity?"

Table 6.6
Bivariate OLS Regressions between Level of Party Competition
and Candidate-Directed Interdependence Scales

Activity (Dep. Variable)	Slope	S.E.	R-Square
Strategic Cooperation	.04	.05	.03
Tangible Benefits			
$ Contributions to Candidates	.08	.06	.06
Survey Research	.06	.12	.02
Candidate Seminars	-.02	.08	.01
Media Assistance	.03	.08	.01
Direct Mail	.02	.09	.01

N = > 22 for each item (The N fluctuates due to the varying number of respondents that suggested the LCCs in their state engage in each activity.)
The independent variable is interparty competition, and dependent variables
are cooperation scales. The former is based on the aggregate outcome of a
set of statewide elections; see Beck and Sorauf (1992, 38–39), pp. 38–39. For
more information on the cooperation scales, see Table 6.5.

least regarding contributions to candidates, than in states with modestly funded LCCs.[11]

Overall, the picture to emerge concerning candidate-directed interdependence is muddled. It might suggest that in most states interdependence is limited, particularly with regard to strategic decisions, yet this is not universally true. In some states there is close cooperation on both dimensions. Attempting to sort out these differences with several control variables was only moderately helpful. Perhaps an examination of material interdependence will shed a bit more light.

Material Interdependence

Material interdependence implies the sharing of facilities, equipment, and personnel. Why should both units pay for a headquarters, for example, when the cost could be shared? The same might be said about computers, printers, or support staff. Two questions were used to assess this dimension: whether the units shared the same physical space, and if certain staff worked for both organizations. It was a bit surprising that just 24 percent (eight) of the respondents reported that the state committee and the LCCs were located in the same building. Slightly more respondents noted joint staff (31 percent), but on the whole the results do not appear to support the hypothesis. Material interdependence seems to be the exception rather than the rule. One responded wrote, "No, these committees are strictly state house and senate legislator operations," and another that "there are plans for them to move back in."

Neither relative strength, respondent's party, level of interparty competition, or legal linkages had any significant bearing on this finding. It should be noted also that a few respondents suggest the LCCs in their state were not developed enough to have a headquarters or staff. "There is not a staff, office, etc., for those two committees. Work is done from the state house, home, and party headquarters." A few others suggested that LCC staff were "legislative leadership volunteers."

What makes this finding poignant is the fact that nearly all the state party organizations are located in state capitals, the same cities where the LCCs are found. If LCCs are simply appendages of the state party and were created to augment the party's campaign services, it would be expected that scarce resources would be conserved by sharing facilities and personnel. It is hard to conceive how such a physical separation would be beneficial to the overall party organization. At the very least, they might be in the same building so that communications would be easer. As this is generally not the case, one can only assume LCC autonomy is important to these new units and is worth the cost.

Interdependence and Legislative Professionalization

In the preceding chapter the rapid professionalization of the legislature was found to be a key ingredient in the relationship between LCCs and traditional parties in New York State. This dimension is added here as a further control. Results point to one of the most striking findings in the data set. The relationship between legislative professionalization and project interdependence—both institutional support and candidate-directed—is consistently negative. In other words, the more professional a state's legislature, the less likely the LCCs within that state will interact with the state party committee. Table 6.7 notes the correlations between each of the interaction scales and a legislative professionalization scale—based on member pay, length of session, and staffing levels. Although a few of the coefficients are modest, every one is in a negative direction, and several are quite strong.

This control was also telling with regard to material interdependence. Only 14 percent of the respondents from professional states noted that their organization shared either office space or personnel with the LCCs. Over 50 percent from part-time states suggested this type of cooperation occurred.

Several components might help explain the import of legislative professionalization. Again, Ehrenhalt's argument (1992) that contemporary legislators represent a different breed, primarily because they see their service as a career rather than a temporary stopping ground, may be a key part of the dynamic between LCCs and traditional parties. The more the job is worth keeping, the more channeled the objectives and activities of the LCCs and, consequently, their distance from traditional party organizations.

A second, related possibility is that professionalization places an added emphasis on majority party control. As noted in the New York case study, serving in a professional legislature is much different on the majority side than on the minority side. Moreover, with the expansion of legislative duties and resources comes the growth of professional staff. Instead of being granted their jobs as patronage or working on a part-time basis, as in the past, modern legislative staff are hired for their skills. They are paid very well, hold their jobs at the discretion of caucus leadership, and are not the product of party politics but of universities and graduate schools. Many of these profes-

Table 6.7
Correlation Between Measures of Project Interdependence and
Legislative Professionalization

Activity	Correlation	N*
Institutional Support:		
Fund-raising	-.86	30
Recruiting Candidates	-.81	27
Voter Registration	-.58	8
Voter Mobilization Programs	-.28	10
Candidate Directed:		
Candidate Seminars	-.94	24
Media Assistance	-.86	23
Survey Research	-.63	16
Direct Mail	-.19	19
Strategic Cooperation	-.06	34
Contributing $ to Candidates	-.01	29

*The N fluctuates due to the varying number of respondents who suggested the LCCs in their state engage in each activity.
Legislative professionalization is based on three criteria: legislative pay, length of session, and staffing levels. For a complete breakdown, see Kurtz (1992b).

sionals are involved (at least on a part-time basis) with LCC activities. Not only are their pay checks directly tied to the success of the caucus, but they have few material or ideological links with any party. Interactions with the party, what few there may be, will be calculated from purely an instrumental vantage: that is, what has the party done for us lately?

ACTIVITIES AND OBJECTIVES:
SIMILARITIES AND DIFFERENCES

The scope of linkages between the units is an important piece of the LCC/state committee puzzle. Yet, if cooperative efforts are only a small part of each organization's activities, linkage queries miss something. Perhaps, for example, a state committee works with an LCC on candidate-directed activities but spends a large portion of its time on broader endeavors. As highlighted in Table 6.2, many state committees view voter registration and other general party building projects as important and spend considerable time on them. If LCCs do not work with state committees on these projects, perhaps they conduct them independently. The reader may recall the relevant number of cases for several of the linkage questions were greatly reduced because the respondents did not believe the LCCs in their states engaged in the project under question. This section takes a close look at how the state party chairs perceive the activities and goals of these new units.

Similarly to the interdependence dimension, activities can be divided into two clusters: broad-based projects and targetable services. *Broad-based* activities refer to those projects which help an array of candidates running under the party banner—including voter registration drives, media relations, support for community events, and get-out-the-vote drives. *Targetable services* can be helpful to many candidates or directed to a specific candidate. Examples here are polling, direct mail, or canvassing.

It was speculated that state party organizations would conduct both sets of activities, while LCCs would center nearly exclusively on the latter. Precise targeting strategies, combined with a narrow objective, suggested broad-range activities would be rarely conducted by these new units. Level of party competition may modify this relationship; those states with high interparty competition will have LCCs that are less likely to conduct broad-based activities. It might be also expected for LCCs that are formally linked with state party committees to engage in broad-based activities more often than those that are structurally independent.

Respondents were provided an open-ended question regarding what they see as the principal objectives of LCCs.[12] Nearly every response touched on the election and reelection of state legislative candidates: "[They] recruit candidates, train candidates, provide financial support for candidates, and give advice to candidates"; and "they reelect incumbents and gain new seats in the state legislature." A few others noted a direct link to caucus leadership: "Their objectives are the same as [legislative] leadership's objectives." Answers were coded using the same scheme for a question concerning state committee objectives and a comparison was conducted. To a large extent, LCC objectives appear similar to state party committee goals. Two exceptions are: a greater concern by state committees to structure and organize the overall party, and more LCCs perceived as providing funds directly to candidates.

Party leaders were then asked a series of questions on whether or not LCCs undertook a list of activities. The results are found in Table 6.8. For nearly all the respondents, LCCs seem to concentrate their efforts on campaign finances, fund-raising, and lending a hand to candidates. Considerably fewer are believed to conduct general party activities, such as voter registration and mobilization drives. This is not to say this focus was viewed as altogether a bad thing. As one respondent noted, "The state committee's primary objective is to raise money. That is the reason [LCCs] were formed. In a state with a small population it is much easier for elected officials to raise money than it is of the party. If they stick to that, it's fine with me."

As a group, then, LCCs are seen by state party leaders as geared toward raising money, winning elections, and structuring activities accordingly. While there may be some effort directed toward broad-based activities, this focus is rather limited. Nearly every state com-

Table 6.8

Perception of LCC Activities: Do They Undertake the Following?

Broad-Based Activities:	%Yes	N
Candidate Seminars	74	23
Voter Mobilization Programs	38	12
Voter Registration Drives	13	4
Targetable Projects:		
Fund-raising for Candidates	94	31
Contributing $ to Candidates	97	32
Recruit Candidates	84	27
Provide Media Assistance	74	23
Conduct Direct Mail	57	17
Polling	38	12

The question read: "Below is a list of activities that might be conducted by both the state party committee and legislative campaign committees. Indicate whether the legislative campaign committees conduct each of the activities."

mittee leader suggested his/her organization engaged in voter registration projects, but only four respondents said the LCCs of their states did the same.

Whether or not there was a formal relationship between the units seemed to affect perceptions of LCC activities. Legislative campaign committees legally aligned were thought to be interested in broadbased projects more often than were autonomous units. A state's environment of interparty competition, on the other hand, does not appear to make a difference. Roughly as many LCCs in high competitive states as in moderate and low competitive states are thought to engage in broad-based activities.

In general then, this analysis of perceived LCC objectives and activities finds these new organizations are seen as campaign-oriented. Roughly 80 percent of the state party leaders noted the foremost objectives of the LCCs in their states are either to win elections or to assist candidates. There seems to be little faith in their willingness to engage in less targeted activities—such as voter registration drives. For the most part, this narrow range of goals and activities does *not* seem to be in conflict with state party objectives. There is only modest support for the notion that the two camps have divergent objectives and, as such, engage in distinct activities. We might say that LCCs are perceived to be closer in reality to the rational-efficient model than the responsible perspective, but so (to a large extent) are state party committees. If anything, the narrow range of activities performed by the LCCs may complement the party's focus on campaigns. A few comments are illustrative: "Their main emphasis is winning their elections. We agree with that focus. They have been very supportive of the state chairman in many ways"; "[t]his state party believes general party activities includes winning elections as its number one priority, so we are very compatible"; and "[t]hey have a narrow focus, but we have found it to complement rather than hinder our work on most occasions."

ARE LCCs "PARTYLIKE"?

Respondents were asked how they conceived the LCCs in their state. Do they see them as "partylike" or are they more akin to political action committees or candidate-centered organizations? What effect have these new organizations had on state party committees? Before we objectively label LCC party adaptations and symbols of party resurgence, the subjective views of state party leaders would seem an appropriate area of inquiry.

From what has been learned about the relationship between state committees and LCCs thus far—the fit between their objectives and activities and a few areas of interdependence—it might be expected that party leaders see LCCs, if not a direct extension of the state party organization, certainly "partylike." This does not appear to be the case.

Asked how they view the LCCs in his/her state, only 18 percent said partylike. As Table 6.9 notes, 27 percent found them analogous to political action committees, 24 percent as legislative leadership units, and 24 percent as candidate-centered organizations. Republicans were slightly more likely to see them as PACs and the Democrats a bit more inclined to view them as legislative leadership units.[13]

This question is clearly subjective; there are varying definitions for each of these categories, and we may squabble over which definition is most appropriate. The important point argued here is that, while many political scientists see fit to label these organizations "partylike," party leaders see it otherwise.

Along similar lines, respondents were asked if they believed LCCs in their state were interested in only winning state legislative elections or also in general party activities. This question may well be a soft test of responsible party inclinations. It distinguishes LCCs viewed as concerned *only* about their elections, and those that *also*

Table 6.9
Respondent's View of LCC, Controlled by Party

	Republicans	N	Democrats	N
PACs	27%	6	18%	2
Legislative Leadership Units	18	4	37	4
Partylike	18	4	18	2
Independent Campaign Consulting Firms	13	3	—	—
Candidate Centered Units	18	4	27	3
Other	5	1	—	—
Total		22		11

The question read: "Which of the following best describes how you see legislative campaign organizations in your state?"

heat off the state committees and serves a purpose the state committee sees as legitimate and important. Moreover, legislative leaders are able to tap sources of money that state party leaders cannot. Unless contributions are zero-sum, as a few party leaders imply, there is little conflict with the LCCs. Accordingly, LCC autonomy and their narrow range of activities will seem less troublesome, but these units will still not be viewed as partylike.

It was hypothesized that three conditions would play a part in how state party leaders view these units: the extent to which the LCCs are perceived to engage in broad-based activities; the level of project interdependence; and level of LCC resources. As each would increase, LCCs would more likely be viewed in a positive, helpful light. The first appears to be supported, for example all of the respondents who suggested their state committee had been hurt by the LCCs also said the latter did not assist the party with voter registration drives. Much the same can be said about voter mobilization programs and assistance to other layers of the party. The other two conjectures are less clear. The lack of cooperation around certain activities, such as fund-raising and direct mail, did seem to modify feelings toward these new units in a negative direction, but only moderately. And most, but not all, of the party leaders with ill feelings were from states with poorly funded LCCs. In sum, the degree to which LCCs are perceived to be helpful or harmful may be linked to their financial help and inclination to conduct general party activities, but few other variables seem to matter.

Throughout much of this chapter, the dilemma confronted was: Why is it that in some states LCCs work with the state party committee and are viewed as generally a good thing, but in others they are completely autonomous and perhaps harmful? Legislative professionalization appears to be the answer. Simply put, the more institutionalized the state's legislature, the greater the distance between an LCC and the state party. With the trend toward full-time state legislatures, it is certainly possible that the friendly relationship found between LCCs and state party committees in some states will also become strained. This topic will be taken up in greater detail in the concluding chapter.

Seven

The County-Level Relationship

If state committees are considered the center of the party structure, county-level organizations are the cornerstones. Grass-roots parties screen and select candidates, encourage and promote civic participation, reward party activists, provide services to candidates, and have often altered the course of public policy (at least at the local level). Well-organized local party committees have dominated both the policy and political process in numerous communities, as noted in the case of New York. Because they are instrumental at linking citizens to government, scholars refer to these structures as "key cogs" in the party system (Eldersveld 1982, 141).

Of course, old-style party machines have seen brighter days. In an era of civil service, telecommunications, open-politics, and declining neighborhood associations, much of the wind behind local parties has dissipated. Those who signal the alarm of party decline often point to this level as prima facie evidence. The authors of *The American Voter* found only 10 percent of the respondents had been contacted by a party worker during the 1956 campaign (Campbell, et al. 1960, 426–427). Two decades later, David Broder noted: "For the most part [local parties] are plagued by inadequate finance and the lack of trained, stable cadre of personnel to man the headquarters and provide essential services for the party's office holders and candidates" (1971, 26). More recently, scholars such as Kaden and Mahe (1985) argue that modern modes of communication have replaced the need for local party activists—thereby weakening grass-roots structures.

With this said, however, local party organizations continue to exist and perform important functions. Recall an earlier review of Cotter et al.'s (1985) survey of 7,300 county organizations during the early 1980s. They find local committees—primarily county organizations—are as healthy as they have been for several decades. More recent studies suggest the same (Frendreis, et al. 1994; Beck and Haynes 1994). Additionally, although the heyday of party machines

137

may well be over, numerous city and county organizations today mirror, in some respects, those of earlier periods.

This chapter examines the relationship between legislative campaign units and county party committees. In a way, it represents the apex of the project. Legislative campaign committees will have the most impact on traditional party organizations when they are involved in campaigns, working in the trenches. As implied in the discussion of the Plattsburgh Special, when LCCs enter a district to help a candidate, they often invade a political domain overseen by a local party. Discord may occur over strategy, tactics, and/or the delegation of campaign responsibilities. In the New York case, it was found that if an LCC had targeted a race, local party leaders from that county were less inclined to view them in a party light. The county level also may be where the party will be most involved in state legislative races. Any interactions, cooperation, or hostility between LCCs and the party will surface at this level.

In another way, our examination of the partylike inclinations of LCCs might best proceed from a county-level vantage. Many of the functions performed by traditional parties occur here. Recruiting a full slate of candidates and providing an outlet for the fulfillment of perceived civic duties, for example, are important services generally provided at the grass-roots. Unlike state party committees, where most activities surround organizational maintenance and strategy, LCCs *implement* projects as well; they descend to the local level. The question, therefore, is to what degree these activities translate into traditional party functions.

On the other hand, because LCCs generally target their effort to a small number of races, many county party leaders have had limited exposure to them. Areas dominated by one party will rarely see LCC operatives. Perceptions of them in these areas—particularly in states where LCCs are new or underdeveloped—will be based on a more diffuse set of criteria. Project interdependence naturally will be minimal. And consistent with findings in New York, these county chairs may have optimistic views of LCCs.

Surveys were sent to 667 county party chairs in four states in the spring of 1993. The instrument (found in Appendix C) is divided into two broad sections; the first deals with the objectives and activities of the respondent's organization, and the second concerns the party organization's relationship and interactions with the LCCs of that state. Roughly 27 percent of the county chairs returned the instrument, making a sample of 169 respondents. Quotes throughout the rest of this chapter not otherwise cited are comments by county chairs in response to questions in Appendix C or follow-up telephone interviews.

The chapter begins with a review of the criteria for choosing the four states, followed by a brief look at the political culture of each. Similar to the preceding chapter, findings for the four areas of inquiry then will be examined.

SELECTING THE FOUR STATES

Each LCC state, and each branch of the legislature within those states, will have unique campaign organizations. Some are more extensive than others, inclined to provide services in addition to direct contributions, fund incumbent campaign races more than challenge and open-seat races, and so on. These differences are based on a number of variables—including the partisan distribution of the state's voters, the division between the minority and majority in the legislature, the cost of campaigns, the level of legislative professionalization, and so on.

Because each LCC is somewhat unique, it may be tempting to treat them separately. Unless, however, it is possible to study all of the states with LCCs in depth, or the researcher is not concerned with generalizable findings, some criteria must be established to group them. Two dimensions were selected for this purpose: level of LCC resources, and the strength of party organizations in each state.

As suggested above, many LCCs are just beginning to take root while others are well financed and have been operating since the 1970s. Differences in LCC resources are believed to have a strong bearing on their interactions with traditional parties. To divide the states along this dimension, one can refer to Gierzinski's (1992) and Jewell and Olson's (1988) data on LCC finances.

The second criteria refers to traditional party vitality. Whether the state holds vibrant party organizations, units ready and willing to assist state legislative candidates, will certainly play a role in the relationship between LCCs and the party. Strong party committees may stand on an equal footing with aggressive LCCs. Perhaps, as earlier findings seem to suggest (Chapter 6), strong party organizations interact more frequently with LCCs than do relatively weak ones. Cotter, et al.'s data (1984) and Mayhew's (1986) narratives were used to rank states along this dimension. Considerations of both state and local party strength were utilized.

Figure 7.1
Dimensions Used to Select the Four States:
LCC Resources and Party Organization Strength

Level of LCC Resources*

		High	Low
Party Organization Strength**	High	Illinois **Ohio** New Jersey New York Michigan	**Indiana** Maine New Mexico Washington Wisconsin
	Low	California Connecticut **Florida** Minnesota	Arizona Missouri Oregon **Tennessee**

*Gierzynski's (1992) and Jewell and Olson's (1988) data on LCC resources are used to assess this dimension; both works refer to LCC operating budgets. Because their analyses are restricted to 18 states, 22 LCC states are not included.

**Cotter et al.'s (1984) state and local party organization rankings are used to assess this dimension. See pages 28–29 and 52–53. Because there is some disparity between the two levels of analysis, as well as between parties, this breakdown should be taken as a tentative generalization.

With these two dimensions, states were divided into High and Low categories. One state was randomly selected to fit each cell. As Figure 7.1 indicates, the four states are Ohio (HH), Indiana (HL), Florida (LH), and Tennessee (LL). A brief review of each is provided.[1]

Ohio: Aggressive LCCs and Strong Parties

Mayhew (1986) finds party organizations in Ohio, particularly at the local level, robust and able to exercise real influence in selecting and supporting state legislative candidates. He notes: "Party is the reservoir from which candidates come, the screen through which they must pass, and the object at which their [primary] campaigns are directed" (Mayhew citing Flinn 1973, 237–244). In the recent past, strong, aggressive parties could be found in Hamilton County (Cincinnati), Cuyahoga County (Cleveland), Mahoning County (Youngstown), Summit County (Akron), Jefferson County, and Steubenville, among many other urban and rural areas (Mayhew 1986, 66–73). Although the current import of these units may have declined, the legacy of precinct, ward, city, and county organizations clearly mark this state as party-oriented.

At the state level, Cotter and his colleagues (1984) rank the Ohio Republicans as one of the most virile parties in the nation. Even though the state-level Democrats do not seem to have the same intensity, at the local-party level, both parties are ranked in the top one-third of the scale.

The operating budget for the Ohio Republican State Committee in 1992 was over $3 million. It also maintains several full-time operatives. Similarly, the Ohio Democratic State Committee raised an impressive $4.9 million in 1992. By all counts, these organizations are vibrant and aggressive.

The 1992 election also suggests an atmosphere of party competition and organizational vitality in Ohio. It was considered a swing state by both the Clinton and Bush campaigns, eventually going to the former by two percentage points. John Glenn faced a difficult challenge, as did a number of long-term members of Congress (two were defeated). The state House was the venue of fierce competition. The Republicans picked up fourteen new members in 1992, closing the gap to five short of majority control. Such a change would represent a reversal of over twenty years of Democratic domination.

Very much related to our concerns, Ohio's legislature is considered full-time and professional (Kurtz 1992b). Similar to New York, session runs from January until early summer. Members receive a base salary of $42,247, with extra grants of approximately $2,000 for leadership posts. Each branch maintains roughly two hundred year-round employees.

Legislative campaign committees in Ohio are also well developed—majority units particularly so. The House Democrats collected nearly $5 million, and the Senate Republicans gathered approximately $2 million in 1992.[2] Although they are legally separate from the state party committees, three of the units are physically housed in state committee buildings. The Senate Democrats, for example, rent space from the state party.

Indiana: LCCs in the Shadow of Strong Parties

Few would suggest party organizations in Indiana are not some of the strongest, most aggressive in the nation. "Politics in Indiana is a business conducted by men [sic] who devote their living to it" (Mayhew citing Munger 1955, 6). Throughout much of the past few decades, party government was "emphatically an organization enterprise anchored in inducements of state and local patronage" (Mayhew 1986, 94). In fact, during the early 1970s the custom of state, county, and local employees kicking-back a mandatory two percent to the parties was still in effect. In both urban and rural areas, an endorsement by the party has traditionally meant a lock on the nomination. Although the Republicans might have an upper hand overall (particularly at the county level), most areas of the state experience a struggle between long-standing party committees. Cotter, et al. (1985) place only two states higher in local party vitality (New Jersey and Pennsylvania) and only a handful at the state level. Mayhew grants this state his highest ranking (5).

Over the past few years the Indiana Democrats have made significant gains at the congressional and state level. They now control the executive branch, attorney general, office of secretary of state, and seven of ten congressional districts. They raised nearly $3 million in 1992. After losing control of the governorship in 1988, the Republicans, on the other hand, found refuge at having delivered their state to George Bush in 1992. They raised only $1.7 million during that year.

The Indiana State Legislature is divided; the Democrats control the House (fifty-five to forty-five), and the GOP rules the Senate (twenty-eight to twenty-two). Session generally lasts sixty-one days in odd-numbered years and thirty days in even-numbered years. Each member is paid $11,600 per year, with $101 per diem reimbursement during session. While noted as a hybrid with regard to legislative professionalization (Kurtz 1992b), we might place the Hoosier State toward the bottom of this group.[3]

That Indiana has only a moderately institutionalized legislature allows its poorly funded LCCs to be better understood. Recall in New York, another strong party state, that the combined resources of the LCCs was far greater than the state party committee's budgets. Although LCCs in Indiana also date back to the mid-1970s, they have but one-half the resources of their respective state party budgets. Each of the four committees raised similar amounts in 1992, roughly $500,000.

In sum, while Indiana has energetic, virile traditional party committees, the LCCs are relatively weak. This might be explained, in part, by the low level of legislative professionalization.

Florida: Weak Parties and Hidden LCCs

Florida hosts weak party organizations. In the Sunshine State, "[p]arty organizations have always been too weak to deserve much notice" (Mayhew citing Angelo 1984, 162). In fact, Mayhew finds Florida to be one of the weakest party organization states in the Union (1986, 120–121). Although there is some variation between the parties—the Democrats being a bit more organized—Cotter and his colleagues also place this state at the bottom of their index. County level Republicans are believed to be almost nonexistent.

Accounts taken during the 1970s and even the early 1980s, nevertheless, may not speak to contemporary party activity in Florida. Republicans argue their organization is on the rise; recent voter registration has been heavily in their favor, turnout during off-year elections is higher for Republicans, and they were successful in seven out of the last ten special elections. Although they have not broken the Democratic's hold on county sheriffs and other local-level offices, competition at the state level is considered fierce. The GOP's operating budget for 1992 was roughly $5.5 million, a healthy sum in any state.

The Democrats suggest they, too, are doing well. They compiled $8.5 million in 1992 and have recently undertaken an extensive grassroots training program. Their emphasis is on building the organization from the ground up. Clinton's narrow victory here may prove to be an organizational plus.

Of the 149 seats in the Florida House, only forty-nine are held by Republicans. The Senate, on the other hand, is evenly divided between the parties with twenty seats each. Control of the Senate (President Pro Tempore) is switched each year. Session runs roughly sixty days per year, and members are paid $18,000 ($25,000 for top leadership). There are also approximately 1,500 state legislative employees (Florida Division of Legislative Library Services 1993). As such, it is considered moderately professional.

The structural relationship between LCCs and the state parties in Florida is somewhat unique. Prior to 1989, each caucus (in each branch of the Legislature) formed a leadership fund-raising committee. These units aggregated monies from members and outside sources and distributed it according to need, as well as other criteria.

In many respects, like most LCCs in their early stages, they were mere reelection finance mechanisms. State party committees played little or no role in allocation decisions. On the heels of a public outcry over the influence of leadership PACs during the 1980s, these units were outlawed in 1990. It is now illegal in Florida to construct or maintain distinct legislative campaign organizations.

This is not to say these structures have disappeared altogether, but simply moved. Both state party committees now host groups specifically geared to state House and Senate elections. They maintain separate financial ledgers, thereby keeping track of contributions and expenditures for each branch. For the Democrats these accounts are called Victory House 1994, and Victory Senate 1994. Similar units are used by the Republicans. It was made clear during telephone interviews with leaders from both parties that the LCCs are *not*, in a legal sense, separate organizations. Moreover, all state committee resources and staff are controlled by the state committee. It was not possible, for example, to discern the exact portion of the state committee's budget set aside for state legislative elections.[4]

The political reality, regardless, seems to be that the state committees are holding pens for the LCCs. Legislative leaders "suggest" where and how the state committee should use funds and maintain control over certain staff on the state committee. Although the new Republican State Chair is determined to break the influence of legislative leaders on the state committee, by all counts he faces an uphill battle.

It will be interesting to explore the differences and similarities between county chairs where the LCCs are legally autonomous, such as in Indiana and Ohio, with those where they are structurally analogous with the state committees, as in Florida. Does the complete merging of legislative campaign activities with the state committee move the perceptions of LCCs by TPO leaders in a partylike direction? Are the views of county chairs in Florida who held their posts prior to 1989 unique from those who were recently elected?

Tennessee: Weak LCCs and Weak Parties

While also a southern state, Tennessee has some history of party organization activity. During much of the last century, aggressive, patronage-based parties were found in several of the larger cities. By the 1970s, few had remained significant. Both Mayhew (1986) and Cotter, et al. (1984) rank the Volunteer State near the bottom of their respective scales. Today, both parties have moderately active state committees; the Democrats raised $489,000 and the GOP $925,000 in 1992. Organizations at the county level are less assured.

Tennessee's legislature is considered moderately professional. The state constitution limits legislative days to ninty per biennium. Rank-and-file members consider their jobs part-time; they receive $16,500 per year. Caucus leaders, on the other hand, are granted $49,500 per year. Democrats control both branches comfortably. The entire Legislature maintains only two hundred year-round employees.

It is not surprising that LCCs in Tennessee are nominally developed. Their operating budgets in 1992 ranged from $225,000 for the House Democrats to $39,000 for the House Republicans. None of the four LCCs maintain a headquarters or any paid staff during nonelection periods. There are no formal linkages between these units and the state party committees, in short, Tennessee fits the bill of being a weak party, weak LCC state.

Summary of Selected States

The goal of choosing these four states was to highlight two important conditions in the LCC/TPO dynamic. To this aim, states were selected with varying levels of party organization strength and LCC vitality. As will be shown, other relevant distinctions also emerge.

The population of county chairs in the four states was mailed questionnaires. Response rates by state are as follows: Ohio fifty-four (32 percent); Indiana fifty (26 percent); Tennessee thirty-three (18 percent); Florida twenty-seven (19 percent).[5] That Ohio and Indiana have the highest response rates may add support to their being placed in the strong party states category. On the other hand, only 19 percent of the chairs from Florida, a state believed to have weak local party organizations, returned the survey.

The reader should keep in mind throughout the analysis to follow that, for the most part, the data represents *one* sample. The goal here is to examine the county-level relationship and perhaps begin to make generalizations. The respondent's state (the dimensions outlined above) is used as a control variable, rather than as one of four distinct samples.

EXPOSURE AND COMMUNICATIONS

Several measures were used to assess the respondent's exposure to the LCCs in his/her state. An initial question asked if "[LCCs] had ever been involved in a campaign in [their] county while [they] were active with the party?" If they answered yes, a follow-up question asked in how many races they had been involved. Overall, 64 percent answered in the affirmative, with the average number of races being 2.9. A third question utilized a ten-point, level-of-contact scale (1 indicated very little contact and 10 denoted a great deal of contact). The mean response was 4.4.

Table 7.1 notes the results of these questions, controlled by the respondent's state. Ohio stands out as having the highest level of LCC involvement; nearly nine of ten respondents noted an LCC had been active in their county at least once. Being that Ohio was selected as a strong LCC state, this finding is not surprising. That just one-half of the respondents in Florida noted LCC involvement, however, was somewhat unexpected. Prior to the 1990s, these units were very active, boasting budgets of well over $1 million. Perhaps their activities were focused in only competitive, urban areas. Or, because they are closely aligned with the state party committees, the county chairs were not able to distinguish LCC activity from state committee involvement.

It was also interesting to find level of interparty competition having little to do with exposure. A series of questions was used to assess the number of close state legislative races and competitive seats in the respondent's county. Correlations between these figures and the

Table 7.1
Exposure to LCCs, Controlled by State

	Ohio	Indiana	Tennessee	Florida
Have LCCs Ever Been Involved in Your County While You Were Chair?				
(% Answering Yes)	86%	71%	67%	55%
If Yes, How Many Times? (Mean # of Campaigns)	2.9	3.4	1.4	2.1
Level of Exposure Scale (Mean Response)*	5.2	4.4	3.5	4.1
N	54	35	50	27

* Level of Exposure Scale ranges from 1 (very little contact) to 10 (a great deal of contact).

level of exposure scale are modest. Several other variables, such as the size and affluence of the county committee, the tenure of the respondent, if he/she had ever served on the state party committees, and the county committee's relationship with the state committee all appear to be better predictors.

The limited role electoral competition plays in explaining exposure to LCCs is perplexing. It is likely, as in New York, that certain counties comprise only a portion of state House and Senate districts. Even if a county is within a competitive district, LCCs may limit their activities to the more populous areas. Accordingly, larger, more affluent county committees (generally ones in populated areas) may be exposed to LCCs more often than rural party organizations, even though both are part of the same competitive district. This line of reasoning seem to be supported by the data. When the size of the county committee is controlled, interparty competition is a better predictor of exposure to LCCs. "We are a small rural county," noted one respondent, "and have virtually no contact with legislative committees." The same respondent noted both a competitive House and Senate seat in his county.

An important, yet rarely discussed, topic in the parties' literature is the health of *rural* party organizations. We know that urban machines have withered and many of the suburban structures have taken hold over the past few decades. Much less is known about the vitality of rural structures. This finding suggests that, even if we were to link LCC growth to traditional local party organizations, rural units may be left out in the cold. These new units target their activities not only to competitive areas, but *highly populated* competitive areas. A comment from a rural Indiana county chair is telling: "The future of our party [organization] is dimmer. It could be a lot better if the state legislative campaign committee would get down to the grass-roots level. I don't even like going to state committee meetings because I feel very out of place."

For those chairs who had workings with the LCCs, it was asked how often during elections members of the county committee communicated with LCC staff. The average response was a few times per month, but the mode answer was hardly ever (29 percent). The number stating "hardly ever" from Indiana was 39 percent. While these numbers may not appear especially low, those who have been involved in highly contested campaigns (the type of races LCCs become involved in) are familiar with the fervent level of communication between members of a campaign team. In this light, these figures are quite modest.

Finally, an open-ended question asked what the county chairs thought legislative campaign committees do in their state. One-fifth said they were unsure. This portion is roughly the same for three of the four states, with Ohio being slightly lower, and is consistent with findings in New York. Legislative campaign committees in these four states have been around for several years and, in at least two, are the heavy hitters. Yet approximately 20 percent of the county party leaders in these states could not begin to say what they do.

PROJECT INTERDEPENDENCE

Three questions were used to assess the extent of financial interdependence. It was first asked if the county committee had ever contributed money to these organizations. Slightly lower than at the state level, here 34 percent reported that they had. This number increased to 45 percent in Ohio but stays at roughly the one-third mark for the other states. Party differences were minimal.

The picture is even bleaker when the direction of the assistance is inverted. Only 11 percent of the respondents said the LCCs have contributed money to their organization. "I can't imagine that they would do so," suggested a Republican from Indiana. Another query was whether, during the past two years, they had worked with the LCCs on joint fund-raisers. One-forth replied in the affirmative. While the respondent's party had no significant impact, there was some variation between the states; over 30 percent of the respondents from the strong party states (Ohio and Indiana) answered "yes," but less than 20 percent in the other two.

A brief anecdote conveyed in a follow-up conversation is worth repeating. A County committee in Ohio was pressured by the state party to raise $5,000 for the 1992 presidential election. In exchange, committee members were told they would receive technical and strategic help for their state senate candidate from the LCC. They raised the money, but when the election approached they received a cold shoulder from the LCC. "We were told the race was simply not winnable and that little assistance would be forthcoming. . . . They didn't know what the blazes I was talking about. We would have kept some of the money if I would have known."

With regard to project interdependence more generally, 31 percent of the county committees in the sample conducted joint activities with the LCCs during the last election. In Ohio, this figure is increased to 44 percent, but it is less than 20 percent for both Tennessee and Florida. "I tried to," noted a Democrat from Florida, "but they didn't feel my candidates could win so they stayed out." Most of the joint endeavors seem to be labor intensive projects such as telephoning, literature drops, and GOTV drives. Another frequently noted activity was arranging guest speakers. "They helped us bring in John Glenn," noted an Ohio Democrat.

Only 23 percent (thirty-seven) of the respondents *asked* the LCCs in their state for assistance during the last election. Of that amount, less than one-half received the help they requested. "They helped us raise money and get out the vote," wrote a Florida Democrat, but another Democrat from Ohio said "zilch—they are selfish and work to elect their own." In total, then, 9 percent (fourteen) of the 169 county party committees in the sample asked for and received assistance from an LCC. In Ohio, the strongest LCC state in the sample, only thirteen respondents (24 percent) asked the LCCs for help during the last election. Of that amount, eight received the aid they were looking for. Most of these activities were related to technical support and finances.

Even within a diffuse party structure, the lack of assistance directed to county party organizations is significant and speaks to the office-specific nature of LCC activity. It says a good deal about the extent and direction of the LCC adaptation process. If these new units have been a boon for parties, it is hard to see how this is true at the county level. As will be seen, most respondents believe these units have had little impact on their organization.

Based upon the county-level analysis in New York, as well as the scant communications between the county committees and LCCs in these four states, it is not surprising that strategic cooperation is also meager. Table 7.2 notes the frequencies of two strategic cooperation questions, controlled by state. The first deals with how much influence the county committee has in deciding *which* candidates the LCCs will support, and the second on *how* resources will be spent. Both use a ten-point scale, with 1 indicating "very little influence" and 10 being "a great deal of influence." Even though chairs in Ohio may have a slightly larger say, it appears that, on the whole, county party committees play a very limited role in LCC decisions.[6]

As modest as it appears, strategic cooperation is further lowered by high levels of electoral competition. That is, the more competitive

Table 7.2
Levels of Strategic Cooperation, Controlled by State
(Means on Ten-Point Cooperation Scales)*

How Much Influence Does the County Committee Have on:

	Overall	Ohio	Tennessee	Indiana	Florida
Which Candidates the LCCs Support?	3.7	4.2	3.3	3.7	3.8
	(2.8)*	(2.5)	(3.6)	(2.8)	(3.1)
How to Spend LCC Resources?	3.0	3.5	2.2	3.0	2.7
	(2.4)	(2.2)	(1.9)	(2.4)	(1.9)

N = 136
*One indicates "very little influence," and ten denotes "a great deal of influence." Standerd Deviations are noted in parentheses.

the county's state legislative seats, the lower the cooperation means. This seems especially true with regard to the second dimension—how the LCC should spend resources. This finding supports an earlier supposition that interdependence, if it occurs at all, generally will be focused around specific projects rather than tactical judgments.

Larger county committees, however, may have a greater say in LCC decisions. The correlation between the annual operating budget of the county committee and cooperation on which candidates to support is .38; for how these units should spend money it is .31. Using a multivariate regression, the size of the county committee and the annual operating budget of the county committee explain roughly 20 percent of the variance in strategic cooperation. In other words, county committees with a good deal to offer, both in resources and volunteers, seem to have a greater say in LCC decisions.

The overall low level of strategic cooperation is quite illustrative. Units in the traditional party structure are generally autonomous, particularly when it comes to their roles in campaigns within their immediate jurisdiction. A state committee would never dream of telling a county party organization how to run a race for sheriff, nor would it conduct activities in that county without the chairs' approval. It is only when districts transcend party committee boundaries, such as congressional and state legislative districts, that cooperation takes place, particularly when it comes to strategic decisions.

This does not seem to be the case with LCCs, as most county chairs are removed from the strategy council. It is little wonder they have a hard time distinguishing these new units from independent campaign consulting firms—as will be seen below.

Moving from strategy to the implementation of projects, Table 7.3 notes the results of two questions regarding a list of activities—both institutional support and candidate directed. Similar to the state level instrument, chairs were first asked to indicate whether the LCCs in their state conducted each project and, if so, to use a ten-point scale to assess the level of coordination with the county committee on that activity.

One finding to emerge is the modest portion of respondents who believed the LCCs conduct party-oriented institutional support projects. Only one-half said the LCCs in their state conduct voter registration programs and GOTV drives. Fewer yet are believed to produce newsletters for rank-and-file party activists. Fund-raising, however, was seen as an important LCC enterprise by two thirds of the chairs.

A second point concerns the overall low level of teamwork. The mean cooperation score for nearly every project is less than 5.0, with the exception of GOTV drives at 5.8. Several dimensions, i.e., contributing to candidates and polling, are below 4.0. The latter is particularly surprising because it can be a labor-intensive project, where local volunteers can be a great help. What is also puzzling is the low level of collaboration on candidate recruitment. We might assume that if LCCs were looking for candidates they might first check with the county party chair. Traditionally, this has been the nearly exclusive province of the party leader.[7]

An account from a Democratic chair is perhaps informative in this regard: In the spring of 1990 both the respondent's county committee and the LCC of his state had discerned the incumbent was vulnerable and were gearing up for a strong race. The county committee had settled on a prominent county legislator from the largest urban center of the district. She was also Vice-Chair of the county party committee. "I couldn't imagine a better candidate." The LCC, on the other hand, recruited a wealthy Republican who had run against the incumbent in two previous primaries, narrowly losing. They assured him that if he switched his loyalties he would get the nomination without a primary battle and receive matching funds during the general election. When the county Democrats heard of this, they were aghast and vowed an all-out battle. "The guy was a staunch Republican his

Table 7.3
County-Level Project Interdependence
(Percent Noting LCCs Conduct Activity and Cooperation Scale, Controlled by State)

	Total		Ohio		Tennessee		Indiana		Florida	
	%	Scale	%	Scale	%	Scale	%	Scale	%	Scale
Institutional Support										
GOTV Drives	55	5.8	67	6.2	46	5.0	55	6.1	48	5.3
Voter Reg.	47	4.9	61	5.1	39	3.2	46	5.5	36	5.3
Newsletters	36	4.5	32	4.4	30	3.9	49	5.4	32	3.7
Fund-raising	68	4.2	77	4.5	68	4.1	66	4.1	52	3.8
Candidate Directed										
Polling	58	3.6	69	3.8	39	3.4	64	4.0	48	2.4
Media Help	70	4.6	83	5.1	55	3.8	68	4.5	64	4.3
Direct Mail	70	4.9	83	6.2	49	2.9	79	4.6	52	3.7
Recruit Candidates	61	5.1	81	5.4	40	4.7	64	5.6	44	3.4
Seminars	63	4.8	87	5.0	40	4.4	66	4.9	40	3.9
Giving $ to Candidates	69	3.9	73	4.2	68	3.6	75	4.1	52	3.2

The first column represents the percent of respondents that indicated the LCCs in their state conducted the activity.

If "Yes" to the first query, respondents were asked to rank the level of cooperation between the LCCs and their county committee for each activity. The scale ranges from 1 (very little coordination) to 10 (very close coordination).

whole life and I was furious. . . . Unfortunately, our candidate got the jitters and decided to stay out of the primary. To be perfectly honest, she was intimidated by the amount of money [the former Republican] was going to spend." In the end, the county committee joined forces with the LCC. The campaign spent over $100,000, losing by less than one percent of the total vote.

Finally, with regard to material interdependence, just 22 percent noted their organization had shared a headquarters with an LCC. This figure is a bit higher in Ohio (34 percent), followed by Indiana (24 percent). The disparity between states may be as much a function of local party strength as it is a measure of LCC/county committee interdependence. In other words, if a county committee is not vigorous enough to maintain a headquarters, then it cannot possibly share one with an LCC. The data supports this claim; more affluent county committees are more likely to have shared a facility with an LCC than moderately funded ones.

Explaining Interdependence Using a Multivariate Model

Project interdependence is a complex notion. There can be degrees of assistance—the direction of which may tell as much about the process as the extent of cooperation. Findings thus far imply county party committees infrequently join forces with the LCCs. Yet this is not true for all county committees, and the correlation between each of the interdependence measures is high: either the county committee (generally speaking) cooperates with the LCCs on a set of projects, or not at all.

What types of committees cooperate with LCCs more than others? An answer to this puzzle suggests that certain variables matter (such as the size of the county committee), and others do not (such as the respondent's party). In order to be a bit more comprehensive, each of the ten-point scales of interdependence have been grouped into two areas: 1) institutional support activities, and 2) candidate-directed projects. A composite scale was then created for each: the former ranges from 4 to 40, and the latter from 6 to 60. They were then introduced as dependent variables. As for independent variables, increased party competition is believed to lower institutional support cooperation but, at the same time, increase candidate-directed linkages. The extent of LCC resources and the strength of the county committee also may be telling. If the respondent has a close relationship with the state party committee, it may spill into workings with the LCCs. The chair's tenure may have an effect as well. Finally, the

Table 7.4
Multivariate OLS Regressions, with Institutional Support and
Candidate-Directed Interdependence as Dependent Variables

Independent Variables	B	Beta	Sig T
Institutional Support Model:			
Interparty Competition	6.70	.18	.50
Relationship with State Committee	1.19	.38	.16
Legislative Professionalization	-1.48	-.07	.78
Chair's Tenure	.35	.23	.36
County Committee Resources ($)	-.12	-.04	.85
Number of LCC Races in R's County	.10	.06	.78
Size of County Committee	.01	.17	.58

Constant = 6.8

R-Square = .33

Candidate-Directed Model:			
Interparty Competition	4.55	.09	.57
Legislative Professionalization	3.84	.08	.62
Relationship with State Committee	1.24	.21	.20
Number of LCC Races in R's County	.76	.23	.16
Chair's Tenure	.59	.25	.22
County Committee Resources ($)	.33	.06	.77
Size of County Committee	-.04	.01	.95

Constant = 8.9

R-Square = .25

N = 136 for both models

case study of New York tells us that level of exposure and legislative professionalization should have a significant bearing on linkages.

Table 7.4 notes the findings of two models—one for each of the dependent variables. For institutional support linkages, the chair's relationship with the state committee seems to be the most telling, followed by his/her tenure. It appears that, the closer the county committee is to the state committee and the longer the chair has held that post, the higher the level of institutional support interactions. As expected, legislative professionalization seems to lower interdependence, but only modestly. On the other hand, unlike chairs in New York, the level of exposure has little impact, as does interparty competition. Altogether, these seven variables explain one-third of the variance. (This figure remains at roughly 30 percent with the two least significant variables dropped.)

As for candidate-directed interdependence, the chair's tenure is the most significant, followed by the number of state legislative races in the respondent's county and his/her relations with the state committee. Here, however, legislative professionalization has a positive slope, and level of exposure to the LCCs seems to make a difference. The r-square for this model is a bit lower at .25.

Efforts to sort out the influences leading to interdependence are a bit disappointing. None of the coefficients are statistically significant at the 95 percent confidence level, but the relatively small sample makes this criteria somewhat ridged. Perhaps other variables, such as the internal dynamics of each county committee and its willingness to work with and accept direction from outsiders, are the key components. Adding to this puzzle is the candidate; is she, for example, closer to the county committee or LCC operatives? And what about the political history and norms of each county? Considering the complexity of this topic, one might be somewhat satisfied explaining one-third of the variance with only five variables.

A COMPARISON OF ACTIVITIES

In the preceding chapter, state party committees were found to be more election driven than expected. There seemed to be little effort directed towards party-building activities, such as voter registration programs and mobilization drives. The distance between perceived LCC goals/activities and state committee objectives/activities was rather narrow. This does not appear to hold true at the county level.

Respondents were asked to list the three most important objectives of their party organization. Table 7.5 reports the results of this query. While winning elections was the most frequently cited objective, this figure is roughly one-half of that at the state level. Here, helping candidates barely makes the scale. In fact, if all the objectives considered broad-based were combined, it would extend to well over the 50 percent mark.

Although recruiting candidates may appear election-centered, this is not necessarily the case. A follow-up question asked how important it was for the county committee to run a full slate of candidates each election. A robust 60 percent thought it was very important, and another 27 percent said it was important. We also know that many local and state-level elections are noncompetitive. As such, recruiting candidates may be as much an organizational mandate as an election-based activity. The same might be said about "helping candidates."

Moving beyond the goals of the organization to specific activities, again a less rational-efficient picture emerges. Chairs were asked to use a ten-point scale to note the amount of effort their organizations

Table 7.5
Objectives of County Party Committees
(Percent Citing as 1st, 2nd, and 3rd)

	1st	2nd	3rd
Win Elections	30%	12%	12%
Recruit Candidates	21	15	7
Register Voters	11	6	7
Raise Money	10	24	17
Develop/Strengthen Party	9	9	16
Encourage Participation	6	9	12
Help Candidates	3	7	4
Other/Missing	10	18	25

N = 166

Respondents were asked: "What would you say are the three most important objectives of your county committee?"

spent on a list of activities. Dividing these projects into broad-based activities and candidate-specific projects, and comparing the aggregate mean scores suggests an equal, if not greater, emphasis on the

Table 7.6
Amount of Effort Respondent's County Committee Places
on Certain Projects

	Mean Ranking	S.D.
Broad-Based Activities:		
Fund-raising	7.4	2.5
Recruiting a Full Ticket	7.2	3.1
Voter Registration Drives	6.7	2.6
Working with Other Layers of Party	5.9	2.8
GOTV Drives	5.6	2.6
Party Newsletters	4.4	2.9
Candidate-Directed Services:		
Assisting Candidates with Advertising	6.7	2.9
Providing $ to Candidates	5.8	2.5
Mailings for Candidates	5.2	3.1
Running Telephone Banks	4.9	3.1
Survey Research	3.3	2.7
Campaign Seminars	3.8	2.8
Community-Based Activities:		
Working on Community Problems	6.6	2.7
Local Media Relations	6.2	2.7
Holding Community Events	6.0	2.8

N = 169
S.D. = Standard Deviation
Respondents were asked to use a ten-point scale (1 being "very little" and 10 being a "great deal") to note how much effort their committees spent on each item.

former. As Table 7.6 suggests, voter registration drives and fund-raising, in particular, lay at the center of county party activity.

Clearly two activities extraneous to purely election-driven parties are community-based projects and social events. Using the same scale, the mean score for questions regarding endeavors directed at supporting community events and working to solve problems in [respondent's] county were 6.0 and 6.6, respectively (see Table 7.6). These means are even higher than for giving money to candidates, running telephone banks, and producing mailings during elections. What is more, 94 percent of the committees conduct social events—most events being dinners, picnics, dances, and the like. Sixty-two percent hold these events at least every six months.

Finally, asked directly if the county parties conducted activities unrelated to political campaigns, 74 percent of the chairs answered in the affirmative—the average number of activities being 1.9 per year. A few of these activities include: dedication of a flag and flag pole, talking with teenagers about the importance of voting, visiting senior citizen centers, selling daffodils for the American Cancer Society, volunteering for the United Way and Salvation Army, assisting veterans and their dependents, Earth Day activities, good government projects, chamber of commerce activities, recycling projects, and many others.

Perceptions of LCC Activities

The next step was to analyze how the county chairs perceive the goals and activities of the LCCs. It was noted that voter registration drives appear to be an important activity for county committees. Nonetheless, 15 percent of the respondents believed it would be very likely that the LCCs in their state would provide assistance for this type of project. Nearly one-half thought it would be either unlikely or very unlikely.

Even for more specific election-centered activities, most chairs were pessimistic concerning LCC aid. Asked if these new units would help their county organization with a local election, 16 percent thought it would be very likely and 18 percent likely. Conversely, more than 50 percent did not believe the LCCs would provide help. Neither the respondent's party nor state had much of a bearing on this finding.

Table 7.7 notes the correlation between the amount of effort spent by the county committees on a list of projects and the perceived interest LCCs have in the same activities. The list refers to either broad-based party endeavors or nonelection projects.[9] Unfortunately, interval scales were not used to measure each unit's concern for items such as winning elections and helping candidates. It is assumed that the correlation would be high. As noted in Chapter 4, winning elections also lies at the center of TPO objectives. The question confronted here is the degree of shared interest in less rational-efficient projects. Not surprisingly, only one of the coefficients is statistically significant at the.05 level: being accessible to the media.

An open-ended question was then used, calling upon chairs to comment on the fit between the goals of their organization and LCC objectives. Many of the remarks are rather approving:

- [LCCs] do not appropriate any funds or provide help in the way of support/concern for local parties. That's okay, they have to concentrate on legislative races.

- They are concerned with state legislative races and they do

Table 7.7
Correlation between County Committee Concerns
and Perceived LCC Interests

Activity	Correlation Coefficient
Running a Full Slate of Candidates	.05
Support of the Entire Party Ticket	-.05
Providing Services to Local Communities	.18
Being Accessible to the Media	.24*
Working with Layers of the Party	.20
Getting People Involved in Politics	.23
Holding Social Events for Party Regulars	.13
Working on Community-Based Issues	.07

*Significant at the .05 level.

N = 136

Referring to the LCC, respondents were asked "How much time and energy do legislative campaign committees in your state put into the following?" This scale ran from 1 (very little) to 5 (a great deal). For the county committee measure, a similar five-point scale was used.

interact with state party officials. They should not focus their limited resources on local elections; that's our job.

- I perceive the legislative caucus as providing a supplement to our overall efforts by injecting funds and promoting their candidates, which relieves the local organization somewhat.

- They do what they can—they must take care of their objectives first.

- They probably care only about winning their legislative seats. . . . They feel that by creating interest in the legislative seat that this spurs interest in other races and thus helps to elect other candidates to office. I agree.

But an equal number were more critical:

- There have been occasions when they will shun the head of the ticket if they believe it will hurt them. In the Dukakis campaign they walked away—in the Clinton campaign they embraced the candidate.

- They are geared *only* to their elections. However, the closer to election day, the more important the county chair becomes, i.e., 'take me to your voters, have a meeting and let me speak, have a fund-raiser for me, get out the vote for me, etc., etc.'

- It is my opinion that they use the county parties only for their best interest—to get to know the people and lay of the land. . . .

- I do not know of one county committee they have helped.

- They care only about a limited area, and preserving (or enhancing) the power of their leadership. The "party" is but a symbolic umbrella given lip service.

ARE LCCs PART OF "THE PARTY"?

A final analysis looked at how the TPO leaders see LCCs fitting into the overall party structure. While a majority of *state* party leaders believe these new units are *not* part of their organizations, most *county* chairs believe they are. Roughly 65 percent said the LCCs in their state are part of the overall party structure. The respondent's party does not seem to alter this finding, but which state they are from does. Eighty-five percent of the chairs from Indiana put them in this category, 64 percent from Ohio, and 60 percent each from Tennessee and Florida.

Being that a large number of respondents place these units within the party framework, it was most surprising to find that only a small portion conceive of them as partylike. Table 7.8 notes the results of a closed-ended question concerning how LCCs are envisioned, controlled by state. In each state a large portion—roughly 33 percent—noted "candidate-centered organizations," followed by "legislative leadership units." "Partylike" organizations ranks third. Unlike the state chairs, few (about 10 percent) said they resemble political action committees.

Why would a solid majority of state party chairs, the level of the party where legal linkages with the LCCs are to be found, suggest these units are *not* part of the overall organization—while most county-level leaders say they are? Moreover, if they are thought to be an element of the party, why do so few county chairs see them as partylike?

The answer may lie in looking closely at the core implication of each question. The first pertains to a structural facet and the second to a functional dimension. State party chairs have more information regarding the locus of LCCs in their organization. County chairs, on the other hand, may simply view them as state-level units, emerging from somewhere in the legislature. They would simply assume they

Table 7.8
How County Chairs See LCCs in Their State
(Percent Noting the Following, Controled by State)

Category	Ohio	Tennessee	Indiana	Florida
Candidate-Centered Organizations	38	26	36	32
Legislative Leader Units	26	10	24	14
Partylike	20	35	29	22
PACs	10	16	5	14
Campaign Consulting Firms	4	7	4	14
Other/Missing	2	6	—	4
N = 139				

The question asks: "Which of the following best describes how you see legislative campaign organizations in your state?"

are a limb of the state committee. When it comes to the activities performed by these units—the second query—county chairs have more
information; many have worked with them on campaigns. In this light,
they are viewed as distinct from party units. The data adds support
to this conjecture. Chairs having more contact with LCCs are less
likely to see them as partylike than are chairs with little exposure.

The final two questions on the instrument ask whether these new
units have helped or hurt their organization, and if the future of local
party organizations is brighter or dimmer because of them. Thirty-
eight percent noted they have been a help. Most comments suggest
their financial assistance frees county party money for other endeavors: "They have helped. Most legislative districts are either multi-
county or multidistrict counties where the county chair and his/her
party organization need to concentrate their efforts on local races." A
very small portion (roughly 10 percent) suggested they have been
harmful: "I think they hurt when they get people from your county to
run for state office and will not support them financially." Another
noted: "They reduce the power and prestige of the county organization." Most respondents (roughly 40 percent) from each of the four
states said they have had little or no impact: "Maybe they have
helped strengthen the state party, but they have not seemed to make
a difference on what we do."

As for the future, the percentages are roughly the same. Approximately 35 percent said it is brighter, 14 percent dimmer, and 29 percent that they will have little impact. Three comments are worth noting: "It's brighter," suggested an Indiana Democrat, " ... [LCCs]
provide another dimension to our campaigns. The overall goal of the
local organization is to elect more Democrats, and we are certainly
complimented in that area by the assistance of the legislative caucuses." But an Ohio Republican noted: "Anytime someone else picks
up party responsibilities we lose power." And an Ohio Democrat
writes "strong-arm politics has hurt good Democrats—hard work
only pays off if you kiss ass!"

What might explain why certain chairs have a more benevolent,
optimistic view of these new units than others? First, those who view
LCCs within the party structure are clearly more sanguine about
them. Second, respondents who suggested they have a close relationship with the *state* committee also have a more positive view of their
state's LCCs. As perhaps expected, legislative professionalization
may have a negative impact; that is, respondents from Ohio are more
likely to view LCCs as harmful and removed from the party structure

than are chairs from the other states. Respondents from Indiana, the state with the least professional legislature in the sample, seem to be closer to these new units; 85 percent believed they were a branch of the state party, and most (roughly 50 percent) believed they have been helpful.

Fourth, and perhaps most importantly, chairs who believed LCCs are concerned with general party-building activities were considerably more likely to see them as helpful. Table 7.9 notes the correlations between a set of activities and a ten-point scale measuring how close the chair believed his/her organization was to the LCCs. As each coefficient is positive and statistically significant at the .05 level, it may be argued that how traditional party leaders feel about these new units is closely tied to the perceived scope of LCC activities.

Table 7.9
Correlation of LCC Involvement in General Party-Building Activities
and Relationship Between Party and LCC

Activity	Correlation Coefficient
Getting People Involved in Politics	.55**
Working with Layers of the Party	.51**
Organizing Groups Behind the Party Banner	.51**
Providing Services to Local Communities	.48**
Supporting a Party Platform	.48**
Being Accessible to the Media	.45**
Support of the Entire Party Ticket	.43**
Running a Full Slate of Candidates	.25*
Holding Social Events for Party Regulars	.21*

*Significant at .05 confidence level.
** Significant at .01 confidence level.
The two questions are: "How much time and energy do legislative campaign committees in your state put into the following?" and "County party chairs have had different experiences with legislative campaign organizations. On a ten point scale, where 1 is very distant and 10 is very close, how would you rank your relationship with these new organizations?"

Finally, the degree to which LCCs and party committees cooperate on projects is strongly related to overall perceptions of these new organizations. One must be cautious here, however, not to infer causation. It is not clear that interactions lead to positive evaluations or that positive evaluations contribute to interdependence. It may be enough to say that the county committees that work with the LCCs have a more optimistic view of them.

Perhaps the most significant finding of this chapter is that county parties focus on broad-based and frequent nonelection activities. County committees are very much concerned with tickets, slating, civic participation, local issues, augmenting the party, and providing social rewards for activists—perhaps as much as they are interested in winning elections. This implies that there is a large, important dimension to local parties *not* shared by these new organizations. Therefore, growth and adaptation at one level may not impact, or may even negatively effect, units on another level. To follow through on concern about the vitality of community-based party organizations and the functions they provide, one may have to look beyond LCCs for encouragement. A case can be made (and is in the final chapter) that by shifting the locus of state parties from the traditional stratarchy to narrow, legislative election spheres, grass-roots parties are set adrift. In an age of modern communications, high-priced campaigns, and sophisticated campaign technologies, the future of our key cogs may be less certain.

Eight

Conclusion

LCCs AND TRADITIONAL PARTY ADAPTATION

Champions of responsible parties have had little to applaud over the last several decades. Because they seemed fixed on the endangered species list, many scholars backed away from the strong party model and embraced a more procedural-based, rational vista. Here parties are seen as but one player, at best the largest, in the pluralist pressure system. Many trained in the 1950s and 1960s, the period when responsible party advocacy was at its height, find themselves questioning, in their quieter moments, the ability of political parties to link the governed with the governors. Others schooled during the party decline period of the 1970s and 1980s find it difficult, indeed challenging, to preach the old doctrine. Responsible party advocacy, although never disappearing, certainly has been out of vogue during the past decade.

It is only in the last few years that writings on the rebirth and import of parties have emerged. A new generation of scholars has once again called our attention to the individual and systemic benefits of strong parties. In one of the most widely used undergraduate texts, for example, Larry Sabato lays out "The Case for Parties" (1988, 5–30). If it is unfashionable to favor normative, strong party arguments, Sabato has either not heard of it or simply does not care.

But if "The Party's Just Begun" has been the headline over the last decade, "adaptation" and "evolution" have been the subtext. Candidate-centered campaigns, PACs, campaign consultants, high-technology communications, and a different legal environment are challenges to traditional parties not likely to disappear. If parties are to survive, scholars argue, adaptation is the key. Many suggest this process continues to occur. Bibby writes: "In the face of a changing and often unfriendly environment, political parties in the American States have demonstrated adaptability and resilience. This capacity to cope

165

with the forces of political change has meant, of course, that the parties have undergone substantial alteration" (1990, 21).

Perceived by many at the forefront of this adjustment are state legislative campaign committees. The question lying at the heart of this project, however, is whether traditional party units are part of this evolution. And, if they are, has this turn so transformed parties that the functions they once performed—the very functions spelled out by Schattschneider in the 1940s and Sabato in the 1980s—are no longer possible. Because LCCs target resources to close races (unlike PACs), provide help to a set of candidates (unlike candidate-centered units), and are, in one way or another, linked to legislative caucus leaders, does that necessarily imply a party development? Are responsible party scholars so anxious for resurgence that change is valued on its face? Does growth in one sphere imply adjustment in another and, if so, at what cost?

LCCs AS DISTINCT, NONPARTY ORGANIZATIONS

Two suppositions guided this research. The first was that LCCs are independent of traditional party organizations, and the second, that LCC activities are narrower than TPO activities. That is, it was hypothesized that LCCs are autonomous, election-driven machines. Time now to assess the validity of these claims.

LCCs as Independent Units

The principal finding of this project is that state LCCs should be considered distinct organizations, at best nominally linked to traditional geographic party organizations (TPOs). The consequences of each, and their place in contemporary politics, must be assessed independent of the other. This was established by examining several dimensions.

The first step was to look at why LCCs were created. Legislative campaign committees are generally conceived as a response to waning party organizations and a more competitive political environment. From this functionalist view, one would expect LCCs to have developed where the cost and style of campaigns have changed and party organizations have declined. This does not appear to be the case; the correlation between LCC vitality and TPO strength was found to be positive, not negative. Another shortcoming of this perspective is that it assumes they were created by those in direct need of assistance, that is, rank-and-file members. It is concluded, however that the modern political environment—particularly the profession-alization of legislatures and a flood of state-level special interest money—helped legislative *leaders*, as political entrepreneurs, estab-lish LCCs. A final criticism of the fuctionalist view concerns the rela-tionship between minority and majority units. Little data was found to suggest minority party LCCs—the ones, according to this approach, with the greatest incentive to innovate—developed first or are more extensive. Just the opposite seems to be the case.

Understanding why LCCs were created is a vital aspect of this project; it speaks directly to the their autonomy, as well as to the party adaptation question. There is inadequate evidence to believe that they were devised by or for parties. It even may be the case that they were forged as a response to *strengthening* state-level party orga-nizations—units generally controlled by the executive. LCCs repre-sent a means for legislative leaders to control external resources—to collect and control campaign funds, to free their members of damag-ing elements of the party, and to augment their caucus regardless of the party's status in other branches. There are clearly interactions between these new units and party committees, more in some states than in others. The important point is that they were not devised to augment party committees, and any interaction will be calculated by LCCs strictly from a utilitarian point of view; how will it help win state legislative elections.

The next step was to examine the formal, or structural, linkages. If there is reason to suggest these units are coupled with state party organizations, it might be from this strict constructionist vantage: roughly one half of the state committee chairs surveyed noted some type of formal relationship. Nevertheless, this tie was found to be soft—if not irrelevant. In most cases, it carried no practical import, New York being a case in point.

With regard to project interdependence, findings also point to LCC autonomy. This was first evident in the case study of New York. This state hosts one of the most institutionalized legislatures in the nation. The creation of in-house policy and budgetary units over the last few decades has helped that body stand on an equal footing with a traditionally powerful governor. This is coupled with an exceed-ingly strong leadership structure within the legislature. Not surpris-ingly, there appears to be considerable distance between LCCs and TPOs. Neither of the state parties interact with the LCCs on institu-tional support activities or candidate-directed services. Nor do they share physical space or staff. Few county chairs said their organization had ever worked with these new units. In fact, a surprisingly large number of respondents have had no contact with them at all. Although a number of controls were introduced, exposure to the LCCs stood out as the most telling. Simply put, the more the county chair has worked with these new units, the greater the perceived distance between organizations.

New York holds several of the components believed to be important in this new relationship, not the least of which is *both* strong LCCs and vibrant traditional party organizations. The Empire State was one of the first to develop LCCs and today may have the most sophisticated/advanced units. Coupled with an increasingly uncertain electorate, it is perhaps easy to see why LCCs might be perceived as autonomous.

On the other hand, New York sustains powerful state committees and robust local party organizations. If LCCs were conceived and ripened as adaptations of the party, arguably it would have occurred here. Dwyer and Stonecash, in their examination of New York State campaign finances, suggest as much: "It is not sufficient to examine only the traditional state party committees . . . [but] all party organizations in [New York] to assess the condition of the state party" (1992, 340). By all party organizations, they refer to LCCs as well. Yet very few linkages were found.

Moving beyond New York, project independence was found to be modest, if not altogether lacking, in the sample of state party committees. Teamwork, what little was found, is mostly project-centered rather than strategic. These new units use state committee resources, but are hesitant to share strategic control.

Several controls produced noteworthy findings. Legislative campaign committees in noncompetitive areas are just as likely to work with state parties as are those in highly competitive states. This seems to contradict Schlesinger's notion that electoral competition brings campaign nuclei together. As in New York, levels of party organizational strength did not significantly modify overall findings. Perhaps the most telling for every dimension examined, respondents from states with professional legislatures noted a larger gap between their organization and the LCCs.

The modest interdependence found in both New York and at the state level was further supported at the county level in four additional states. Most respondents conceive of these units as distinct from the traditional party structure. Cooperation along any dimension was somewhat sparse. Again, most interactions centered on the implementation of labor intensive projects.

Are LCCs Similar to Parties?

To suggest state LCCs are independent of traditional party organizations is not to say they are different than parties or that they do not provide partylike services. The second core supposition was that these new units undertake a set of activities and maintain goals dissimilar to TPOs. There are two ways to address this issue: by fitting them into a theoretical construct, or by comparing their characteristics with what are believed to be the realistic attributes of TPOs.

As discussed at length in Chapter 3, theoretical views of party range from the rational-efficient to the responsible party perspective. At first glance, LCCs appear to fit the former. Their objectives seem restricted to winning elections, and they put a premium on efficiency. Their structure is professional and incentives are material, and they are quickly becoming the principal mechanism for recruiting viable candidates. The only area where LCCs *may* lean toward the responsible party model is their role in government. This conjecture is, to this point, simply that. More study needs to be done in this area.

It appears reasonable, then, to label LCCs partylike from a rational-choice perspective, and certainly most scholarly writings reflect this characterization. By distributing resources to close races rather than simply reelection campaigns, and by providing a host of campaign services, they may well be "very similar to typical political party organizations" (Gierzynski 1992, 58). Much of the research presented here would bolster this notion; TPO leaders perceive LCC interests and activities as very narrowly fixed on winning their elections.

But *even* within this restricted theoretical framework, LCCs may not demonstrate party affinity. Downs (1957) speaks of a united pursuit of controlling government—not merely a single branch of the legislature. Urban party machines seek to dominate city hall, not simply a wing of the city council. It may, therefore, be unsettling, and even descriptively inaccurate, to tag these units merely rationally-driven party organizations.

It is true that many state party committees have neglected state legislative campaigns in their pursuit to control the governor's mansion, and that most of a state's patronage can be gained by attaining that one goal. Are these state committees also less partylike? Two points can be raised in retort: First, even when it appears that state committees are narrowly fixed on gubernatorial campaigns, broad activities/concerns are undertaken. For a party to win a gubernatorial election party leaders must mobilize their core constituencies, and this helps the entire party ticket, including state legislative candidates. There are voter registration drives, platforms, get-out-the-vote efforts, joint press appearances, notions of tickets, and so on. There is always some concern for the long-range interests of the party, no matter how focused a state committee may appear to be. And a state committee would never dream of running down other members of the ticket simply to win the gubernatorial election.

It was once reported that a disgruntled New York State Assembly candidate approached a party leader and complained that all the party's efforts were being directed to the gubernatorial candidate and none to his race. He was told:

> You see the ferry boats come in? You see them pull into the slip? You see the water suck in behind? And when the water sucks in behind the ferryboat, and all kinds of dirty garbage comes smack into the slip with the ferryboat? Go home. Al Smith is the ferryboat. This year you are the garbage (Ware 1985, 143, citing Tolchin and Tolchin 1971, 18–19).

Second, if a state party committee were to focus *all* of its efforts on the gubernatorial election, at the peril of other members on the ticket, they would quickly be criticized for being candidate-centered instead of a "party" organization. This censure would come from party activists, journalists, and academics alike.

In brief, at first glance we might tag LCCs partylike by relying upon a rational-choice view of party. But on closer inspection even this notion is tenuous. Units designed to capture seats only within one branch of a legislature, holding little or no affinity for board-based or long-range activities, may strain even the most inclusive view of "party."

Another approach is to move beyond theoretical models to a close inspection of how LCCs compare to actual party organizations. The first step was to review how LCCs are structured, how they operate, and how they choose to distribute resources (Chapter 2).

A key facet of these new organizations is their use of legislative employees during campaigns. This practice affords LCCs considerably more weight than finance disclosures reveal. A more important point for the present concern is that these people do *not* engage in campaign activities because of an affiliation with, or concern for, the traditional party organization or even a particular candidate. Rather, LCC operatives are part of the new breed of campaign consultants whose interests extend no further than the election at hand.

It was further noted that, even though rank-and-file legislators may be products of—and therefore beholden to—local party organizations, most have little say over LCC activities. Legislative *leaders* bestow LCC operatives with a mission, and these professionals conduct their activities accordingly. Because operatives are transient (they move from one campaign to the next), it was argued that local sensibilities and political norms may be ignored. Organizational maintenance, purposive and social incentives for party regulars, slating, and many other important pieces of local party activities are irrelevant and perhaps even irrational to LCC personnel.

While early LCCs spent their resources primarily on incumbents, modern units target services to close races—either incumbent, challenge- or open-seat campaigns. Few resources are spent on nonlegislative candidates or general party-building activities. More importantly than risking inefficiency, an inclusive set of activities might link LCC candidates to adverse national or state trends and to unpopular executives seeking reelection. Support for board-based party programs also would make reliance on local issues and personalized campaigns more difficult.

It was argued at several points that many of the important functions provided by parties are a product of activity unrelated to winning elections. By recruiting a full slate of candidates (even within noncompetitive seats), local parties provide voters a choice. By getting out the vote, they encourage participation, and, by holding meetings and organizing community events, they give citizens an avenue to fulfill their civic duties. By maintaining a political socialization mechanism, they also serve an important screening function.

Findings support this conjecture. Data from each of the three samples suggest party organizations (particularly at the county level) place significant emphasis on activities *not* directly coupled to winning elections. The same party leaders do not see these broader concerns shared by legislative campaign committees.

Fundamentally, the goals of LCCs appear dissimilar to traditional party objectives. Legislative campaign committees are generally perceived to be concerned only with winning *their* elections and augmenting *their* caucus. TPOs, on the other hand, are interested in a broader range of topics as well. They are concerned as much about controlling branches of government as capturing more seats in any one of them, long-term party development as well as immediate electoral success, and what goes on in communities as well as in legislative districts.

Although it could never be claimed that traditional party organizations are unconcerned with winning elections, or that they distribute resources randomly, notions of tickets are relevant. They are important, not simply because of the teamlike orientation of parties, but because controlling the material benefits of state government, as well as a concern for policy alternatives, implies an emphasis on tickets. In order to get legislation passed into law, support is needed from *both* branches of the legislature and the executive. Parties, unlike candidate-centered nuclei, seek to bridge this "constitutional obstruction" (Key 1964). Again, will a house LCC, firmly entrenched in the majority, aid a senate LCC of the same party struggling to capture the majority? Will LCCs of either branch help a gubernatorial candidate of the same party? Both aggregate data and interviews with LCC officials conducted by others suggest, generally speaking, no. And this sentiment was echoed by party leaders in this study.

Traditional party organizations certainly shift resources from lost causes to close elections. But an important difference is that they do not openly distance members from unpopular candidates on the party ticket in order to secure the election of another—a practice characteristic of LCCs. Divided government is a sign of weak *parties*, not an indication of divergent LCC resources. Who controls the *other* branch of the legislature may be important to rank-and-file members, but it is of little concern to LCC officials. Does it really matter to LCC operatives or the caucus elite that the government is divided, as long as they are in the majority? The same might be said about the articulation and support of a set of policy alternatives, e.g., a party platform.

It is simply not enough to say that, because LCCs distribute resources according to need and provide in-kind services along with direct contributions, they are typical party organizations. Labor PACs are more inclined to contribute to open-seat races and provide volunteers than are corporate PACs (Eismeier and Pollock 1986, 203; Sorauf 1988, 102). Does that mean the former are more partylike than the latter? To define party activities with such a criteria at best stretches the rational approach, and more likely negates reality and belittles traditional party functions. Parties are, and have been, more than election-driven machines.

ARE LCCs HARMFUL?
AND OTHER RESEARCH QUESTIONS

An important question touched upon but not fully addressed by this research, is whether LCCs are in competition with traditional parties. While LCCs may be independent and hold a much more restricted set of activities, does it follow that they are harmful to parties? For a number of reasons, the answer is less than clear. More respondents in the samples found them helpful than damaging. On the other hand, an equal number said they have had no effect, and numerous others expressed strong negative sentiments. It is also difficult to suggest LCCs have been harmful to TPOs, as the latter have experienced a resurgence over the last several decades, the very period when LCCs emerged.

Certainly one advantage granted TPOs from these organizations is electoral success. Nothing can spark a party committee like winning a seat previously held by the other party, or even running a close second. Being involved in a race, otherwise noncompetitive if not for LCC involvement, can trigger organizational vitality. Along similar lines, the recruitment of good candidates (candidates with money to spend) is now becoming the province of LCC officials. This may bring new people and life to party organizations. Overall, the expansion of interparty competition may contribute to party vigor and cohesion.

Another way LCCs can be helpful is by cooperating with party committees. Recall how the Locals and the Republican LCC worked in tandem during the Plattsburgh Special (See Introduction). Interdependence, particularly around fund-raising, was noted by a sizeable portion of respondents at the state level. Conceivably, LCCs may work closely with the state party and certain local-level units (generally the larger ones). This is likely to happen in states with part-time legislatures more often than in ones with institutionalized bodies.

A third form of assistance—the one most frequently cited by party leaders in the sample—is financial. State legislative elections will certainly become more expensive, so much so that traditional parties may become increasingly irrelevant. If candidates perceive LCC assistance coming from the party, state and local committees may gain access and influence with candidates/legislators. If the distance between LCC officials and TPO leaders is perceived to be narrow, PACs and other large donors may channel their contributions through the parties. Additionally, a division of labor, where LCCs furnish the expensive parts of a campaign and the Locals provide the workers may be mutually beneficial. Local parties need not concern themselves with large treasuries, only membership, and they can divert scarce resources elsewhere.

Legislative campaign committees may reinforce party cohesion within legislatures as well, thereby helping to create divergent policy alternatives. Clearly defined, meaningful platform differences always have been at the heart of strong party organizations and partisanship. If legislative caucus leaders choose to use campaign assistance as a reward or punishment, party-in-government structures may become stronger.

Unfortunately, LCC maturation may represent as many, and perhaps more, harmful possibilities than positive developments. For one thing, these units may compete for resources. Conceivably more damaging than candidate-centered campaigns, contributors might find the biggest bang for the buck with LCCs. And why not; these units are extensions of caucus leadership, the very group that controls the flow of legislation. If one is interested in influencing policy or gaining favor with decision makers, it would be irrational to send money to TPO leaders rather than to LCC officials. As the power of these new units increases, they become even more attractive to contributors.

Their focus on winning elections may lead LCCs to recruit and select candidates based on a narrow set of criteria—principally their mass appeal. Such a process would undercut much of the internal incentive/promotion structures of local party organizations. Not unlike direct primaries, potential candidates would not need to work their way through party meetings and pot-luck dinners. They would only have to demonstrate their appeal to the general election voters. Candidates chosen by LCCs would not *even* need to be registered in that party. It should also be kept in mind that LCCs will do little or nothing to recruit candidates and foster competition in districts where their party is badly outnumbered.

The short-range perspective of LCCs may bode poorly for party organizations. Their goal is to win the election at hand. They may demand, for example, running opposed to an unpopular candidate on the ticket or using unconventional tactics (recall the Genovesi's use of direct mail in the Plattsburgh Special). Adherence to platforms may be seen also as electorally inefficient. This might divide loyalties among party activists, thereby destroying a sense of collective purpose. As any TPO leader knows, active party membership is fragile— easily shaken by dissention, particularly over purposive goals.

Even though moving into a district and infusing a race with massive resources may spark local party involvement, the opposite may also occur. One of the most important organizational incentives for any group is to make sure members have a sense of purpose. They must feel as though they are involved and necessary. Since LCCs often use state-of-the-art campaign techniques, grass-roots projects may be viewed as subordinate, if needed at all. Party regulars will have little input into the direction of campaigns, and their labor seen as ancillary. Even if party regulars are called upon to assist in labor intensive projects, they may feel used rather than part of the campaign team.

Finally, because LCCs show little concern for united party efforts, party control of state governments will remain irregular. At the very least, LCCs' myopic set of concerns will do little to unify state governments and the public will find it hard to make accountability judgments. In this light, no different than in a candidate-centered environment, partisanship becomes confusing and scarce, and the public becomes alienated and distrustful.

In summary, it may be too early to suggest that these new structures represent either a helpful or harmful turn for traditional parties. There are a number of potential benefits, not the least of which is financial. But there are also a number of likely hazards. This is not to suggest LCCs have, or will, single-handedly lead to party decay. Declining partisanship, for example, may be as much a reason for LCC growth as it is a product of their myopic objectives. Nor can it be said that LCCs have, independently, led to declining party influence with candidates and elected officials. And what might the alternatives be; is it not preferable to have candidates beholden to caucus leaders instead of PACs and fat cats, and to have LCC operatives running elections instead of campaign consulting firms? The implication of this project is that their growth does not automatically suggest a boon for traditional party organizations. Those concerned with the survival of party structures, and the important functions they provide, might take notice of these potential implications.

Other Areas of Research

The ramifications of state LCC growth may stretch far beyond party organizations. As noted throughout this project, their impact on party-in-government may be another area. At the national level, scholars have begun recently to examine the role of the Hill Committees in promoting party discipline. Do LCCs, for example, seek out candidates who will tote the party line, or is their mass appeal the sole criteria? From another angle, do legislators consider LCC support before they cast controversial votes? Precisely when we expect party coherence in legislatures to dissipate, brought on by the professionalization and atomization of service (Jewell and Lynn 1994), the opposite seems to be occurring. Party-in-government is getting stronger. Have LCCs had a hand in this or are other forces at work? There will be considerable difficulty in answering such questions. For one, the interplay of forces leading to a legislator's vote choice is complex—as congressional scholars have come to recognize all too well. At the very least a time-series model would be necessary.

Another area of inquiry is the impact of LCC money on candidates. In the Plattsburgh Special, Bob Garrow, the Democratic candidate, was torn between his allegiance to local party organizations, his friends and family, and the resources and personnel supplied by DACC. How do candidates—particularly nonincumbents—perceive LCC assistance? A few works have begun to highlight the struggle between Hill Committees and candidates (Fowler and McClure 1989), but little has been done at the state level. What happens when candidates are denied support? Whom do they blame: legislative leaders, the state party, or the LCC?

Several studies have been directed to where LCC money comes from, but few have been focused on what contributors expect in exchange. Why would a large donor send money to an LCC rather than to a candidate or the party committee? Do LCCs modify PAC contribution strategies?

No study has addressed the role of LCC operatives. These people are a critical element of this new puzzle. What impact will publicly employed campaign professionals have on state politics? Can traditional party organizations, stripped of patronage, compete with this type of activity? How extensive is this practice, and how do LCC operatives perceive their role?

Because these units are extensions of caucus leadership, has their import in elections altered the focus to include a referendum on legislative leadership? In the Plattsburgh Special, Republicans did their best to convey to the voters precisely who was behind their opponent's campaign and use the resultant anti-Downstate sentiment to their advantage. Perhaps in high profile campaigns, voting for a candidate may be as much a notice of support or rejection of legislative leadership as it is a choice of legislator.

Another area worthy of close attention is the impact of LCCs on other elements of the traditional party tripod: the relationship between party organizations, party-in-the-electorate and party-in-government. The evidence behind the new orthodoxy of party organization resurgence is compelling, but a number of scholars are beginning to examine the relationship between organizational adjustments and other, perhaps more relevant, questions (Coleman 1994; Hames 1994; Reiter Ch. 3, 1993). We might inquire, for example, why organizational maturation has coincided with declining voter turnout and growing split-ticket voting. It is just a coincidence that, at the same time legislative caucus leaders are as influential as ever, partisanship among the electorate is weakest? Should we congratulate parties for responding while a growing number of people do not vote, disdain party labels, and hold even less affinity for governing institutions? Will parties of the twenty-first century be measured only in terms of the extent of services they provide candidates? It may be time to reconceptualize the party system or, at the very least, seek integrative models that link components of the tripod.

What role do these new organizations play in the transformation of direct political communications to impersonal, high-technology techniques? Many believe that traditional party organizations perform an important intermediary function. Average citizens are linked with elected officials by communicating and interacting with party members. This discourse is an even exchange—parties listen as well as inform. Legislative campaign committees, as transient election machines, are part of, and perhaps fueling, a movement toward one way, impersonal communications. They seek to reach voters with the most cost-efficient means available, often by direct mail, radio, and television. And when the election is over they depart, maybe returning for the next election. Little emphasis is put on feedback during campaigns and even less on listening to voters during off-election years.

It is not the intent to lay the burden of changing campaign technologies on the doorstep of LCCs. This transformation has advanced independently of these new units and will continue regardless of them. Yet impersonal campaign techniques are generally viewed juxtaposed to local party organizations. Scholars should recognize, at the very least, the qualitative differences between a party worker chatting with a citizen on a front porch and a piece of literature in that citizen's mailbox. They may be hesitant to characterize units that rely solely on the latter as helpful to grass-roots parties.

Finally, this topic should draw close scrutiny not only from party scholars but, more generally, students of American government. Precisely why citizens feel increasingly alienated from government and politics is as complex as it is disquieting. One cause may be the disappearance of mechanisms by which citizens are pulled into the political process in a meaningful, consistent way and elected officials are linked into a coherent, knowable group. Historically, this has been a function provided by parties. Perhaps this is why any apparent expansion of party activities is welcomed by many scholars with open arms. The efforts of LCCs during campaigns increase competition and thus encourages average citizens to become involved. Interest in politics is greatest when elections are contested and meaningful. Moreover, the fervent level of campaigning augments the level of political information citizens hold, thereby creating a more informed electorate. In this light, there is much to applaud about these new organizations.

But if LCCs rely upon impersonal campaign techniques, support only candidates with a good chance of winning, disappear after election day, and have little affinity for issues, tickets and platforms, it is hard to see how LCCs serve democracy. It is likely they have added fuel to the fire. In close tandem with candidate-centered politics, LCCs are telling the voter: support our candidate, but what you do for the rest of the ticket is of little concern to us. When the policy process is mired by the automization of politics, and when divided government becomes the norm, voters are left puzzled and frustrated. Again, who are the "ins" and who are the "outs"? Thus, LCC activity may push citizens away from politics and contribute to a sense of distrust toward government. At the very least, close attention must be paid to the way LCCs conduct their business and how it affects the attitudes and behavior of voters. By abandoning noncompetitive districts, thereby contributing to one-party dominance in those areas, for example, is the political system ripe for the ills so amply spelled out by V. O. Key some 45 years ago (1949)? What will happen to turnout in these areas? And what about the concerns of minorities and the have-nots in one-party communities?

We may also wonder whether the transition to permanent, high technology campaigning, of which LCCs are a full participant, will distort the voter's ability to make thoughtful, retrospective evaluations. Many find alarm in interest group and candidate-centered politics because, among other things, they reduce long-term partisan loyalties, thereby contributing to volatile turns in public opinion. The loss of a minimal sense of consistency in the way we see politics leads to confusion and mistrust. What will stop politicans from putting together self-contradictory coalitions and jumping from one side of the ideological fence to the other? In the end, politics becomes particularized, yet remote; our elected officials are sufficient, but all politicians and governing institutions are corrupt.

Much of this, of course, is open to speculation and study. However, we must be prepared to accept the idea that while parties have historically aided the democratic process and enhanced the role of the average citizen, LCCs may serve opposite ends.

It seems clear that there are numerous areas of inquiry yet to be examined. Many of these topics, like the focus of this research, address larger democratic issues such as representation, fair elections, and the nature of politics. One cautionary note should be made: there may be shortcomings in relying on LCC officials, legislative leaders, or LCC operatives for information. Those who control LCCs may wish them to be seen as benign, party organizations. There is certainly an air of secrecy, particularly in states with professional legislatures. The use of state employees as operatives is common but perhaps improper (if not illegal). One can recall the 564-count indictment against New York State Senate Minority Leader Manfred Ohrenstein (Chapter 2). Second, the reason why LCCs have become so powerful in many states is because of their fund-raising capabilities. In an era of open government, the notion of special interests channeling capital to legislative leaders suggests, at best, access—and, at worst, direct influence. As noted in previous chapters, party committees have been granted, in both state and federal law, advantages over nonparty organizations. LCC leaders may wish to maintain this edge and therefore would be hesitant to say that their organization is truly independent from the state party committee. Lastly, our political system is dominated by a pervasive sense of localism. The idea of organizations created to infuse campaigns with external resources may appear to run counter to this norm. This is not to suggest that fruitful information cannot be obtained by LCC officials, only that the researcher must proceed with caution. This is a new phenomenon, the contours of which are not fully known.

THE FUTURE OF LCC
AND PARTY ORGANIZATIONS

This concluding section provides a few speculative thoughts about LCCs and TPOs down the road.

Legislative Professionalization

If LCC autonomy is the principal finding of this project, the weight of legislative professionalization is a close second. Every state with a highly institutionalized/professional legislature has LCCs. And these units are more likely to be viewed as independent, rational-efficient campaign machines than are LCCs in part-time states.

At the same time, legislative professionalization is a strong current in contemporary politics. States that are not already institutionalized may be heading in that direction (Chubb 1988; Rosenthal 1990). There is reason to suggest this movement will push (keep) moderately autonomous LCCs from the party. State legislators and caucus leaders in professional states will pursue protective strategies. This means keeping LCCs as *their* organizations. This movement also implies that states yet to develop LCCs will soon do so.

Term Limits

Nearly four out of ten states now limit the terms of state legislators. What effect will frequent turnover and large numbers of open seats have on LCCs?

One possibility is that term limits will change the incentives, norms, and expectations of individual legislators—pushing the institution in an amateur direction. Knowing their stay will be brief, ideological and policy incentives may supersede long-term career goals. Legislators may thus look to the party caucus not for election assistance but policy guidance. If reelection becomes less important relative to policy platforms, LCC influence could diminish.

On the other hand, because their short stay will not allow them to cultivate their constituency, members may never feel safe (Benjamin and Malbin 1992, 210–212). Policy enactment often takes longer than one term, making reelection an imperative. What is more, even if state legislators do not see their *current* positions as a career, they may still want to be career politicians. Many will always have an eye to their next election, knowing that nothing can kill political careers quicker than electoral defeat. For career legislators, the need to win big is only intensified by limited terms. All this suggests LCCs will be viewed as critical to reelection and as boosts up a political career ladder.

Another possibility is that term limits will destroy strong leadership structures. There is little reason to believe members, again knowing their stay will be brief, will fall neatly behind a caucus leader.

Also, if potential contributors do not perceive leadership as being able to control members, there is no reason for them to contribute to the LCCs. In other words, much of the power of these new organizations is linked to the perceived ability of legislative leaders to control members and thus legislation. If they cannot do this, contributors will go elsewhere (most likely back to the candidates directly).

Along similar lines, if leadership structures are weakened by term limits, much of the power that professional state legislatures have gained over the past few decades, relative to the executive, will diminish. One possibility is that governors will cherish their renewed domination. However, as suggested by others (Benjamin and Malbin 1992, 213–217), executives also hold a stake in stable legislative coalitions. If term limits destroy caucus structures, they may wish to fill that void. To do so, they may reinvigorate state party organizations. Members would thus come to the state party committee (the governor) for campaign assistance. In short, LCCs in states with professional legislatures and term limits may fall under the shadow of stronger state committees.

Finally, and conceivably the most likely, term limits may create uncertainty—both for the member and caucuses. This may occur not simply because of the large number of open seats but due to the electoral frailty of novice incumbents. Electoral security comes only after members are able to interact with constituents for some time. This means running scared each election. Apprehension may be even more powerful where majority control carries tremendous perks—particularly in professional legislatures.[1] In order for members to hold on to their jobs and for caucuses to remain secure, emphasis on winning elections is even more pivotal. Obviously, the import of LCCs (and their autonomy) is sharpened.

Statutes Limiting LCC Activity

That LCCs are the new muscle in state legislative campaigns in many states has not altogether escaped the attention of the media and general public. Much of this acclaim has been in a negative direction.

As noted in Chapter 7, Florida passed a law in 1989 outlawing LCCs. California passed a similar statute a year before; Proposition 73, passed in 1988, set limits on fund-raising activities and restricted the transfer of resources between party committees (Gierzynski 1992, 64–65). The intended target of the law was Willie Brown's enormous House LCC treasury. Early in 1991, California's highest court nullified the statute. Its decision was based primarily on disparities between challenger and incumbent fund-raising restrictions. LCCs were effectively absolved and have since been revived.

By all indications, during the period when his campaign committee was interrupted, Brown's influence was only marginally deflated. In fact, his powerful fund-raising capabilities continued to dominate legislative politics. Although not directly collecting contributions, during this period Brown was able to channel money to needy candidates. By attending a candidate's fund-raiser, for example, a sign was given to PACs and others that the seat was high on Brown's priority list.[2]

It is likely that, in some states, concerned citizens or good-government groups will take notice of the vast resources controlled by LCCs. As implied above, perhaps part of the reason some LCCs are legally linked to a state party committee is to insulate their actions from the public. Because they centralize contributions and forge an implied influence mechanism there is little reason to suggest these organizations will not continue to receive critical review. This may be especially true when they are seen as independent units, rather than party appendages. Conversely, as long as party scholars contribute to the notion that LCCs are party appendages, there will be few reform suggestions coming from their quarter.

It is hard to see how legislators or legislative leaders would be willing to curtail their own reelection organizations. The difficulty in passing other campaign reform statutes is no less to the point. Perhaps only in states where referenda are frequently used, such as California, will LCCs be significantly restricted. Moreover, even if they are legally banned, their practical import may be only moderately reduced—as our review of the Florida LCCs suggests (Chapter 7). Because they are powerful and because they help keep legislators in office, nothing short of term limits are likely to prevent LCCs from remaining an integral part of state legislative politics.

The Cost of State Legislative Elections and Public Financing

Currently, twenty-two states have programs of tax-assisted funding for state parties and candidate campaigns. Of these, only two (Minnesota and Wisconsin) have significantly extended public financing to state legislative elections (Alexander 1992, 141–142). Nevertheless, one might speculate how public monies, for both state legislative candidates and TPOs, would impact LCCs. Keeping in mind that any public financing of state elections would, in all likelihood, follow the *Buckley v. Valeo* (1976)[3] decision and thus be voluntary, there is little reason to believe LCCs will wane in this environment. Instead, a change may occur in LCC spending patterns: specifically, more money being directed to incumbents. The first goal of these organizations is to hold their own. Public financing will likely provide a larger pool of viable challengers. Incumbents will feel less secure and fall back on their centralized campaign committee for help. Additionally, as campaigns become even more competitive, the import of campaign professionals (LCC operatives) will be heightened.

If, however, public financing is directed towards the traditional party committees, the relative strength of LCCs may decline. With help from tax dollars perhaps state party committees can retain (or recapture) their place in state legislative elections. Unfortunately, because of the current dualism between LCCs and party organizations in many states, it is possible that the new source of funds will be directed to other campaigns—primarily gubernatorial races. Legislative campaign committees may simply continue to do their own thing regardless of TPO strength.

LCCs at a Lower Level?

A final question is whether LCCs will spread to county- and local-level offices. These new units were created and continue to grow because of new environmental pressures and because they are effective. There are, thus, compelling reasons to suggest they will move into the local electoral context—particularly if elections at this level become expensive and service in these bodies becomes professional. And why not; they provide centralized fund-raising, economies of scale, and target vast resources to the most needy. They also link paid professionals to a campaign organization—similar to old-style political machines.

If they do spread to this level, what will it mean for local parties? The answer to this question is again hard to say. In the face of a rapidly changing social and political order, local party committees have demonstrated surprising resilience. This study, nevertheless, should provide a warning sign. Party organizations, especially at the local level, are key components in our democratic system. Their displacement by myopic, level- and office-specific campaign organizations might bode poorly for popular governance. Among many other notable functions, local party committees are one of the last direct, personal links between citizens and elected officials in a highly technical, complex world. Before a rush to congratulate the adaptability of parties, it should be considered what LCCs imply. This may not be the "party" we had in mind.

Appendix A
The New York State Instrument

This survey was conducted over the telephone between February and April of 1991.

Before beginning the survey, note the following:

Survey number _____

Name of chair _____
Telephone number _____
Date and time of call _____
County of chair _____
County code _____
Sex of the chair _____
Party of chair _____
Were other arrangements set? If so, note below:

Introduction:

Hello, is _____ at home? My name is Dan Shea. I'm conducting research at the State University of New York at Albany on local political organizations; you may have received my letter. If it's possible, I would like to ask some questions regarding the _____ county committee—it shouldn't take more than fifteen to twenty minutes.

I want to stress that all your responses will remain confidential.

If, at any point during the interview, you would like to elaborate on a topic, or if something is unclear and you don't understand what i'm asking, please feel free to stop me. If you can't recall an item or you are unfamiliar with something, that's completely fine. I want the interview to be as informal as possible.

I'd like to begin with some background information:

1) How long have you been (or were you) county party chair?

_____ years

98) other_____

99) refused/don't know (dk)

2) Have you ever served in another elected position on the county committee?

1) yes
2) no
8) other_____
9) refused/dk

IF YES,

What position was that, and how long did you serve?
Position(s) How long did you serve?

3) How long have you been active with your present county committee?

_____ years

98) other_____
89) refused/dk

4) Have you ever served on the *state* (Republican/ Democratic) committee?

1) yes
2) no
98) other_____
99) refused/dk

IF YES,

In what capacity, and for how long?
Position(s) How long did you serve?

Now I would like to ask you about the activities of your county committee. Some of the questions may be hard to give exact amounts—here your closest recollection would help.

5) How many people do you have on the county committee at this time?

_____ people

98)other _____

99)refused/dk

6) How many committeemen would you say are very active, that is, how many make up the core of the organization?

_____ people

98) other _____

99) refused/dk

7) How many times during the last year did your committee hold *full* meetings?

_____ number of times

98) other _____

99) refused/dk

8) Approximately how many people attended these meetings?

_____ people

2nd_____ 3rd _____4th _____

98) other_____

99) refuse/dk

9) Does your committee currently have a year-round headquarters?

1) yes

2) no

98) other _____
99) refused/dk

10) Are there any paid staff positions on your county committee? (PROBE: ask about chair)

    1) yes
    2) no
    8) other _____
    9) refused/dk
IF YES, list positions:

11) How much money would you estimate your county committee spent on all activities last year, including the 1990 elections. (IF HESITANT, read list)

    1) less than $1,000
    2) $1,001 to $2,500
    3) $2,501 to $5,000
    4) $5,001 to $7,500
    5) $7,501 to $10,000
    6) $10,001 to $15,000
    7) $15,001 to $20,000
    8) $20,001 to $30,000
    9) $30,001 to $40,000
    10) $40,001 to $50,000
    11) $50,001 to $75,000
    12) $75,001 to $100,000
    13) over $100,000
    98) other_____
    99) refused/dk

12) Which of the following campaigns would you say your committee worked the *most* on during the 1990 election?

    1) the gubernatorial campaign
    2) a state Senate campaign
    3) a state Assembly campaign
    or
    4) a congressional campaign

5) all about the same
98) other_____
99) refused/dk

13) In your own words, how would you describe your relationship with the state DEMOCRATIC/REPUBLICAN Committee?

14) Roughly speaking, how often do you communicate—either by phone or in person—with leaders of the New York State DEMO-CRATIC/REPUBLICAN Committee? (read list)

   1) more than once a week
   2) about once a week
   3) several times a month
   4) about once a month
   5) a few times a year
   6) hardly ever
   98) other _____
   99) refused/dk

15) Do your communications with the state committee greatly increase during campaign periods, or is it generally about the same throughout the year?

   1) greatly increase
   2 slightly increase
   3) about the same
   4) decrease
   8) other _____
   9) refused/dk

16) While some chairs feel their county committee has a close rela-tionship with the state commmittee, others do not. On a scale of 1 to 7, with 1 being very *distant* and 7 being very *close*, how would you describe your committees' relationship with the state committee?

_____ rank

   98) other _____
   99) refused/dk

17) If someone in your county was interested in running for the state Senate or Assembly—and that person came to you for help—is there anyone at the state level you might talk to about this race?

    1) a state party leader_____
    2) a legislator_____
    3) a legislative leader _____
    4) a legislative campaign committee person_____
    5) no
    98) other _____
    99) refused/dk

18) Have you ever talked with leaders of the state Senate or state Assembly about things in your county?

    1) yes
    2) no
    98) other _____
    99) refused/dk

IF YES, what kinds of things do you talk about most frequently?

19) As you may know, there are organizations that become involved in state Senate and state Assembly campaigns: the DEMOCRATIC/ REPUBLICAN *Senate* Campaign Committee and the DEMOCRATIC/ REPUBLICAN *Assembly* Campaign Committee.
These organizations get involved in some races and not in others. Do you recall if either was involved in a race in your county while you were chair? Is so, which race comes to mind?

97) unsure if they were ever involved
98) other_____
99) refused/dk

Although these organizations may not have been involved in a race in your county, have you ever had any workings, contact, or communications with either one? (IF NO, GO TO 20)

    1) yes (Go to 25)
    2) no (Go to 20)

98) other _____

99) refused/dk

IF NO: Do you know anything about these organizations? (IF NO, end survey) (IF YES, probe)

IF YES: What were these communications about?

20) In general terms, what kinds of things do these organizations do?

21) In your own words, how would you describe your relationship with the (these) organizations?

22) If you could use a scale of 1 to 7, how would you rate your overall impression of these units? One indicates very *un*favorable, and 7 indicates very favorable.

_____ rank

98) other _____

99) refused/dk

23) A number of county chairs have felt legislative campaign organizations _____. While others have said that _____.
(ALTERNATE)

1) are only geared toward winning elections, and in general don't care about *party* activities.

or

2) Although they concentrate on state legislative races, they *are* concerned about party activities.

Which is closest to your impression: do these organizations generally care about party activites or only winning elections?

24) If there is anything further you might want to say about your experiences with the legislative campaign organizations, I would really appreciate hearing it.

Thanks again, and have a nice evening.

25) During that campaign, did the legislative campaign organizations send people into the district?

    1) yes
    2) no
    98) other _____
    99) refused/dk

26) How often during the campaign would you say that you, or other members of the county committee, talked with staff members of the legislative campaign organization?

    1) at least once per day
    2) once per week
    3) several times per week
    4) a few times per month
    5) hardly ever
    98) other _____
    99) refused/dk

27) In general, what parts of that race were the legislative campaign organization mostly responsible for?

28) When it came to selecting the candidate to run for that seat, what role did legislative organization play? Were they...

    1) very involved
    2) somewhat involved
or
    3) not at all involved
    4) unsure
    98) other _____
    99) refused

IF YES (EITHER 1 OR 2), what did they do?

Was it your understanding that the legislative campaign organiza-tion's involvement in selecting the candidate represented the wishes of the state party organization, the state party leadership, or was it acting as an independent unit?

   1) state organization
   2) state leadership
   3) independent
   98) other _____
   99) refused/dk

29) Given your experience with legislative camnpaign organizations, do you think they should become involved in selecting candidates, or is that something which should be left up to local party committees or state party leadership?

30) Thinking back to that race, which of the following would you say was in charge of the overall campaign?

   1) the candidate
   2) the local party committees
   3) a professional hired by the candidate
   4) a local volunteer
or
   5) the legislative campaign organization
   98) other _____
   99) refused/dk

31) I'm going to read you a list of activities. Please tell me which activities the county committee was significantly involved in during that campaign and which ones the legislative campaign committee was significantly involved in during that campaign?
1 = county comm only 2 = LCC only 3 = both 4 = unsure 8 = other 9) refused

   _____ 1) recruiting the candidate
   _____ 2) circulating petitions
   _____ 3) providing people for grass-roots activities, such as handing out leaflets and stamping envelopes
   _____ 4) direct mail production and costs
   _____ 5) electronic media; radio and TV production & cost
   _____ 6) giving money directly to the candidate
   _____ 7) phone banks

_____ 8) press releases and putting together media events
_____ 9) printing material such as flyers, bumper-stickers and posters
_____ 10) conducting polls
_____ 11) getting out the vote
_____ 12) poll watching
_____ 13) strategic planning such as targeting groups of voters
Have I missed any projects?_____

32) During that campaign, did your county committee work together with the legislative organization on projects?

   1) yes
   2) no
   98) other
   99) refused/dk

IF YES, tell me about these projects; what were they?

In your own words, how would you describe the relationship between your committee people and the legislative committee staff, I mean, was it friendly, unfriendlly, or what?

33) I would like to measure how much you think the legislative campaign organizations listened to the local party's input during the campaign. Please use a seven-point scale where 1 indicates they never listened to you and 7 indicates they always listened to your input.

   _____ rank
   98) other _____
   99) refused/dk

34) Were there times during the last election when your committee asked the legislative campaign organization for help on a project? If so, what projects, and did you get the help you needed?

35) Suppose you were to ask one of the legislative organizations for help on a project, and that project was unrelated to the race that they were involved in—for example, putting together a voter registration drive—how likely do you think it would be that you would get the help you needed?

1) very likely
2) somewhat likely
3) somewhat unlikely

or

4) very unlikely
98) other _____
99) refused/dk

36) Did your committee work together with the legislative campaign organization to raise money for candidates?

37) Do you recall any campaign activities or projects that were funded jointly by your committee and the legislative campaign organization? In other words, did you pool resources at any time?

38) If, as county chair, you approached one of the legislative campaign committees and asked for money to help fund a local party activity, how likely do you think it would be that you would get the money you needed?

1) very likely
2) likely
3) unlikely

or

4) very unlikely
98) other _____
99) refused/dk

39) County chairs throughout the state have had a number of different experiences with state legislative campaign organizations. Some have felt their committees operated independently from the legislative organization, while others felt they worked closely with them.
On a seven-point scale, where 1 represents a very *distant* relationship and 7 indicates a very *close* relationship, how would you rank your workings with these organizations?

_____ rank

98) other _____
99) refused/dk

40) In your own words, please tell me how you see legislative campaign committees fitting into the state party organization.

41) A number of county chairs have felt legislative campaign organizations ____. While others have said that____.
(ALTERNATE)

> 1) are only geared toward winning elections, and in general don't care about *party* activities.
> or
> 2) Although they concentrate on state legislative races, they *are* concerned about party activities.
>
> Which is closest to your impression, do these organizations generally care about party activites or only winning elections?

42) Finally, many party chairs feel legislative campaign committees are unhealthy to local political parties in that control over campaigns is often removed. Others, however, argue that these organizations help local parties by providing resources and technical assistance. What's your feeling? In a very general sense, are legislative campaign organizations helpful or harmful to local party committees?

43) If there is anything further you might want to say about your experiences with the legislative campaign organizations, I would really appreciate hearing it.

44) Finally, in what year were you born?

> _____ year
>
> 98) other _____
> 99) refused/dk

Thank you for your time. The information you have provided has been most insightful. If, by chance, you think of something else you might want to add, please feel free to give me a call. My telephone number is (518) 869-3474.

Thanks again, and have a nice evening.

Appendix B
State Party Chair Survey

This survey was conducted through the mail to the population of state party chairs in December of 1992.

State Party Survey

Please be assured that all answers will be kept confidential. Your thoughtful comments would be greatly appreciated.

Part I:

1) What is your position with the state party committee?
   1) State Party Chair
   2) Executive Officer
   3) Other (please explain)_____

2) How long have you held this position?_____

3) Have you held any other position on the state committee?
   1) Yes
   2) No
   If yes, what was that position and how long did you serve?

4) Is your current position 1) full or 2) part time?_____Is it 1) paid or 2) volunteer?_____

5) What would you say are the principal objectives of your state committee?

6) Do *county* committee chairs serve on the state committee in your organization? If so, in what capacity?

7) Using the broad categories listed below, what was the state committee's total operating budget for 1992?

1) less than $100,000	5)$750,000 to $1 million
2) $100,000 to $250,000	6)$1 million to $1.5 mill
3) $250,000 to $500,000	7)$1.5 million to $3 mill
4) $500,000 to $750,000	8) over $3 million

8) What were the primary *sources* of state committee funds during 1992? Please list them in rank order:

9) Please describe the principal activities performed by the state committee during the past year.

10) Using a scale of 1 to 10—where 1 means very little and 10 means a great deal—note how much effort your committee spent on the following activities during the past year:

1 --- 2 ---3--- 4 --- 5 ---6--- 7 ---8----9--- 10
Very Little   A Great Deal

_____voter mobilization programs
_____polling operations
_____issue development
_____state committee newsletters
_____fund-raising
_____contributing directly to candidates
_____producing direct mail for candidates
_____running telephone banks
_____recruiting candidates
_____conducting candidate seminars
_____developing and distributing mailing lists
_____assisting candidates with their advertising

11) Although it's probably hard to generalize, who did your committee assist the *most* during the past election?

1) congressional candidates
2) state Senate candidates
3) state House candidates
4) the U.S. Senate candidate
5) the presidential candidate

6) the gubernatorial candidate

7) other (please explain)_____

12) Generalizing again, what portion of your total operating budget did your committee spend directly on *state legislative* candidates in 1992?

1) less than 5 percent

2) between 5 and 10 percent

3) between 10 and 20 percent

4) between 20 and 30 percent

5) between 30 and 50 percent

6) over 50 percent

7) other (please explain)_____

13) At some point in the future, I may look closely at a few state legislative races in each state. Could you please list several of the closest, most highly contested *state Senate* races in your state during the last election. (It makes no difference which party's candidate won. Several races would be helpful):

14) What were some of the most highly contested *state House* races?

Part II. Relationship With State Legislative Leaders:

15) When it comes to making important decisions, how much influence do state legislative leaders (of your party) have on the state party committee? Please use the ten-point scale noted below (circle one).

1--- 2 --- 3----4--- 5 ---6--- 7 --- 8 ---9--- 10
Very Little Input   A Great Deal of Input

16) Using the same scale, how much influence does the state party committee have on the decisions made by state legislative leaders of your party?

1--- 2 --- 3----4--- 5 ---6--- 7 --- 8 ---9--- 10
Very Little Input   A Great Deal of Input

17) In your own words, how would you describe the relationship between state legislative leaders of your party and your state party committee?

Part III. Legislative Campaign Committees:

In many states there are now *legislative campaign committees*. Sometimes referred to as "legislative campaign caucuses," or "house/senate reelection committees," these new organizations are generally run by legislative leaders, and they assist state legislative candidates. In some states they provide an array of services, while in others they give only financial help.

18) Are there legislative campaign committees in your state? If so, are they found in both houses and for both parties?
If there are *no* legislative campaign committees in your state or if you are unsure, you have completed the survey. Please enclose all of the pages in the return envelope and mail it as soon as possible. Thank you for your assistance!

19) In general, what do these legislative campaign organizations do?

20) Who controls their activities?

21) Do you know if there is any *formal* or legal relationship between these organizations and the party state committee? If so, what is this relationship?

22) Are these organizations located in the same building as the state committee? _____Yes _____No

23) Do the people who work for these organizations *also* work for the state party committee? Explain.
24) Which of the following best describes the "fit" between these legislative organizations and the overall *party* organization in your state?

    1) they *are* part of the overall party structure
    2) although you work for the same candidates, they are *not* part of the party structure
        3) other_____

25) Which of the following best describes how you see legislative campaign organizations in your state:

    1) partylike
    2) independent campaign consulting firms
    3) political action committees
    4) legislative leadership units
    5) candidate-centered organizations
    6) other_____

26) What is the financial relationship between the state committee and these organizations? That is, does the state committee contribute money to these organizations?
    1) yes
    2) yes, but only a very small portion
    3) no
    4) other

Do these organizations contribute funds to the state party committee?
    1) yes
    2) yes, but only a very small portion
    3) no
    4) other _____

27) When it comes to *raising* revenues, does the state committee work with the legislative campaign organizations, or does each unit raise money separately? Together _____ Separately _____

28) On the whole, what would you say is *the* principal objective of legislative campaign committees in your state?

Does this objective differ from the state committee's? If so, how?

29) When legislative campaign committees select *who* to spend its resources on, and *how* to spend it, does the state party committee have influence in these decisions? Please use the ten-point scale.

    1--- 2 --- 3----4--- 5 ---6--- 7 --- 8 ---9--- 10
    Very Little Influence   A Great Deal of Influence

30) Below is a list of activities that might be conducted by both the state party committee and legislative campaign committees. *First,* indicate with a check whether the legislative campaign committees conduct each of the activities. *Second,* if they do, please use the ten-point scale to describe the degree of cooperation between the state committee and the legislative campaign committee for each project. In other words, do you work together on the activity? The scale is as follows:

1 --- 2 --- 3 --- 4 --- 5 --- 6 --- 7 --- 8 --- 9 --- 10
Very Little Coordination   Very Close Coordination

Do These Organizations Do This level of Coordination
With State Committee

	YES	NO
_____Get-Out-the-Vote Drives	_____	_____
_____Polling Operations	_____	_____
_____Fund-raising	_____	_____
_____Contribute Funds Directly to Candidates	_____	_____
_____Recruit Candidates	_____	_____
_____Candidate Seminars	_____	_____
_____Media Assistance	_____	_____
_____Direct Mail	_____	_____
_____Voter Registration	_____	_____

31) With regard to the entire party ticket, which of the following best describes legislative campaign committees in your state?

    1) they care *a great deal* about the entire party ticket
    2) they care *a moderate* amount about the entire party ticket
    3) they care *very little* about the entire party ticket
    4) other_____

32) With regard to the party platform, which of the following best describes legislative campaign committees in your state?

    1) they care *a great deal* about the party platform
    2) they care *a moderate* amount about the party platform
    3) they care *very little* about the party platform
    4) other_____

33) One function performed by many party leaders is being accessible to the media in order to answer questions about candidates, issues, and party activities. Which of the following best describes legislative campaign committees in your state?

     1) they care *a great deal* about media relations
     2) they care *a moderate* amount about media relations
     3) they care *very little* about media relations
     4) other_____

34) As a leader of the state party, if you approached one of these legislative campaign committees and asked for help on a state party activity, such as a get-out-the-vote drive, how likely do you think it would be that you would get the assistance you need?

     1) very likely
     2) likely
     3) unlikely
     4) very unlikely
     5) other _____

35) How likely do you think it would be that you would get the assistance you needed if you asked for help on a *gubernatorial* election?

     1) very likely
     2) likely
     3) unlikely
     4) very unlikely
     5) other_____

36) State party chairs have had different experiences with legislative campaign organizations. On a ten-point scale, where 1 is very distant and 10 is very close, how would you rank your workings with these new organizations?

     1--- 2 ---3----4--- 5 ---6--- 7 --- 8 ---9--- 10
     Very Distant   Very Close

37) A number of state chairs have felt legislative campaign organizations are geared only to winning their elections and care very little

about general party activities (such as get-out-the-vote drives). Still others feel that, although they concentrate on elections, they are also concerned about general party activities.

Which is closest to your impression? Do these organizations generally care only about winning their elections, or do they also care about general party activities? Please explain.

38) In the space remaining, please describe what you feel has been the impact of legislative campaign committees on *your* party organization. Have they helped, hurt, modified, or had no impact on what you do? In what ways?

Thank for you help! Check here _____ if you would like a copy of the findings mailed to you.

Appendix C
County-Level Instrument

This survey was conducted through the mail in March and April of 1993.

County Party Survey

Please be assured that all answers will be kept confidential. Your thoughtful comments would be greatly appreciated.

Part I. Background Information:

1) How long have you held your position as county committee chair? _____ years.

2) Have you ever served on the *state* party committee? If so, in what capacity?

3) How many *active* members do you have on your county committee at this time? _____

4) Does your committee currently have a year-round headquarters?
_____

5) Does your committee have any paid staff positions? If so, how many? _____

6) What would you say are the *three* most important objectives of your county committee?

7) Using the broad categories listed below, what was *your* committee's total operating budget for 1992?

1) less than $1,000   6) $10,000 to $15,000
2) $1,000 to $2,500   7) $15,000 to $20,000
3) $2,500 to $5,000   8) $20,000 to $40,000
4) $5,000 to $7,500   9) $40,000 to $75,000
5) $7,500 to $10,000   10) over $75,00

8) Using a scale of 1 to 10—where 1 means very little and 10 means a great deal—please note how much *effort* your committee spent on the following activities during the past year:

1 --- 2 ---3--- 4 --- 5 ---6--- 7 ---8----9--- 10
Very Little   A Great Deal

_____voter mobilization programs
_____creating and distributing committee newsletters
_____fund-raising
_____contributing money directly to candidates
_____producing mailings for candidates
_____running telephone banks
_____recruiting a full slate of candidates
_____public opinion polling
_____conducting candidate training seminars
_____working with other party committees
_____assisting candidates with advertising
_____voter registration drives
_____supporting community events
_____sending press releases and other material to the local media
_____working to solve problems in your county

9) Does your committee hold social events—such as dinners, dances, or picnics? If so, what are these events, and how often do you hold them?

10) There are many ways a county party organization could spend its time and resources. How often does your committee engage in activities that are *unrelated* to political campaigns? (circle one)

1 --- 2 ---3--- 4 --- 5 ---6--- 7 ---8----9--- 10
Hardly Ever   Very Often

What are some of these nonelection activities?

11) I would like to ask a few questions about *state* Senate and *state* House elections in your county. First, how many districts (or portions of districts) fall within your county?

_____House_____Senate

How many of these districts are currently held by *Republicans*?

_____House_____Senate

In how many of these districts did the winner of the last election receive *less than 55%* of the vote?

_____House_____Senate

In the last election, how many of these districts had incumbents running for reelection?

_____House_____Senate

If *all* of the current state legislators in your county chose *not* to run for reelection, in how many of these districts, generally speaking, would the winner receive less than 55% of the vote? In other words, how many districts would have close elections?

_____House_____Senate

12) Some county committees have a close relationship with their state party organization, while others do not. On a scale of 1 to 10—1 being very *distant* and ten being very *close*—how would you rate your committee's relationship with the state committee? (circle one)

1--- 2 --- 3----4--- 5 ---6--- 7 --- 8 ---9--- 10
Very Distant   Very Close

Part II. Legislative Campaign Committees:

In most states there are now *legislative campaign committees*. Sometimes referred to as "legislative campaign caucuses," or "House/Senate reelection committees," these new organizations are generally run at the state level. In some states they provide an array of services, while in others they give only financial help.

13) In general, what do legislative campaign committees do in *your* state?

14) Some county chairs have had a great deal of workings with state legislative campaign committees, while others have had very little contact. Using the scale noted below, how would you categorize your level of contact with these organizations? (circle one)

    1 --- 2 ---3--- 4 --- 5 ---6--- 7 ---8----9--- 10
    Very Little Contact   A Great Deal of Contact

15) These organizations get involved in some races and not others. Do you recall if they have ever been involved in a campaign in *your* county while you were chair? If so, how many _____

16) How often during the last election did you, or other members of the county committee, talk with legislative campaign committees staff?

    1) at least once per day
    2) several times per week
    3) about once per week
    4) a few times per month
    5) about once per month
    6) hardly ever
    7) other (please explain)_____

17) Does your county committee contribute money to these organizations? _____

18) Do legislative campaign committees contribute funds to your county committee? _____

19) During the last two years, did your committee work with a legislative campaign committee to raise money. In other words, did you hold joint fund-raisers? _____

20) On the whole, what would you say are the principal objectives of legislative campaign committees in your state?

21) During the last election, did your county committee work together with legislative campaign committees on projects? If so, what were these projects?

22) Has your committee ever shared a campaign headquarters or office space with one of these units?_____

23) If you have worked with these organizations, how would you describe the relationship between your county committee and the legislative committee staff?

    1) very unfriendly
    2) friendly
    3) very friendly
    4) other (please explain) _____

24) When legislative campaign committees select *which candidates* in your area to spend its resources on, how much influence does your county committee have in these decisions?

    1--- 2 ---3---4--- 5 ---6--- 7---8 ---9--- 10
    Very Little Influence   A Great Deal of Influence

25) Once they have decided who to spend its resources on, how much influence does your committee have on *how* they spend it?

    1--- 2 ---3---4--- 5 ---6--- 7---8 ---9--- 10
    Very Little Influence   A Great Deal of Influence

26) Were there times during the last election when your committee asked a legislative campaign committee for help on a project? If so, what projects were they, and did you get the help you needed?

27) If you approached one of these legislative campaign committees and asked for help on a local party activity, such as a voter registration drive, how likely do you think it would be that you would get the assistance you need?

    1) very likely
    2) likely

3) unlikely
4) very unlikely

28) Below is a list of activities that might be conducted by your county committee *and* legislative campaign committees. *First*, indicate with a check whether or not the legislative campaign committees do each of the activities. *Second*, if they do, please use the ten-point scale to describe the degree of cooperation between your organization and the legislative campaign committee for each project. In other words, do you work together on the activity? The scale is as follows:

1 --- 2 ---3--- 4 --- 5 ---6--- 7 ---8----9--- 10
Very Little Coordination   Very Close Coordination

Do These Organizations Do This Level of Coordination
with County Committee

	YES	NO
____Get-Out-the-Vote Drives	____	____
____Polling Operations	____	____
____Fund-raising	____	____
____Contribute Funds Directly to Candidates	____	____
____Recruit Candidates	____	____
____Candidate Seminars	____	____
____Media Assistance	____	____
____Direct Mail	____	____
____Voter Registration	____	____
____Producing/Distributing	____	____
____Party Newsletters	____	____

29) Please use the scale noted below to answer the next seven questions. (Please choose only one)

1 = they care *a great deal*
2 = they care *a moderate amount*
3 = they care *very little*

How much do legislative campaign committees *care* about:
* the entire party ticket_____
* the party platform_____
* providing services to local communities_____

* getting people involved in the political process _____
* organizing groups behind the party banner _____
* being accessible to the local media _____
* running a full slate of candidates _____

30) How likely do you think it would be that you would get assistance from a legislative campaign committee for a *local* election, such as a county legislative race?

    1) very likely
    2) likely
    3) unlikely
    4) very unlikely

31) Which of the following do you think best describes the "fit" between legislative campaign committees and the overall *party* organization in your state?

    1) they *are* part of the overall party structure
    2) they are *not* part of the party structure
    32) Which of the following best describes how *you* see legislative campaign organizations in your state:

1) partylike
2) independent campaign consulting firms
3) political action committees
4) legislative leadership units
5) candidate-centered organizations
6) other_____

33) County party chairs have had different experiences with legislative campaign organizations. On a ten point scale, where 1 is very distant and 10 is very close, how would you rank your relationship with these new organizations?

    1--- 2 ---3----4--- 5 ---6--- 7 --- 8 ---9--- 10
    Very Distant   Very Close

34) A number of county chairs have felt legislative campaign organizations are geared only to winning their elections and care very little about general party activities (such as get-out-the-vote drives). Still

others feel that, although they concentrate on their elections, they are also concerned about general party activities.

> Which is closest to your impression? Do these organizations generally care only about winning their elections, or do they also care about general party activities? Please explain.

35) Please describe what you think has been the *impact* of legislative campaign committees on *your* party organization. Have they helped, hurt, modified, or had no impact on what you do? In what ways?

36) Finally, do you think the *future* of local party organizations is brighter or dimmer because of legislative campaign committees? Please explain.

Notes

INTRODUCTION

1. New York State Election Law does not label these lines parties, but rather "independent bodies." They last for only one election.

2. It is not clear whether the aggregate total of two or three party lines is greater than a single line. In other words, do you add to your vote total or simply disperse the ones you already have over a number of party lines? It might be argued that additional lines allow the candidate to suggest he/she has broader support than mere Democrats or Republicans. They are often used to associate a candidate with a particularly strong issue, i.e., "The Lower Taxes" line.

3. This comment was made by a local party official interviewed as part of this research in the spring of 1991.

4. As a matter of fact, because the mailings were produced and mailed by DACC, by state law its name had to be found on each mailing—as well as its Albany return address. This information was, of course, noted with very small type in the corner of each piece.

5. This suggestion was made by Edward Rollins, Director of the Republican Congressional Campaign Committee, in a letter to Republican members of the House regarding the President's 1990 budget agreement with congressional leaders. See *The Washington Post*, October 25, 1990, p. A21; *The New York Times*, October 26, 1990, p. A22.

CHAPTER 1

1. A few states, such as Maine and Missouri, have LCCs in only one branch of the legislature. Others, such as Virginia and Maryland, have joint House and Senate committees.

2. The extent to which committees of the same party work together is an important criteria in evaluating their partylike nature. Evidence from prior research suggests they interact very little

(Gierzynski 1992). This issue will be addressed in further detail in subsequent chapters.

3. It is important to note this claim is from the perspective of LCC officials. Whether or not other players, such as traditional party officials, view LCCs as independent will be examined in detail below.

4. This finding was especially true for competitive party states such as Indiana, Illinois, New York, Connecticut, and Pennsylvania.

5. For a review of the charges against Ohrenstein, see *The New York Times*, September 17, 18, 19, 20, 25 (1987). On the New York State Supreme Court upholding his conviction, see *The New York Times*, November 23 (1989). And on the Court of Appeals' decision to overturn the conviction, *The New York Times*, November 28, 29, 30 (1990).

6. Herrnson (1989) found this to be true with regard to the Democratic Congressional Campaign Committee.

7. Eldersveld (1964, 1–13) notes three major clusters of factors affecting party structure: 1) environmental pressures, such as socioeconomic factors and political history; 2) internal dynamics such as personal orientations and styles; and 3) a chronological component—how long the structure has been in existence.

8. Jones and Borris (1985) reject this argument. They find the correlation between competitive races and PAC contributions in state legislative races to be low. PACs give to sure winners—incumbents. I would argue, however, that the centralization of campaign resources during the last decade (the creation of LCCs) has established another vehicle for PACs to seek access with legislative leaders. Additionally, this strategy may be used more often in strong caucus states than in decentralized ones.

9. O'Neill was, of course, the Democratic Speaker of the House during this period.

10. For a telling illustration of the propensity for candidates to distance themselves from adverse national trends, see Adam Clymer, "Many Candidates Run Happily Ignoring Bush." *The New York Times*, October 19, 1992, p. A10.

CHAPTER 2

1. Mayhew's comprehensive study is based upon academic and journalistic writings of the local and state party organization in each

state. Although much of his information refers to the party system prior to the 1980s, he provides a rather good account of each state's party system immediately prior to LCC development, and that this is precisely what we are interested in. That is, the conditions leading to LCC evolution.

2. Their analysis is based upon two dimensions: institutional support mechanisms and candidate directed services. It should be kept in mind that these scales refer to party organization strength and not level of party competition. The latter is frequently used to reflect the closeness of elections or partisan divisions in the legislature. Such measures are somewhat spurious to our discussion, since a weak party organization state also may have very close legislative and gubernatorial elections. Again, the concern here is with the level of support the party committee provides candidates.

3. This figure gives us a neat measure of the relative strength of the LCCs in his study but unfortunately says little about in-kind expenditures and nothing about the remaining twenty-four LCC states not part of his analysis. Also, this data is similar, but certainly not identical, to LCC operating budgets. It does not include, for instance, in-house expenditures or staffing allotments.

4. Although there are several ways one might operationalize this dimension, for our purposes Kurtz's 1992 scale is used. He combines three measures (legislative pay, length of sessions, and staffing) into one scale.

5. The states with strong and weak state party organizations are virtually the same as those cited in Mayhew (1986).

6. This group of scholars includes David Breaux, Anthony Gierzynski, Bill Cassie, Keith Hamm, Malcolm Jewell, Gary Moncrief, and Joel Thompson.

7. It should be noted that partisan competition and marginal seats have a .61 correlation.

CHAPTER 3

1. They argue this increase is significant even when changes in the consumer price index are considered. See pages 16–18 Cotter, et al., 1984.

2. Wolfinger (1972) is a notable exception.

3. James Sundquist (1983) also takes exception to this view. He writes: "While the attachment of some voters to their parties may derive from an attachment to the party organization, it is surely true of other voters that they identify with a party in the absence of any association at all with the organization—or even when they are repelled by the formal party structure (399)."

4. At this writing, in-depth analysis of this claim has not been conducted. One might argue that the increase in the number of state houses controlled by the Democrats, as well as additional Senate seats, points to increased straight-ticket voting. Another indicator is the declining number of first-time voters not enrolling in a party (independents). Although it is difficult at this stage to make the assertion that dealignment has bottomed out, it would seem that voters disdain for partisan labels may be no longer in vogue.

5. Portions of this review are extracted from Mayhew's definition of traditional party organizations (1986, 19–20).

6. One might divide party functions into manifest—the more overt, immediate, and consciously performed tasks—and latent functions—the more indirect and remote contributions parties make to the operation of the political system. For the time being we shall be concerned only with manifest functions.

CHAPTER 4

1. As noted in Chapter 2, Gierzynski (1992) is a notable exception. His analysis, however, is from the perspective of LCC leaders and not traditional party leaders—the focus of this study.

2. Such as the "stay the course" program in 1982 and the pro-Republican/anti-House Speaker Thomas P. (Tip) O'Neill media campaign prior to the 1982 election.

3. For example, both state and county party chairs were asked to assess their organization's effort on a range of activities. A social desirability effect was certainly possibility; every party leader wishes to be seen as active. Although actually viewing each committee's activities may have produced more factual data, such a method is, of course, excessively time consuming.

4. The reader may recall that while TPOs are not thought to be rational-efficient units, their foremost goal is to win elections. The dif-

ference between LCCs and TPOs is that, while the former holds winning as their sole objective, TOPs hold a larger set of concerns as well.

5. At various points throughout the analysis, survey and aggregate data are supplemented with qualitative illustrations. In order to fully understand this new relationship, and to get a flavor of the feelings and attitudes of the party leaders, we go beyond a strict empirical discussion. Numerous follow-up discussions with state and local party leaders produced telling information. Bits of these conversations will be inserted in the data analysis were appropriate. In short, although this study is empirical, qualitative material is inserted with the hope of painting a more complete picture.

CHAPTER 5

1. According to Warren Moscow, "this was Al Smith's way of describing money paid out 'in lieu of' expenses" (1948, 181).

2. *Anderson V. Regan* (1981) [442 NYS 2d 404; 53 NY 2d 356; 425 NE 2d 792].

3. It should be noted that party cohesion in the legislature is at least in part due to what Howard Scarrow calls "natural communities." That is, the Legislature reflects a geographical pattern of electoral support, where Democrats come from New York City and Republicans from Upstate. Similar constituencies, he argues, lead to similar voting patterns. See Scarrow 1983, 18–23.

4. He also goes on to note "the tradition in New York State has not been one of restrained leadership discretion but quite the reverse (Hevesi 1989, 170).

5. This study also finds over 30 percent of campaign contributions for state legislative races going to the two majority party LCCs (Citizen Action of New York, December 1992; 30).

6. Non-allocable expenditures are defined as neither housekeeping nor direct candidate contributions. An example here would be the production of a generic get-out-the-vote mailing.

7. Admittedly, much of the decline attributed to party organizations is due to lowering partisanship and the growth of split-ticket voting. As suggested in Chapter 3, the two may not be related, and

perhaps even run in opposite directions. Nevertheless, these urban organizations have seen a decline in organizational vitality as well. Fewer active members, infrequent social functions, and declining budgets are all symptoms of this trend.

8. They find the Democratic state party as "moderately weak," and the Republican state committee as "moderately strong" (Cotter, et. al., 1984, 28–29).

9. Several current illustrations bolster their data findings with regard to New York. The Madison County Republican Committee holds four committee meetings and numerous social functions each year. They consistently carry a full slate of committeepersons, are involved in diverse community activities, and work aggressively for their candidates. The St. Lawrence County Democrats, under the leadership of Sam Burns, provide services and are conducting activities unthinkable in recent years. By defeating an incumbent County Executive (Patrick Halpin) and a prestigious congressional incumbent (Tom Downey), the Suffolk County Republican organization is also feeling its oats.

10. Two of these defeats were due to reapportionment; two sets of legislators were placed in the same district. However, the remaining six is equal to or greater than the number of defeats in the four previous elections. In fact, only one incumbent lost in 1986, three in 1988, and four in 1990. Although these figures may not represent a trend, we can simply note that state legislators in New York may not be any safer today than in the past two decades.

11. In many respects this chapter is exploratory. It represents the first stab at assessing this new relationship. As such, meetings with state party leaders were somewhat unstructured and, at times, resembled more of a chat than an official interview.

12. Nelson Rockefeller was an exceedingly strong Republican governor, who served from 1963 to 1975. Warren Anderson was Majority Leader of the Senate for sixteen years during the 1970s and 1980s. An outspoken, aggressive leader, Anderson retired in December of 1988.

13. *Baker v. Carr* 369 U.S. 186 (1962).

14. *Reynolds v. Simms* 377 U.S. 1 (1964).

15. Powers was not elected State Chair until after the 1990 elec-

tion; therefore, his recollections of project interdependence must be taken with caution. He was, however, Vice-Chair of the State Committee and also Rensselaer County Republican Chair immediately prior to his election.

16. No mention was made as to how the proceeds were divided.

17. See, for example, *The New York Times*, October 22, 1986, II, 1:2; July 9, 1986, I 31:6; September 8, 1990, I, 26:1; October 27, 1990, I, 27:1.

18. Each chair was assured that his/her responses would remain confidential. Consequently, no reference will be made to specific chairs or counties.

19. Dependent variable is seven-point relationship scale. Pearson's Correlation Coefficient is.045, with Sig. F=.697.

20. An obvious shortcoming of the three-part division is the vast disparities of LCC involvement in campaigns and in counties. A large, evenly partisan county may have a number of highly contested Assembly and Senate races each year. LCCs may be involved in as many as five campaigns in such counties. On the other hand, smaller counties often compose only a small section of Assembly and Senate districts. Also, legislative districts frequently cut into a narrow section of a county. The extent and type of exposure to LCCs in the more populated counties may be vastly different from more rural ones. The variation of specific knowledge of "High Group" chairs concerning the activities of the LCC in their counties also reflects the diverse levels of exposure within this single category.

21. Most of the linkage queries were only applicable to those chairs who have had campaign interactions with the LCCs—the High category. Therefore, the sample is lowered to thirty-nine respondents.

22. Numerous variables might affect the degree of project interaction, including the geographic dispersion of the district, the strategic importance of the county, the strength of the county committee, the relationship of the candidate to the county committee, and the level of LCC involvement. Nevertheless, the number of chairs who said their committees worked extensively with the LCC on a number of projects was small.

23. Unlike linkage measures, most of the questions dealing with perceptions were asked to chairs in the Moderate group, as well as in High group.

24. Democrats = 0 and Republicans = 1.

25. We are again hesitant to place too much stock in these findings, as they are not statistically significant at the.95 percent confidence interval. It is, however, exceedingly difficult to achieve statistical significance with such a small sample size. See Lewis-Beck 1980, 35–37.

CHAPTER 6

1. Because this distribution is clearly not optimal, a close eye will be kept on party as a control.

2. As noted in Chapter 4, respondents were asked to provide both perceptual and *some* factual information. This set of questions, as well as several others to follow, deals with the latter. There are certainly other ways of collecting this information—including a review of all one hundred state party bylaws. The slight advantages of such a method are, however, far outweighed by the costs.

3. Level of legislative professionalization was divided into three groups: full time, hybrid, and part time. This was determined by length of session, legislative pay, and staffing levels. For a state-by-state breakdown, see Kurtz (1992B).

4. This was an open-ended question which read: "Who controls their activities?"

5. It is tempting to conclude that these small groups are indeed composed of legislative leaders.

6. The latter was created by combining Gierzynski's (1992) data with Jewell and Olson's (1986) figures. Combined, twenty (of thirty-four) LCC states have aggregate figures—twelve of which are included in our sample.

7. The latter was compiled from an ACIR Report (Fall 1984).

8. Again, party differences were minimal. Legal connections between the units also had little impact. In fact, of the state committees with legal links to the LCCs, more worked independently to raise money than together.

9. It is based upon the aggregate outcomes of several statewide elections. The more evenly divided the totals (between the two major

parties), the higher the interparty competition ranking (see Bibby 1990).

10. One limit to this control is the difficulty in defining minority or majority party status. Three components should be considered: the party's position in the House; the party's status in the Senate, the party of the Governor. Consequently, the sample was divided into three groups: respondents whose party controls all three components (majority), respondents whose party controls none of the components (minority), and respondents from mixed party states (mixed). From these calculations, of the one hundred state party committees, sixteen are majority units, sixteen are minority units and sixty-eight are mixed. In the sample, four are majority, seven are minority, and twenty-five are mixed.

11. Respondent's party was also introduced as a further control. Overall, Republicans are more likely to work together on giving money to candidates. Adding party as a dummy variable (0=Republican and 1 = Democrats) produced a partial slope of -3.5. The coefficient of determination is increased to .50, suggesting party and LCC strength explain one-half of the variance in the dependent variable (contributing funds to candidates).

12. The question read: "On the whole, what would you say is *the* principal objective of legislative campaign committees in your state?"

13. Neither structural linkages or level of interparty competitions, however, had any bearing on this finding.

CHAPTER 7

1. Much of the information was compiled from board of election data and informal telephone interviews with party leaders and LCC officials. In places, the state-level survey is also referenced.

2. Both the minority units, the Senate Democrats and the House Republicans, raised roughly $500,000 during 1992.

3. In fact, as will be seen, it is the least professional of the states within the sample.

4. When it was possible (pre-1990), LCCs in Florida were quite strong. In 1985, for example, these units spent over $1.2 million (See Jewell 1986, 11).

5. Four additional instruments were returned with the state code missing.

6. The two questions are highly correlated:.65.

7. Contrary to expectations, neither the extent of LCC resources nor levels of party organization strength appear to modify levels of interdependence.

8. The reader may recall that, of the four states in sample, only Ohio is considered by Kurtz (1992) to have a professional legislature. Each of the others is thought to be a hybrid. For purposes here, a scale between the states was created, using legislative pay and length of session. The resulting order (from the most professional to least professional) and the value they were assigned is as follows: Ohio (4), Florida (3), Tennessee (2), and Indiana (1). I recognize that this simple ranking may also capture dimensions other than legislative professionalization.

CHAPTER 8

1. This assumes, of course, that the rules for distributing perks remains the same.

2. Much of the discussion on Proposition 73 was collected from a telephone interview with Richard Clucus, of the University of Wisconsin, Eau Claire. Clucus had recently written an article on Brown's organization. See Clucus (1992).

3. Among other things, this case held that public funding of presidential elections was constitutional, so long as it remained voluntary.

Bibliography

Associated Press. September 20, 1988. "Senator Marino Uses Pull to Stall Fund-raising Rules Change." *Middletown Times Herald Record.*

Adamany, David. 1984. "Political Parties in the 1980s." In Michael J. Malbin, ed. *Money and Politics in the United States: Financing Elections in the 1980s.* Chatham, NJ: Chatham House.

Advisory Commission on Intergovernmental Relations. 1986. *The Transformation of American Politics: Implications for Federalism.* Washington, DC: Advisory Commission on Intergovernmental Relations.

———. 1984. "State Parties in the 1980s." *Intergovernmental Perspective.* Washington, DC: Advisory Commission on Intergovernmental Relations. 10:6–14.

Alexander, Herbert E. 1992. *Financing Politics: Money, Elections and Political Reform,* 4th ed. Washington, DC: Congressional Quarterly.

American Political Science Association, Committee on Political Parties. 1950. *Toward a More Responsible Two-Party System.* New York: Rinehart.

Agranoff, Robert. 1976. *The New Style in Election Campaigns.* rev. ed. Boston: Holbrook.

Arterton, Christopher F. 1982. "Political Money and Party Strength." In Joel L. Fleishman, ed. *The Future of American Political Parties: The Challenge of Governance.* Englewood Cliffs, NJ: Prentice-Hall.

Beck, Paul Allen. 1974. "Environment and Party." *American Political Science Review.* 68:1229–44.

———, and Frank Sorauf. 1992. *Party Politics in America.* 7th ed. New York: Harper-Collins.

———, and Audrey Haynes. 1994. "Party Effort at the Grass Roots: Local Presidential Campaigning in 1992." Paper delivered at the Midwest Political Science Association, Chicago.

Benjamin, Gerald, and Michael J. Malbin, eds. 1992. *Limiting Legislative Terms.* Washington, DC: Congressional Quarterly Press.

————, and Robert T. Nakamura, eds. 1991. *The Modern New York State Legislature: Redressing the Balance.* Albany, NY: The Rockefeller Institute of Government.

Bibby, John F. 1990. "Party Organization at the State Level." In Sandy L. Maisel *The Parties Respond: Changes in the American Political System.* Boulder CO: Westview Press.

————. 1987. *Politics, Parties, and Elections in America.* Chicago: Nelson-Hall.

————. 1980. "Party Renewal in the National Republican Party." In Gerald M. Pomper, ed. *Party Renewal in America: Theory and Practice.* New York: Praeger.

————, Cornelius P. Cotter, James Gibson, and Robert Huckshorn. 1990. "Parties in State Politics," In Virginia Gray, et al., eds. *Politics in the American States.* Boston: Little, Brown and Company.

Blumenthal, Sidney. 1980. *The Permanent Campaign: Inside the World of Elite Political Operatives.* Boston: Beacon Press.

Brady, David, Joseph Cooper, and P. Hurley. 1979. "The Decline of Party in the U.S. House of Representatives 1887–1968." *Legislative Studies Quarterly.* 4:381–407.

Broder, David S. 1971. *The Party's Over: The Failure of American Politics.* New York: Harper and Row.

Burnham, Walter Dean. 1982. *The Current Crisis in American Politics.* New York: Oxford University Press.

————. 1989. "The Reagan Heritage." In Gerald M. Pomper, et al. *The Election of 1988.* Chatham, NJ: Chatham House.

————. 1970. *Critical Elections and the Mainsprings of American Politics.* New York: Norton.

Caldeira, Gregory A., and Samuel C. Patterson. 1982. "Bringing Home the Votes: Electoral Outcomes in State Legislative Races." *Political Behavior.* 4:33–67.

California Commission on Campaign Financing. 1985. *The New Gold Rush: Financing California Legislative Campaigns.* Los Angeles: Center for Responsive Government.

Campbell, Angus, Phillip E. Converse, Warren E. Miller, and Donald E. Stokes. 1960. *The American Voter.* New York: John Wiley and Sons.

Cassie, William E., Joel A. Thompson, and Malcolm E. Jewell. 1992. "The Pattern of PAC Contributions in Legislative Elections: An Eleven State Analysis." Paper delivered at the American Political Science Association, Chicago.

Chubb, John E. 1988. "Institutions, the Economy, and the Dynamics of State Elections." *The American Political Science Review.* 82:133–154.

Citizen Action of New York. 1992. "Fueling New York's Incumbency Machine: Campaign Contributions to the New York State Legislature in 1990." Albany, NY: Citizen Action of New York.

———. 1993. "Citizens Coalition Calls for Legislature to Overhaul Rules." (Press Release) Albany, NY: Citizen Action of New York.

Clausen, Aage. 1973. *How Congressmen Decide.* New York: St. Martin's Press.

Clucas, Richard. 1992. "Campaign Support as a Leadership Resource: A Case Study of Two California Assembly Speakers." *Legislative Studies Quarterly.* 17:265–283.

Coleman, John J. 1994. "The Resurgence of Party Organization? A Dissent from the Orthodoxy." In Daniel M. Shea and John C. Green, eds. *The State of the Parties: The Changing Role of Contemporary American Parties.* Lanham, NY: Rowman and Littlefield.

Costikyan, Edward N. 1966. *Behind Closed Doors: Politics in the Public Interest.* New York: Harcourt, Brace, and World, Inc.

Cotter, Cornelius P., James L. Gibson, John F. Bibby, and Robert J. Huckshorn. 1984. *Party Organizations in American Politics.* New York: Praeger Publishers.

Council of State Governments. 1990. *State Elected Officials and the Legislatures, 1989–1990.* Lexington, KY: Council of State Governments.

Crotty, William J. 1984. *American Parties in Decline.* Boston: Little, Brown.

———, ed. 1986. *Political Parties in Local Areas.* Knoxville, TN: University of Tennessee Press.

Davidson, Roger, ed. 1992. *The Post Reform Congress.* New York: St. Martin's.

Dennis, Jack. 1976. "Trends in Public Support for the American Party System." *British Journal of Political Science.* 5:187–230.

Downs, Anthony. 1957. *An Economic Theory of Democracy.* New York: Harper and Row.

Duverger, Maurice. 1954. *Political Parties.* Barbara and Robert North, trans. New York: John Wiley and Sons.

Dwyre, Diana. 1994. "Party Strategy and Political Reality: The Distribution of Congressional Campaign Committee Resources." In Daniel M. Shea and John C. Green, eds., *The State of the Parties: The Changing Role of Contemporary American Parties.* Lanham, New York: Rowman and Littlefield.

———, and Jeffrey Stonecash. 1992. "Where's the Party? Changing State Party Organizations." *American Politics Quarterly.* 20:326–344.

———. 1990. "The Rise of Legislative Party Campaign Committees in New York." Paper delivered at the New York State Political Science Association. April 20–21.

Ehrenhalt, Alan. 1992. *The United States of Ambition: Politicians, Power, and the Pursuit of Power.* New York: Times Books.

Eldersveld, Samuel. 1982. *Political Parties in American Society.* New York: Basic Books.

———. 1964. *Political Parties: A Behavioral Analysis.* Chicago: Rand McNally.

Eismeier, Theodore J., and Philip H. Pollock III. 1986. "Strategy and Choice in Congressional Elections: The Role of Political Action Committees." *American Journal of Political Science.* 30:197–213.

Epstein, Leon D. 1986. *Political Parties in the American Mold.* Madison: University of Wisconsin Press.

Fenno, Richard F. 1978. *Homestyle: House Members in Their Own Districts.* Boston: Little, Brown.

———. 1973. *Congressmen in Committees.* Boston: Little, Brown.

Fine, Terri Susan. 1994. "Proclaiming Party Identity: A View from the Platforms." In Daniel M. Shea and John C. Green, eds., *The State of the Parties: The Changing Role of Contemporary American Parties.* Lanham, New York: Rowman and Littlefield.

Fiorina, Morris P. 1989. *Congress: Keystone of the Washington Establishment.* 2nd ed. New Haven, CT: Yale University Press.

———. 1977 *Congress: Keystone of the Washington Establishment.* New Haven, CT: Yale University Press.

Fowler, Linda, and Robert McClure. 1989. *Political Ambition: Who Decides to Run for Congress.* New Haven, CT: Yale University Press.

Francis, Wayne. 1985. "Leadership, Party Caucuses and Committees in U.S. State Legislatures." *Legislative Studies Quarterly.* 10:243–264.

Frendreis, John P., James L. Gibson, and Laura L. Vertz. 1990. "The Electoral Relevance of Local Party Organizations." *American Political Science Review.* 84:225–35.

———, Alan R. Gitelson, Gregory Flemming, and Anne Layzell. 1994. "Local Political Parties and Legislative Races in 1992." In Daniel M. Shea and

John C. Green, eds. *The State of the Parties: The Changing Role of Contemporary American Parties*. Lanham, NY: Rowman and Littlefield.

Garand, James C. 1991. "Electoral Marginality in State Legislative Elections, 1968–86." *Legislative Studies Quarterly*. 16:7–28.

Gibson, James L., John P. Frendeis, and Laura L. Vertz. 1989. "Party Dynamics in the 1980s: Changes in County Party Organizational Strength 1980–1984." *American Journal of Political Science*. 32:67–79

———, Cornelius P. Cotter, John F. Bibby, Robert J. Huckshorn. 1985. "Whither the Local Parties? A Cross-Sectional and Longitudinal Analysis of the Strength of Party Organizations." *American Journal of Political Science*. 29:139–160.

———. 1985. "Assessing Party Organization Strength." *American Journal of Political Science*. 27:193–222.

Gierzynski, Anthony. 1992. *Legislative Party Campaign Committees In The American States*. Lexington, KY: University Press of Kentucky.

———, and David Breaux. 1991. "Money and Votes in State Legislative Elections." *Legislative Studies Quarterly*. 16:203–217.

Giles, Michael W., and Anita Pritchard. 1985. "Campaign Expenditures and Legislative Elections in Florida." *Legislative Studies Quarterly*. 10:71–88.

Gruson, Lindsey. 1992. "How Gain (Partisan) Became Loss (Universal)." *The New York Times*, July 1:B1.

Hames, Tim. 1994. "Confusion in the Analysis of American Political Parties." In Daniel M. Shea and John C. Green, eds., *The State of the Parties: The Changing Role of Contemporary American Parties*. Lanham, New York: Rowman and Littlefield.

Herrnson, Paul S. 1989. "National Party Decision–Making, Strategies, and Resource Distribution in Congressional Elections." *Western Political Quarterly*. 42:301–317.

———. 1988. *Party Campaigning in the 1980's*. Cambridge:Harvard University Press.

———. 1986. "Do Parties Make a Difference? The Role of Party Organizations in Congressional Elections." *The Journal of Politics*. 48:589–615.

Hevesi, Alan G. 1985. "The Renewed State Legislature." In Peter Colby, ed.*New York State Today*. Albany, NY: SUNY Press.

———. 1975. *Legislative Politics in New York*. New York: Praeger Publishers.

Huckfeldt, Robert, and John Sprague. "Political Parties and Electoral Mobilization: Political Structure, Social Structure, and the Party Canvass." *American Political Science Review.* 86:70–86.

Huckshorn, Robert J., and John F. Bibby. 1982. "State Parties in an Era of Political Change." In Joel L. Fleishman, ed. *The Future of American Political Parties: The Challenge of Governance.* Englewood Cliffs, NJ: Prentice-Hall.

Jacobson, Gary. 1987. *The Politics of Congressional Elections, Second Edition.* Glenview, IL: Scott, Foresman.

———. 1987. "The Marginal Never Vanished: Incumbency and Competition in Elections in the U.S. House of Representatives, 1952–82." *American Journal of Political Science.* 31:126–141.

———. 1985. "Money and Votes Reconsidered: Congressional Elections 1972–1982." *Public Choice.* 47:7–92.

———. 1985. "Party Organization and Distribution of Campaign Resources: Republicans and Democrats in 1982." *Political Science Quarterly.* 4:603–625.

———. 1985. "Parties and PACs in Congressional Elections." In Lawrence Dodd and Bruce Oppenheimer, eds. *Congress Reconsidered.* Washington, DC: Congressional Quarterly Press.

———. 1980. *Money in Congressional Elections.* New Haven, CT: Yale University Press.

———. 1992. *The Politics of Congressional Elections,* 3rd ed. New York: HarperCollins.

———, and Samuel Kernell. 1983. *Strategy and Choice in Congressional Elections.* 2nd ed. New Haven, CT: Yale University Press.

Jewell, Malcolm E. 1986. "A Survey of Campaign Fund Raising by Legislative Parties." *Comparative State Politics Newsletter.* 7:9–13.

———, and David Breaux. 1989. "The Effect of Incumbency on State Legislative Elections." *Legislative Studies Quarterly.* 13, no. 4:495–510.

———, and David Olson. 1988. *Political Parties and Elections in American States.* 3rd ed. Chicago: Dorsey Press.

———, and David M. Olson. 1978. *American State Political Parties and Elections.* Homewood, IL: Dorsey Press.

———, and Marcia Lynn Wicker. 1994. *Legislative Leadership in the American States.* Ann Arbor, MI: University of Michigan Press.

Johnson, Richard R. 1987. "Partisan Legislative Campaign Committees: New Power, New Problems." *Illinois Issues.* (July):16–18.

Jones, Ruth S. 1984. "Financing State Elections." In Michael Malbin, ed. *Money and Politics in the United States: Financing Elections in the 1980s.* Chatham, NJ: Chatham House.

———, and Thomas J. Borris. 1985. "Strategic Contributing in Legislative Campaigns: The Case of Minnesota." *Legislative Studies Quarterly.* 10:89–105.

Kayden, Xandra, and Eddie Mahe, Jr. 1985. *The Party Goes On: The Persistence of the Two Party System in the United States.* New York: Basic Books.

Key, V. O., Jr. 1964. *Politics, Parties, and Pressure Groups.* 5th ed. New York: Thomas Y. Crowell Company.

———. 1956. *American State Politics.* New York: Knopf.

———. 1949. *Southern Politics in State and Nation.* New York: Knopf.

Kingdon, John. 1989. *Congressmen's Voting Decisions*, 3rd ed. Ann Arbor: University of Michigan Press.

Kirkpatrick, Jeane J. 1979. *Dismantling the Parties.* Washington, DC: American Enterprise Institute. In Daniel M. Shea and John C. Green, eds., *The State of the Parties: The Changing Role of Contemporary American Parties.* Lanham, NY: Rowman and Littlefield.

Klinker, Philip. 1994. "Party Culture and Party Behavior." In Daniel M. Shea and John C. Green, eds., *The State of the Parties: The Changing Role of Contemporary American Parties.* Lanham, NY: Rowman and Littlefield.

Kolbert, Elizabeth, and Mark Uhlig. 14 July 1987. "Albany's Discret Budget: A Tool for Political Ends." *The New York Times.*

Kurtz, Karl T. 1992a. "The 1992 State Legislative Election in Perspective." *APSA Legislative Studies Section Newsletter.* 16:10–14.

———. 1992b. "Assessing the Potential Impact of Term Limitations." *State Legislatures.* 18 (January 1992).

Ladd, Everett C., and Charles D. Hadley. 1978. *Transformation of the American Party System.* 2nd ed. New York: Norton.

———. 1970. *American Political Parties: Social Change and Political Response.* New York: Norton.

Lee, Calvin B. T. 1967. *One Man One Vote: WMCA and the Struggle for Equal Representation.* New York: Charles Scribner's and Sons.

Lewis-Beck, Michael S. 1980. *Applied Regression: An Introduction.* Newbury Park, CA: Sage.

Lipset, Seymour, and Stein Rokkan. 1967. *Party Systems and Voter Alignments.* New York: Free Press.

Loftus, Tom. 1985. "The New 'Political Parties' In State Legislatures." *State Government* 58:108.

――――. 1994. *The Art of Legislative Politics.* Washington, DC: Congressional Quarterly.

Lowi, Theodore. 1963. "Toward Functionalism in Political Science: The Case of Innovation in Party Systems." *American Political Science Review.* 57:570–583.

Maisel, L. Sandy. 1987. *Parties and Elections in American: The Electoral Process.* New York: Random House.

Malbin, Michael J. 1987. "Factions and Incentives in Congress." *The Public Interest.* 86:91–108.

Mann, Thomas E. 1978. *Unsafe at Any Margin.* Washington, DC: American Enterprise Institute.

Mayhew, David R. 1986. *Placing Parties in American Politics: Organization, Electoral Settings, and Government Activity in the Twentieth Century.* Princeton, NJ: Princeton University Press.

――――. 1974. *Congress: The Electoral Connection.* New Haven, CT: Yale University Press.

――――. 1974. "Congressional Elections: The Case of the Vanishing Marginals." *Polity.* 6:295–314.

Merton, Robert K. 1945. "Sociological Theory." *American Journal of Sociology.* 72–82.

Michels, Robert. 1962. *Political Parties: A Sociological Study of Oligarchical Tendencies of Modern Democracies.* New York: Crowell-Collier Books.

Moncrief, Gary. 1992. "The Increase in Campaign Expenditures in State Legislative Elections: A Comparison of Four Northwest States." *Western Political Quarterly.* 45:549–558.

Moscow, Warren. 1948. *Politics in the Empire State.* New York: Alfred A. Knopf.

Neumann, Sigmund. 1956. "Toward a Comparative Study of Political Parties." In Sigmund Neumann, ed. *Modern Political Parties,* Chicago: University of Chicago Press.

New York Democratic State Committee. 1994. *Rules of the Democratic Party of the State of New York.* Albany, NY: New York State Board of Elections.

New York Republican State Committee. 1993. *Rules of the New York Republican State Committee.* Albany, NY: New York State Board of Elections.

New York State Board of Election. 1993. *Reports on Financial Activity, 1990–1992.* Albany, NY.: The State of New York.

Nie, Norman H., Sidney Verba, and John Petrocik. 1976. *The Changing American Voter.* Cambridge: Harvard University Press.

Niemi, Richard G., and Laura R. Winsky. 1987. "Membership Turnover in U.S. Legislatures: Trends and Effects of Districting." *Legislative Studies Quarterly.* 12:115–124.

Ohio Board of Election. 1993. *Financial Disclosure Reports.* Columbus: Ohio Department of State.

Ostrogorski, M. 1964. *Democracy and Organization of Political Parties.* Garden City, NY: Doubleday.

Pitney, John J. 1982. "Leaders and Rules in the New York State Senate." *Legislative Studies Quarterly.* 52:491–506.

Polsby, Nelson W. 1983. *Consequences of Party Reform.* New York: Oxford University Press.

Pomper, Gerald M. 1980. *Party Renewal in America.* New York: Praeger Publishers.

Price, David E. 1984. *Bringing Back the Parties.* Washington, DC: Congressional Quarterly.

Ranney, Austin. 1976. "Parties in State Politics." In Herbert Jacobs and Kenneth Vines, eds. *Politics in the American States: A Comparative Analysis.* 3rd ed. Boston: Little, Brown.

———. 1975. *Curing the Mischiefs of Faction.* Berkeley: University of California Press.

Redfield, Kent D., and Jack Van Der Slik. 1992. "The Circulation of Political Money in Illinois Elections." Paper delivered at the 1992 Midwest Political Science Association, April 9–11.

Riechley, James A. 1985. "The Rise of National Politics." In John E. Chubb and Paul Peterson, eds. *The New Direction in American Politics.* Washington, DC: Brookings Institute.

Reiter, Howard L. 1993. *Parties and Elections in Corporate America.* 2nd ed. White Plains, NY: Longman.

Rohde, David W. 1991. *Parties and Leaders in the Postreform House.* Chicago: University of Chicago Press.

Rose, Gary L. 1987. "Evaluating the Role of Party Organization in the Nomination of State Legislative Candidates: The Case of Connecticut." Paper delivered to the Annual Meeting of the New York State Political Science Association, April 29–30.

Rosenthal, Alan. 1990. *Governors and Legislatures: Contending Powers.* Washington, DC: Congressional Quarterly Press.

Sabato, Larry. 1988. *The Party's Just Begun: Shaping Political Parties for America's Future.* Glenview, IL: Scott, Foresman.

———. 1981. *The Rise of Political Consultants: New Ways of Winning Elections.* New York: Basic Books.

Sack, Kevin. 1992. "Study Lists Political Action Groups' Spending." *The New York Times*, Dec. 3:B11

Salmore, Barbara G., and Stephen A. Salamore. 1989. "The Transformation of State Electoral Politics." In Carl E. Van Horn, ed. *The State of the States.* Washington, DC: Congressional Quarterly Press.

———. 1989. *Candidates Parties, and Campaigns: Electoral Politics in America.* 2nd ed. Washington, DC: Congressional Quarterly Press.

Scarrow, Howard A. 1983. *Parties, Elections, and Representation in the State of New York.* New York: New York University Press.

Schattschneider, E. E. 1960. *The Semisovereign People: A Realist's View of Democracy in America.* New York: Holt, Reinhart and Winston.

———. 1942. *Party Government.* New York: Holt, Reinhart and Winston.

Schlesinger, Joseph A. 1991. *Political Parties and the Winning of Office.* Ann Arbor: University of Michigan Press.

———. 1985. "The New American Political Party." *American Political Science Review.* 79:1152–1169.

———. 1984. "On the Theory of Party Organization." *Journal of Politics.* 46:369–400.

———. 1965. "Political Party Organization." In James March, ed. *Handbook of Organizations.* Chicago: Rand McNally.

Shea, Daniel M. 1991. "The Myth of Party Adaptation: Legislative Campaign Committees and Traditional Party Units." Paper delivered at the New York State Political Science Association, Albany NY, April 11–14.

————, and John C. Green. 1994. "Paths and Crossroads: The State of the Parties and Party Scholarship." In Daniel M. Shea and John C. Green, eds. *The State of the Parties: The Changing Role of Contemporary American Parties.* Lanham, NY: Rowman and Littlefield.

Simon-Rosenthal, Cindy. 1993. "Partners or Solo Players: Legislative Campaign Committees and State Parties." Paper delivered at the State of the Parties: 1992 and Beyond, Sponsored by the Bliss Institute of Applied Politics, University of Akron, Akron Ohio, September 23–24.

Sorauf, Frank J. 1988. *Money in American Elections.* Glenview, IL:Scott, Foresman.

————, and Paul Beck. 1988. *Party Politics in America.* 6th ed. Glenview, IL: Scott, Foresman.

————, and Scott Wilson. 1991. "Campaigns and Money: A Changing Role for Political Parties?" In Sandy Maisel, *The Parties Respond.* Boulder CO: Westview Press.

State of New York Management Resources Project. 1988. *Governing the Empire State: An Insiders Guide.* Albany, NY: State of New York Management Resources Project.

Stone, Walter J., Alan I. Abramowitz, and Ronald Rapoport. 1989. "Candidate Support in Presidential Nomination Campaigns." Boulder, CO: Center for the Study of American Politics, University of Colorado.

Stonecash, Jeffrey. 1990. "Working at the Margins: Campaign Finance Strength and Party Strength in New York Assembly Elections." *Legislative Studies Quarterly.* 13:477–493.

————. 1991. "Campaign Finance in New York State Legislative Elections and the Significance of House Control." *Comparative State Politics.* 12:2–15.

Sundquist, James L. 1983. *Dynamics of the Party System: Alignment and Realignment of Political Parties in the United States.* Washington, DC: The Brookings Institute.

Tolchin, Martin, and Susan Tolchin. 1971. *To the Victor.* New York: Random House.

Tucker, Harvey J., and Ronald E. Weber. 1987. "State Legislative Election Outcomes: Contextual Effects and Legislative Performance Effects." *Legislative Studies Quarterly.* 22:537–553.

Ware, Alan. 1985. *The Breakdown of Democratic Party Organizations, 1940–1980.* Oxford, England: Clarendon Press.

Wattenberg, Martin P. 1991. *The Rise of Candidate-Centered Politics: Presidential Elections in the 1980s.* Cambridge: Harvard University Press.

———. 1990. *The Decline of American Political Parties, 1952–1988.* Cambridge: Harvard University Press.

———. 1986. *The Decline of American Political Parties, 1952–1984.* Cambridge: Harvard University Press.

———. 1984. *The Decline of American Political Parties, 1952–1980.* Cambridge: Harvard University Press.

Weber, Max. 1967. "Politics as a Vocation." In Gerald W. and Edward G. Janosik. *Political Parties and the Governmental System: A Book of Readings.* Englewood Cliffs, NJ: Prentice-Hall.

Weber, Ronald E., Harvey J. Tucker, and Paul Brace. 1991. "Vanishing Marginals in State Legislative Elections." *Legislative Studies Quarterly.* 27:29–47.

Wilson, James Q. 1962. *The Amateur Democrat: Club Politics in Three Cities.* Chicago: University of Chicago Press.

Witt, Stuart K. 1967. "The Legislative-Local Party Linkages in New York State." Ph.D. Dissertation, Syracuse University.

Wolfinger, Raymond. 1972. "Why Political Machines Have Not Withered Away and Other Revisionist Thoughts." *Journal of Politics.* 34:365–398.

Wright, William E. 1971. "Comparative Party Models: Rational Efficient and Party Democracy." In *A Comparative Study of Party Organization.* Columbus, OH: Charles E. Merrill.

Zimmerman, Joseph F. 1981. *The Government and Poltics of New York State.* New York: New York University Press.

Index

Adamany, David, 11, 50
Advisory Committee on Intergovern-
    mental Relations (ACIR), 52
American Voter, The, 137
Anderson, Warren, 41

Barrett, Patrick, 95
Bibby, John, 6, 50
Broader, David, 137
Brown, Willie, 26, 41, 181–182
Burnham, Walter Dean, 14
Bush, George, 58, 141

California Assembly Democratic
    Committee, 27, 35. See also
    Willie Brown
Candidate-directed activities, 74–75
Center for Political Studies, 52
Coelho, Tony, 41
Clinton, Bill, 58, 141, 143
Clinton County Democratic Commit-
    tee, 2, 80
Colavita, Anthony, 89, 96
"Congressionalization," see legisla-
    tive professionalization
"Constitutional obstruction," 9, 61,
    172
Corning, Erastus, 87
Cotter, Cornelius, 50, 73, 77, 92, 95,
    137, 139–144.
    See also Party Transformation
    Study (PTS)
Crangle, Joe, 87
Crotty, William, 52

Cunningham, William, 98–100
Cuomo, Mario, 30, 93, 99

Data and methods, 81–82, 94–95, 113,
    138–145
Democratic Assembly Campaign
    Committee (DACC), See New
    York State Democratic Assem-
    bly Campaign Committee.
Democratic Congressional Campaign
    Committee (DCCC), 11
Democratic Senatorial Campaign
    Committee (DSCC), 11
Downs, Anthony, 169. See also Politi-
    cal parties, Downsian model
Duverger, Maurice, 72
Dwyre, Diana, 11, 90, 94, 110, 168

Ehrenhalt, Alan, 42
Eldersveld, Samual, 20, 25, 65
Elefante, Rufus ("Ruffy"), 92

Federal Elections Campaign Act
    (FECA), 41
Fenno, Richard, 28
Fink, Stanley, 2, 88
"Fink's Raiders," see New York State
    Democratic Association Cam-
    paign Committee (DACC)
Fiorina, Morris, 28
Florida
    Democratic party, 143
    legislative campaign committees,
    19, 143, 145–168

235

Florida *(continued)*
   legislature, 143–144
   political parties, 143–144
   Republican party, 143–144
Fowler, Linda, 42
Franklin County Democratic Committee, 2
Francis, Wayne, 21
Frendreis, John, 52, 57

Garrow, Robert, 3–5, 176
Genovesi, Tony, 2, 4, 174
Gibson, James, 50, 52, 57
Gierzynski, Anthony, 6, 13, 19, 21, 23, 25, 27–29, 32–34, 43–44, 78, 90, 139
Glenn, John, 141

Herrnson, Paul, 11, 31, 50
Hevesi, Alan, 88
Hill Committees, 12–17, 175. See also Democratic Congressional Campaign Committee; Democratic Senatorial Campaign Committee; National Republican Congressional Committee; National Senatorial Campaign Committee
Huckshorn, Robert, 31–32. See also Party Transformation Study

Indiana
   Democratic party, 142
   legislative campaign committees, 20, 26, 142, 145–168
   legislature, 142
   political parties, 142
   Republican party, 142
Institutional support activities definition of, 73–74

Jacobson, Gary, 4, 28
Jewell, Malcolm, 13, 19, 36, 43, 139
Jones, Ruth, 37, 50

Kayden, Xandra, 56, 137
Key, V. O., 9, 49, 60, 178
Kremer, Arthur, 88
Kurtz, Karl, 44

Legislative caucus campaign committees. See Legislative campaign committees
Legislative elections
   role of political parties in, 35–36, 52, 57, 102, 128–131, 155–160, 169–172
   role of money in, 37–40, 76
Leadership political action committees, 19, 25, 144
Legislative campaign committees (LCC)
   and models of party, 63–64, 169–172
   definition of, 17
   distribution throughout the U.S., 17–19
   explanation for the growth of, ch. 2
   in Florida, 19, 143–144, 181–182. See also Florida
   in Califorina, 17, 32, 181–182
   in Illinois, 17, 18, 20, 23, 26, 28, 35
   in Indiana, 20, 26, 142–177. See also Indiana
   in Maine, 20, 35
   in Minnesota, 17
   in Missouri, 35
   in New Jersey, 35
   in New York, 17, 18, 22, 24, 32, 39, 83–112. See also New York
   in Ohio, 24, 27, 40, 140–142. See also Ohio
   in Oregon, 20
   in Pennsylvania, 41
   in Tennessee, 144–145. See also Tennessee
   in Wisconsin, 17, 20
   leadership of, 41, 176–177
   majority units, 28, 36–37, 127
   minority units, 28, 36–37, 127
   official committee 20–22

operations unit, 22–25, 176
operatives, 22–25, 170–171, 176, 179
organization of, 20–25
role in elections, 25–30, 89–91, 96, 100–112, 118–135, 144–164, 169–175
services provided by, 17–20
staffing, 22–25, 170–171
Legislative professionalization, 14, 42, 85–89, 116–117, 127–128, 133–135, 180
impact on the growth of legislaitve campaign committees, 41–46, 127–128,
Lipset, Seymore, 31
Loftus, Tom, 29, 41
Londan, Herb, 95
Lowi, Theodore, 36

Madigan, Michel, 41
Mahe, Eddie, 56, 137
Margiotta, Joseph, 87, 92
Marino, John, 98
Marino, Ralph, 38
Mayhew, David, 28, 31–32, 33, 139, 141–145
McClure, Robert, 42
Miller, Mel, 88
Monroe County Democratic Committee, 92
Moscow, Warren, 91, 97

Nassau County Republican Machine, 38, 92
National Republican Campaign Committee (NRCC), 11, 12
National Republican Senatorial Committee (NRSC), 12
National Rifle Association (NRA), 30
New York State, 83–112
county party committees, 92, 100–112
Democratic party, 89, 92, 98–100
electoral competition in, 93–94

electoral laws, 84
legislature, 42, 83, 85–89
legislative professionalization, 85–89
legislative campaign committees, 17, 18, 22, 24, 32, 39, 89–91, 116, 167. See also New York State Democratic Assembly Campaign Committee; New York State Senate Republican Campaign Committee; New York State Republican Assembly Campaign Committee
"member items" 87
political parties, 83, 92, 95–100
Republican party, 89, 92, 95–98
New York State Democratic Assembly Campaign Committee (DACC), 2–5, 30, 38, 40, 80, 84, 89–91, 99, 103, 176
New York State Senate Republican Campaign Committee, 89–91
New York State Republican Assembly Campaign Committee (RACC), 2, 5, 89–91

O'Connell, Dan, 100
Ohio
Democratic party, 141
legislative campaign committees, 24, 27, 40, 140–141, 145–164
legislature, 141
political parties, 140–141
Republican party, 141
Ohio Democratic State Committee, 141
Ohio Republican State Committee, 141
Ohrenstein, Manfred, 23, 179
Olson, David, 13, 19, 36, 43, 139
Ortloff, Christopher, 5

Party Transformation Study (PTS), 50–52, 137. See also Cotter, Cornelius

"Plattsburgh Special," 2–5, 11, 25, 75, 80, 138, 174, 176
Political Action Committees (PACs), 7
    at the state level, 38–39
Political parties
    activities, 49–58, 65–66
    as-organization, 47, 49–58, 64, 177
    county committees, 137–139
    decline of, 47–48
    definition of, 47–48
    Downsian model, 48, 54, 59–63
    funtions of, 8–11, 57, 58–63, 65–66, 169–173, 183
    ideological polorization, 57–58
    in-electorate, 47, 49, 177
    in-government, 47–49, 62, 64, 176–177
    machines, 47, 137
    membership in, 63–64
    organizational complexity, 50–51
    rational choice model, 55. See also Political parties, Downsian model
    realignment, 58
    relationship between layers, 50–51
    responsible model, 48–49, 58–63
    resurgence perspectives, 49–58
    state party organizations, 113–115
    theoretical notions of, 48–49, 54–55, 59–63
    traditional geographic party organization, 64–67
Polsby, Nelson, 57
Powers, William, 95–98

Reagan, Ronald, 1
Redfield, Kent D., 28
Riffe, Vern, 24, 41
Rinfret, Pierre, 95, 98
Rockefeller, Nelson, 87, 95
Rollins, Edward, 12, 63
Ryan, Andrew, 1

Salmore, Barbara, 32
Salmore, Stephen, 32
Schlesinger, Joseph, 39, 54–55, 58
Simon-Rosenthal, Cindy, 34, 40
State legislative campaign committees. See Legislative campaign committees.
Stone, Walter, 57
Stonecash, Jeffery, 90, 110, 168
"stratarchy," 65

"tandem jobs," 23
Targetable activities,
    definition of, 77–80
Tennessee
    Democratic party, 144–145
    legislative campaign committees, 144–168
    legislature, 144–145
    political parties, 144–145
    Republican party, 144–145
Term limits, 180–181
Traditional Party Organizations (TPO), 64–67
    definition of, 64–67
    structure of, 64–65
    functions of, 65–66
    goals and incentives, 66–67. See also Political parties

Van Der Slik, Jack, 28
Verta, Laura 52, 57

Webber, Ronald E., 44
Weber, Max, 31, 41
Weisberg, Fran, 92
Witt, Stuart, 92
Wright, William, 59–63

Zimmerman, Joseph, 84